Mimi

With love and very
fond memories of Campbell

Ronnie
May 2006

Challenge to Democracy

Challenge to Democracy

Politics, Trade Union Power and Economic Failure in the 1970s

Ronald McIntosh

POLITICO'S

First published in Great Britain 2006 by
Politico's Publishing Ltd, an imprint of
Methuen Publishing Ltd
11–12 Buckingham Gate
London
SW1E 6LB

10 9 8 7 6 5 4 3 2 1

A CIP catalogue record for this book is available from the British Library.

ISBN-10: 1-84275-157-3
ISBN-13: 978-1-84275-157-2

Printed and bound in Great Britain by St Edmundsbury Press, Bury St Edmunds, Sufolk

For Doreen
with love and gratitude

Contents

List of illustrations

Foreword

The very best diaries exude a special odour – the smell of the times in which they were written. Within these pages you will pick up time and again whiff after whiff of the decay, depression and drift which plunged the high politics of mid-1970s Britain into near despair. At the time Ronnie McIntosh was a seasoned Whitehall veteran and I was a very young Whitehall watcher on the *Times* (and briefly on the *Financial Times*). But our nostrils twitched as if choreographed, only partly because the list of those with whom we lunched and conversed overlapped in several places.

It was, by peacetime British standards, among the worst of times. It was also the most fascinating of times, because one could feel – almost week by week – the rather noble norms of the post-war settlement, the essentials of the Keynesian-Beveridge way of approaching political economy and society, cracking and spiralling under the stresses of raging inflation and mounting industrial strife. And nobody at or near the top in politics and administration had a firm idea of what to do about it, at least until a real collapse came. It was a matter of when, not if, the pound sterling would plummet and many among the normally sober judged some kind of authoritarian rule a possibility among the ruins of both Conservative and Labour attempts to restore stability.

Ronnie McIntosh was wonderfully well placed to observe this period, which, in my view, constituted the slow-motion domestic equivalent of the Suez crisis twenty years earlier, when the realities of the UK's overseas foreign policy and defence position were revealed in stark primary colours. As director general of the National Economic Development Council, Ronnie McIntosh had no illusions about how deep set Britain's relative economic decline was by 1973–4, when a quadrupling of the oil price shone the harshest of neon lights upon the structural and human failings of British industry.

Ronnie provided a discriminating and sympathetic ear to minister and permanent secretary, captain of industry and trade union general secretary alike. And, most nights, the sympathetic ear turned into a deft pen as the McIntosh diary accrued, accumulating a very special record which henceforth no serious historian of post-war Britain will be able to ignore.

I came to know Ronnie McIntosh during these years. I had no idea he was keeping a diary. I am immensely glad that he did. For diaries such as *Challenge to Democracy* bring a period to light in a way that months spent in the official archives cannot. McIntosh's people breathe and fret in these pages in a way no official note taker can capture.

Sir Ronnie himself was and remains a realist rather than a pessimist. He is not a man given to excessive gloom. And there are some light touches within – including the revelation that the Duke of Edinburgh was quite a deft amateur sociologist of Empire and its aftermath. (I won't spoil it; wait until you reach July 1977.)

Those aspiring to a seat in a future Cabinet, or to one of the higher posts in industry or the civil service, should read the McIntosh diaries and discover what governing in *really* hard times was like. And future scholars wishing to know why so many historians of my generation appeared near obsessed by the 'great decline debate' need do no more than to start here.

Peter Hennessy FBA
Attlee Professor of Contemporary British History
Queen Mary, University of London

Preface and acknowledgements

When towards the end of 1973 I decided to keep a diary, I had no thought of doing so for publication. I began it simply because it was by then crystal clear that Britain was heading for a crisis of historic proportions and I knew that circumstances had given me a unique observation post from which to follow its development. Once started, I felt – as I suspect many diarists before me have felt – a compulsive, almost obsessive urge to record the happenings of each day, however late the hour and however tired I was. I kept this up for as long as I remained in my observation post and then quite happily abandoned it.

For more than twenty years the diary remained unregarded, though not forgotten, in my bottom drawer. Then, not very long before his death in 2003, I showed it to Roy Jenkins (by then Lord Jenkins of Hillhead OM), whom I had known since we were freshmen at Balliol before the war. Roy read it through, characteristically annotating it with his comments wherever he thought my recollection or my judgment was at fault, and told me I should seek to get it published. It is a great pleasure to place on record my thanks to Roy for his encouragement – and for the friendship we enjoyed for six decades.

My talks with Roy led in due course to a convivial meeting with three people for whose judgment on contemporary history I have the highest regard: Andrew Adonis, Peter Hennessy and William Keegan. I am most grateful to them for the encouragement they gave me to go ahead with publication, and especially to Professor Hennessy for the engaging foreword he has written for this book. I would also like to thank my friend Peter Unwin for wise advice about the world of publishing.

At Politico's I received great help from Sean Magee and, after he moved on, from Alan Gordon Walker, who, with Jonathan Wadman, edited the book and saw it through to publication. I am much indebted to them all.

In its original form the diary was a lot longer than the published version and the task of typing it from my manuscript notebooks was a heavy one. This was carried out with cheerfulness and skill by Kim Sumner and Mary Caryer, to both of whom I wish to express my warm thanks.

My wife Doreen shared many of the experiences recorded in this book. She was familiar from her own experience of government with the world in which I worked. She knew many of the people who appear in the diary and more than once came to my rescue when my inter-personal skills were found wanting. Her support and companionship, which I have now enjoyed for more than fifty years of married life, have sustained me in good times and bad and I am profoundly grateful to her.

Organisations cited in the diary

ABCC	Association of British Chambers of Commerce
APEX	Association of Professional, Executive, Clerical and Computer Staff
ASLEF	Associated Society of Locomotive Engineers and Firemen
ASTMS	Association of Scientific, Technical and Managerial Staffs
AUEW	Amalgamated Union of Engineering Workers
BAA	British Airports Authority
BIM	British Institute of Management
BSC	British Steel Corporation
CBI	Confederation of British Industry
CEGB	Central Electricity Generating Board
CPGB	Communist Party of Great Britain
CPRS	Central Policy Review Staff
CPSA	Civil and Public Services Association
CSEU	Confederation of Shipbuilding and Engineering Unions
DEA	Department of Economic Affairs
EDC	Economic Development Committee (little Neddy)
EEC	European Economic Community
EETPU	Electrical, Electronic, Telecommunication, Plumbing Union
EPEA	Electrical Power Engineers' Association

FBI	Federation of British Industries
GLC	Greater London Council
GMWU	General and Municipal Workers' Union
IMF	International Monetary Fund
IRC	Industrial Reorganisation Corporation
ISTC	Iron and Steel Trades Confederation
NALGO	National and Local Government Officers Association
NATSOPA	National Society of Operative Printers
NCB	National Coal Board
NEB	National Enterprise Board
NEDC	National Economic Development Council
NEDO	National Economic Development Office
NIESR	National Institute for Economic and Social Research
NIRC	National Industrial Relations Court
NUM	National Union of Mineworkers
NUPE	National Union of Public Employees
NUR	National Union of Railwaymen
NUS	National Union of Seamen
NUT	National Union of Teachers
OECD	Organisation for Economic Co-operation and Development
OPEC	Organization of the Petroleum Exporting Countries
PEP	Political and Economic Planning
PLP	Parliamentary Labour Party
POEU	Post Office Engineering Union
RIBA	Royal Institute of British Architects
SMMT	Society of Motor Manufacturers and Traders
SRNA	Shipbuilders and Repairers National Association
TASS	Technical, Administrative and Supervising Section (of AUEW)
TGWU	Transport and General Workers Union
TSSA	Transport Salaried Staffs Association

TUC   Trades Union Congress
UCATT   Union of Construction, Allied Trades and
           Technicians
USDAW   Union of Shop, Distributive and Allied Workers

Neddy consisted of two separate, linked entities. NEDC comprised the representatives of government, industry and trade unions who were members of the council and took part in its meetings. NEDO consisted of the permanent staff of economists and other specialists who supported the work of the council and the EDCs. The director general, who was a member of the council and head of NEDO, provided the link between the two. The word 'Neddy' was used more or less indiscriminately to describe either or both of NEDC and NEDO. The EDCs were usually called 'little Neddies'.

Introduction

The diary which follows chronicles an extraordinary chapter in the history of twentieth-century Britain. It opens in November 1973 with a state of emergency in force. It goes on to describe a period when British industry was required by law to work a three-day week and a government minister urged people to clean their teeth in the dark in order to save electricity. It tells of candlelight discussions about how soon the elected government would be replaced by an authoritarian regime and records a dramatic meeting which, if handled differently, might have averted the fall of the Heath government. It deals with the two general elections of 1974, a change at the top in both the main political parties and the emergence of Margaret Thatcher as opposition leader. It also covers an extended period when Britain was widely thought to be facing economic collapse, from which it had to be rescued by the IMF; and it records the views, aspirations and prejudices of a now extinct species – the trade union baron.

As the director general of Neddy (as the National Economic Development Council was universally known) I had a unique vantage point from which to observe these tumultuous events. The council was a tripartite body on which the TUC and CBI were represented by their principal office holders and the government by the relevant Cabinet ministers. The director general was one of two independent members of the council, which met monthly under the chairmanship of the Chancellor of the Exchequer or, from time to time, the Prime Minister.

Neddy had been set up in 1962 by Harold Macmillan and his Chancellor, Selwyn Lloyd, who were alarmed by the growing weakness of the British economy. Their hope was that by involving the trade unions in the process of economic policy-making they might enlist their help in curbing wage inflation and raising industrial productivity. Macmillan also saw Neddy as a means of introducing a degree of central planning – along the lines of the French Commissariat du Plan, which was much admired at the time – in order to arrest the economic decline which seemed to be gathering pace year by year.

Neddy was not an executive body. Its purpose was to provide a forum where each of the three parties (government, employers and trade unions) would seek to influence the views and behaviour of the others. The aim was to develop a consensus on how best to tackle the country's economic weaknesses – whether by overcoming specific obstacles to growth and efficiency or, more generally, by encouraging a change in attitudes or policies. It was expected that, once a consensus had been reached on how to deal with a particular problem area, the TUC and CBI would do their best to persuade their members to be guided by it and the government would give effect to any necessary changes in official policy.

The basic concept of Neddy, in which the main interest groups would work together to improve the country's economic performance, was widely welcomed and the council quickly established itself as a going concern. In 1964, in a rare example of political bipartisanship, the incoming Labour government gave it its full support. Some of its functions were transferred to the short-lived Department of Economic Affairs, leaving Neddy to concentrate on efforts to improve productivity through a network of 'little Neddies', which were concerned with the performance of individual industries. This arrangement came to an end in 1969 with the demise of the DEA.

By 1970, when the Conservatives returned to power, Neddy was an accepted and quite popular feature of the national landscape and Edward Heath (who had been a member of Macmillan's Cabinet when Neddy was set up) reaffirmed the government commitment to it. In 1972, following a strike which had secured for the coal miners a 27 per cent wage rise, Heath invested a huge amount of time in direct talks with the TUC in which he tried to reach agreement with them to restrain inflationary pay settlements. These bilateral talks – and similar, though less time-consuming, discussions with the CBI – were held in Downing Street and not round the NEDC table.

In the event the discussions came to nothing. In December the government imposed a ninety-day wage freeze and this was followed in March 1973 by a detailed system of statutory controls over pay and prices, known as Phase 2 of the counter-inflation policy.

While all this was going on, the economy was running into increasing trouble on other fronts. Throughout the world commodity prices were rising steeply; the cost of many basic materials more than doubled in 1973. The trade balance deteriorated sharply as a result and sterling came under continuing pressure. The abolition of credit controls two years earlier had led to a runaway property boom and in July 1973 the Chancellor, Anthony Barber, had to apply the brakes by raising interest rates to the then unprecedented level of 11.5 per cent.

In the autumn the economy took a further downward plunge. War broke out in the Middle East in October and OPEC followed this by a cut in deliveries of oil and a four-fold increase in its price. The impact of these events on an already shaky economy was severely damaging. It also hugely strengthened the hand of the coalminers, whose new claim for a 35 per cent increase in pay was by now well advanced. This made a confrontation between the miners and the government (which had just published an immensely complex set of rules for Phase 3 of the counter-inflation policy) virtually inevitable.

By November the outlook both at home and abroad could hardly have been more sombre and the sense of impending crisis in the country was almost tangible. For the first (and last) time in my life I decided to keep a diary, which was written up in longhand at the end of the day in question or within twenty-four hours of it. It records the events of this turbulent period as I observed or came to know about them and the opinions which I and others involved held about them at the time. By no means all the judgments made in the diary have stood the test of time but I have resisted the temptation to edit them out of the published text.

Barely thirty years have passed since the period covered in the diary, yet it already has a strong flavour of *ancien régime* about it. The issues which preoccupied politicians and industrial leaders in the 1970s – incomes policy, the social contract, control of nationalised industries and the like – are not those which concern their successors today. They were swept away in the revolution ushered in by the first Thatcher government not long after the diary ends, which (for good or ill) transformed so many long-established attitudes and institutions.

This revolution coincided with a changing of the guard in British society as the period in which virtually all the top people in the country had grown to maturity before 1945 came to an end. This generation's mindset was heavily influenced by experience of the 1930s, when an economic system relying primarily on market forces seemed unable to deliver acceptable living standards to large sections of the population. It looked back with approval on wartime habits of co-operation, across the social divide, in pursuit of agreed national goals; and it broadly supported the wide-ranging social and economic reforms introduced by the Attlee government, several of which had been conceived by the wartime coalition.

The post-war ambitions of this generation (to which I myself belong) were difficult to achieve in an economy which had been severely damaged by the war and was subject to the strains imposed by the painful process of dismantling an empire. It took a long time for most people to take on board the scale and intractability of the underlying problems but by the mid 1960s they had begun to be widely recognised. There was, however, no agreement on solutions and, as the diary makes only too clear, successive governments in the 1970s – though containing many very able people – spent much of their time floundering in the face of rapidly worsening economic circumstances. It was, therefore, to be expected that when a new generation of political leaders took over, the change in style and doctrine would be drastic and abrupt.

Perhaps surprisingly, however, Neddy survived the revolution intact. Its status and relevance were affected by the new administration's perception of the proper role of trade unions, but it remained in existence throughout the Thatcher years. In 1992 it was abolished by its last chairman, Norman Lamont, not long before he was himself sacked as Chancellor of the Exchequer by the Prime Minister, John Major. There was an unexpected symmetry in this as thirty years earlier the first chairman of Neddy, Selwyn Lloyd, had been removed from office as Chancellor with equal suddenness by the then Prime Minister, Harold Macmillan.

PART ONE

WHO GOVERNS
BRITAIN?

27 November 1973 to 9 February 1974

The diary opens at a time when, in the words of Douglas Hurd, who was Edward Heath's political secretary at the time, 'the earth moved under the government's feet'.* The outbreak of the Yom Kippur war in early October had profound implications for the world economy and the international trade and payment flows which underpinned it. The effect on the British economy, with its weak balance of payments and in-built inflationary pressures, seemed likely to be especially severe.

At the end of October the government announced the terms of the statutory incomes policy which would govern wage negotiations in the coming winter. A fortnight later the NUM signalled its determination to ignore this policy by introducing an overtime ban in support of a wage claim which would drive a coach and horses through the government's rules. On the following day a state of emergency was proclaimed. From then on it was evident that statesmanship of a high order would be required if the country was to find a safe path through the social and economic minefield which lay ahead.

By this time I had been at Neddy for about four months. My Whitehall experience – in the Department of Economic Affairs and the Cabinet Office under a Labour government and at Employment and the Treasury under the Conservatives – had made me familiar with most of the problems which confronted the country. In particular, immediately before taking up my Neddy post, I had spent two years as chairman of the inter-departmental committee which co-ordinated Whitehall work on incomes policy. From this I learned a great deal about the way in which wage negotiations were conducted in practice and about the factors which determined the behaviour of trade union negotiators.

I was, however, conscious that, whereas I had a wide acquaintance

---

* Douglas Hurd, *An End to Promises* (London: Collins, 1979).

among politicians and the business community, I did not know many trade union leaders well. As I believed that the whole point of Neddy (in line with Harold Macmillan's original vision) was to bring the trade unions closer to the process of economic policy-making, I made it a priority to get to know as many of them as I could. The diary begins, therefore, with my first one on one meeting with the leader of the engineering workers' union. Hugh Scanlon was one of the most influential (and controversial) figures in the trade union movement of the time. He was thought by many to be a wild man of the left but during the time we worked together in Neddy I found him pragmatic and reasonable and a pleasure to deal with.

Wednesday 27 November 1973

Lunched with Hugh Scanlon at Inigo Jones. I began by telling him something about my own background and motivations and what I hoped to achieve at NEDO. He wished me luck but said that although he was a strong supporter of Neddy he didn't think that there could be any really effective work done there so long as Heath remained Prime Minister.

Friday 29 November 1973

Lunch at the Pearson Group, hosted by the chairman, Lord Cowdray. We soon got into a discussion about our present industrial troubles.

Roger Brooke* foresaw a right-wing regime 'with tanks in the streets'. I argued that this was a poor way to run things – we had to find a way of making a reality of Heath's 'one nation' ambitions. But this would involve recognising where industrial power lay and coming to terms with it rather than confronting it – even if this meant big changes in our ideas about relative rewards etc., which many of the better off would find distasteful and hard to accept.

Monday 3 December 1973

I went to see Douglas Allen† to see how he felt about the situation. He agreed about its gravity and for the first time since I have known him I found him uncertain what should be done next. As a rule he knows exactly what ought to be done, though more often than not he says it

---

* A director of the group. He had been deputy managing director of the IRC from 1966 to 1969.

† Sir Douglas Allen was permanent secretary of the Treasury. With a robustly independent mind, he was the ablest mandarin of his time – and one of the nicest.

won't be done because of the politicians' obtuseness or wrong-
headedness. This time he confessed that he not only didn't know what
ministers would do but didn't know what advice he ought to give them.

Tuesday 4 December 1973

I called on John Partridge at noon.[*] I said I thought we were now
living in history. Next year could see a world recession and would
certainly bring with it fundamental changes in the relationship
between the developed countries and the primary producers and in
the pattern of trade and industry throughout the world. If we
entered the new year with our weak balance of payments and in as
divided a condition as we now were, we should come to grief. It
seemed imperative to work again for a consensus between the
government, the employers and the unions and we should use the
Neddy meeting on the following day to inch towards this. Partridge,
who is very sensible and balanced, agreed with all of this and said he
would do anything he could to help.

Earlier in the morning I had been to see William Armstrong.[†] I
found him in a very depressed mood. He said that the situation was
graver than anything we had faced since the war. But he didn't offer
any suggestions for getting out of it.

I went to see Eric Roll[‡] at Warburgs in the afternoon. I spoke as I
had done to Partridge and said I wanted to enlist his support as the

---

[*] Sir John Partridge was chairman of the Imperial Group. A wise and experienced
industrialist, he was a past president of the CBI.
[†] Sir William Armstrong played a key – though not always benign – role in Edward
Heath's prolonged discussions with the TUC in 1972 and 1973. He was Head of the
Civil Service, having previously been permanent secretary of the Treasury. It is
arguable that he was overpromoted in both these posts.
[‡] Sir Eric Roll was chairman of the merchant bankers S. G. Warburg. A former
academic of high intelligence and great charm, who knew everybody who was worth
knowing, he had been permanent secretary of the Department of Economic Affairs
from 1964 to 1966.

only other independent member of Neddy besides myself.

Eric agreed with my analysis. He had just got back from America and said he had found great hostility towards Europe in Washington. This, coupled with the disunity in the EEC, boded ill for a year in which skilled international statesmanship would be needed if we were to get through it without intolerable strains on world trade and the monetary system.

Wednesday 5 December 1973

Neddy meeting at 10.30. All members were present, including two new ones – Willie Whitelaw, who was brought back from Northern Ireland to be Secretary of State for Employment three days ago, and Monty Finniston, the chairman of BSC. Introducing our paper on the economic situation, I said that while up to now it had been not unreasonable to suggest that we could 'grow our way' out of our economic difficulties, this option was no longer open to us because of the physical shortage of oil and the huge addition to our balance of payments deficit which the increased price of oil would produce. I ended on a note of very qualified and restrained optimism – but added that the situation was very fragile and that the possibility of a bad outcome was great. I said I did not want to discuss the coal situation but that, if things became more difficult internationally, we should be very vulnerable because of our weak balance of payments and our troubled industrial situation – and we couldn't rate our chances of dealing with the problems effectively very high unless the three parties on Neddy agreed in advance on the measures required.

Campbell Adamson* followed with a sensible, low-key contribution. He called for a constructive and imaginative approach to a

---

* Director general of the CBI. In 1967, after several years in the steel industry, he had been made chief industrial adviser in the DEA, where we had worked together closely. His time at the CBI was not an easy one but he emerged from it with great credit.

very serious national situation to be worked out round the NEDC table. He added that, while we should not panic, the situation was one of extreme gravity.

This enabled Len Murray* to make a quite effective intervention in which he said we should jointly agree the priorities round the NEDC table. He accepted that the balance of payments would have to be improved and called for a complete reappraisal of policies – including defence policy and the possibility of imposing import restrictions. At all costs deflation must be avoided.

There followed a good general discussion. Tony Barber† said the situation was very serious: when the price of an essential raw material went up sharply and permanently this had a lasting effect on the standard of living of the importing country – he quoted the case of an east African man who had complained to him that because of a change in world commodity markets his country had to export half as many tons of cashew nuts again in order to pay for the same number of tractors.

Dick Marsh‡ made a very effective contribution in which he said we faced the most dangerous situation we had had since the 1930s and stressed that this was not the time to dismantle the prices and incomes policy. This last point was made in reply to Hugh Scanlon,

---

* Lionel Murray (normally known as Len) had been general secretary of the TUC since September 1973. An intellectual, who had been a TUC apparatchik all his working life, he had no direct experience of the shop floor. He was initially overshadowed by the leaders of big unions like Jack Jones but he gained a great deal of authority after the 1974 congress and became an effective and principled leader of the TUC.

† Anthony Barber became Chancellor of the Exchequer when Iain Macleod died a few weeks after the Heath government came to power. It was not an office he had expected or aspired to and my impression was that he was never wholly comfortable in it.

‡ Richard Marsh was chairman of the British Railways Board, having been Minister of Transport under Harold Wilson in the 1960s. His ebullient personality and caustic wit enlivened the longueurs of NEDC meetings.

who said that there was no chance of getting a united approach so long as the government followed a completely inflexible policy on wages.

Alf Allen and David Basnett* both made moderate, statesmanlike interventions. Peter Walker† then made a long, rambling statement about petrol rationing. In the course of it, Dick Marsh whispered to me that Walker must be stopped – otherwise we should lose the chance to take advantage of the constructive line taken by the TUC members. Walker finally stopped and Barber (who had not said a great deal during the discussion) asked me in effect to sum up.

I said that we all agreed that we faced a potentially very grave situation and that the long-term effects of the Arabs' action might be a good deal greater than was yet generally recognised. I said it was clear we could not get through our difficulties so long as we remained divided by industrial conflict; I didn't overrate what Neddy could do but if one didn't use it in a situation like this, one might as well wind it up. We had already had one of the most realistic discussions Neddy had had for years and it was important to continue it soon on the basis of a paper prepared in a smaller group.

My statement seemed to go down well. Campbell immediately suggested that we should meet in emergency session before Christmas and Len Murray weighed in agreeing to this. Barber said that a special meeting might be dangerous if it aroused expectations which could not be fulfilled – but after some discussion it was agreed that we should meet on 21 December 'to take stock of a rapidly developing situation'.

Over drinks after the meeting there was a widespread atmosphere of relief that Neddy had openly recognised the gravity of the situation and had agreed to have a special meeting. Campbell told me

---

* Respectively general secretaries of USDAW and the GMWU.
† Secretary of State for Trade and Industry.

he had waited with bated breath to see if I would say the right things when I summed up. Fortunately (he said) the gods had inspired me to say precisely what was needed.

I then gave a full briefing to a well-attended press conference. I gave a summary of our paper with a reference to my statement that we could no longer grow out of our difficulties. I quoted Barber as saying that the increase in the price of oil would affect our standard of living and repeated his story about the cashew nuts. I got closely questioned by the reporters and spoke pretty fully and freely in reply because I thought the seriousness of the situation warranted it. I stressed that the discussion had been a good, down-to-earth one and that there had been general agreement on the proposal to have a special meeting before Christmas.

Towards the end of the press conference Bill Keegan of the *Financial Times* asked if what I had said meant that we could no longer achieve the target rate of growth of 3½ per cent a year. I said that in my view there was now no chance of our growing at 3½ per cent because of the increased supply constraints.

This was a really good meeting which more than fulfilled my hopes that we should be able to inch things a little closer to some kind of tripartite agreement.

Thursday 6 December 1973

The *FT* had a short piece about the Neddy meeting tucked away on the inside pages. The *Times* had a short, harmless piece on the front page. The *Guardian* made it the lead story but reported it accurately – even the *Daily Mirror* had it on the front page. Unfortunately the *Daily Telegraph* had really gone to town, making it the lead story and quoting Barber as saying that 3½ per cent growth was unattainable now and that our standard of living was bound to fall next year.

About 10.15 a.m. Tony Barber telephoned me to say he would like to see me urgently. I went across to the Treasury, where he was waiting for me with Chris France, his new private secretary. He was very tense and though scrupulously polite throughout he was clearly upset and rattled.

He told me that the PM had read the *Daily Telegraph* just after midnight and had at once got in touch with him. (Why can't politicians read their papers in the morning like the rest of us?) Barber had told him that he had never made the statements attributed to him and that he was sure I had not told the press that he had. The PM, who was clearly very angry, had said that this sort of thing had never happened when Frank Figgures* was DG and that in future Barber had better see the press himself. Barber then handed me a draft statement which he said he thought I ought to issue to put the record straight.

The statement was well drafted and drew largely on the note which I had sent Barber before the meeting. I told Barber that the *Times* and the *FT* had reported accurately what I had said at my press briefing. I had not said that Barber or the council had agreed that 3½ per cent growth was unattainable; I had given this as my own opinion and I would have to make it clear to journalists that my opinion was unchanged. I expressed some surprise at Barber's concern and said that I found it difficult to see how we could maintain 3½ per cent growth with reduced supplies of coal and oil. Barber simply said that if he was going to announce a change in the rate of growth he would not do it in Neddy – but presumably in Parliament. After a very little more talk I said I would issue the statement and Barber went off to the House.

An unfortunate incident. Although it is upsetting, I don't really mind too much about it personally but I hope it hasn't damaged

---

* Sir Frank Figgures was my immediate predecessor, who became chairman of the Pay Board on leaving Neddy.

POCKET CARTOON
by OSBERT LANCASTER

BARBER SPEAKS

"Cheer up, darling!
There'll be no fall in the
standard of living—it's
just that we're all going
to be a good bit worse
off than we expected."

© Osbert Lancaster/*Daily Express*

Neddy's usefulness in the government's eyes. Heath can be vindictive and I shall not be able to make anything of Neddy unless I can keep, to a reasonable degree, the trust of all three of my shareholders.

I was pleased to receive, during what was a thoroughly trying day, a very nice letter from John Partridge warmly complimenting me on what I said at the beginning and end of yesterday's council meeting.

I spoke to Douglas Allen on the telephone and asked him to do what he could to keep the temperature down. He said he would and added that the trouble was that ministers did not realise how bad things were.

Michael Beckett, the *Daily Telegraph* journalist who caused all the trouble, rang this evening to apologise.

Monday 10 December 1973

Lunched with Donald MacDougall* at the Reform. He made some sensible suggestions about the paper for Council on 21 December. I

---

* Sir Donald MacDougall, a distinguished Oxford economist, was chief economic adviser to the CBI. He had held senior posts in Whitehall under both Conservative and Labour governments.

asked him whether he thought the energy constraints would be inflationary and whether, given that consumer demand was slowing down anyway, he thought special measures to reduce demand were needed. Donald thought they were but it was clear he had not thought through the economic effects of the new situation – he said as much, which reassured me as I cannot judge between the conflicting views of economists.

We met John Burgh[*] over coffee. He said he had run into Eric Roll after the council meeting on 5 December. Eric had said that it had been a very good meeting and that 'Ronnie had been magnificent'.

Tuesday 11 December 1973

I went to see Murray at 9.30 a.m. He was subdued and reflective and very obviously could not see the way ahead clearly.

I opened up by saying that the last council meeting had in the event achieved more than I had expected. We must do everything possible to inch our way a bit further forward on 21 December so as to increase the chances of making real progress after Christmas. I said that although a lot might happen between now and 21 December, the next two meetings of Neddy could have an important bearing on the prospects of getting out of our present mess.

Murray did not disagree. He said that the central issue was to establish whether there was anything which the TUC could offer which would enable the government to give up statutory control of wages. From the trade union point of view a return to some form of voluntary collective bargaining was essential although it was just possible that they could agree to the government keeping back up powers on the statute book.

Murray said that he was sure that a majority of the General

---

[*] Deputy head of the CPRS.

Council were in favour of reaching some agreement with the government but that to produce effective results he would need a very large majority. He would also need to call either a special Congress or a conference of delegates and here too a large majority would be needed. He thought it should be possible to work out a package which would bring the TGWU in but the AUEW was much more difficult and even if Scanlon agreed to a package, one could not count on his executive backing him up.

Murray said that the Industrial Relations Act[*] was still very important, though largely for symbolic reasons. He assumed that the government could be persuaded to put it on ice, as part of an otherwise satisfactory package. I said I did not see how the government could give up statutory control of wages at the moment because of the widespread concern here and abroad about inflation. I suggested that one possibility might be for the government to say that they must clearly keep statutory controls in force through this winter (while the worst of the energy crisis was upon us) but that, provided the outcome of the talks with the TUC and CBI was satisfactory, they would be prepared to give them up at the end of April. Murray expressed some interest in this idea.

Dinner at the Tara Hotel with three union general secretaries, Jack Macgougan, Roy Grantham and John Slater.[†] They are all members of the general council, all reasonable and moderate people and I suppose all without influence. We discussed the crisis and I did what I could to urge them to throw their weight on the side of moderation at the next General Council meeting. Macgougan said

---

[*] The Act, which was the centrepiece of the government's legislative programme in 1971, made the trade unions subject to a variety of statutory controls and set up a number of new institutions, including the National Industrial Relations Court, for this purpose.

[†] Their unions were the National Union of Tailors and Garment Workers, APEX and the NUS respectively.

his members, who are low paid, are getting more now than they would under free collective bargaining because Phase 3 acts as a minimum as well as a maximum.

Wednesday 12 December 1973

I saw Campbell Adamson at 9 a.m. and spent an hour and a half with him. He was pleased about a speech his president, Michael Clapham, had made in Newcastle, in which he warned the country that we were on the brink of a precipice and called for strong leadership. Campbell said that in his own speech at Cardiff tomorrow night he would be speaking about the merits of a new approach on the lines discussed in Neddy.

Campbell said that Tony Barber had been to dinner with him last night and had been very cheerful, giving no indication that he thought that the situation was critical. Whitelaw, on the other hand, when Campbell and Michael Clapham saw him on Monday, had taken a very serious view of the situation and appeared to want a new approach to our economic and industrial affairs. Whitelaw had said he had been struck by the fact that both Jack Jones* and Hugh Scanlon seemed almost frightened of the serious prospect ahead.

I told Campbell of my talk with Len Murray yesterday and of the importance he attached to a return to some form of voluntary collective bargaining. As I expected, Campbell stressed that the CBI would not be willing to see Phase 3 called into question – indeed it ought really to be tightened, though this might not be practical politics. He said that he hoped that it would not be discussed at all on 21 December.

---

* As general secretary of the TGWU Jack Jones was the most powerful trade union leader of his day. He was an idealist with a genuine passion for improving the lot of working-class people. He was also very determined and liked to get his own way. I got on well with him personally but, as the diary shows, our working relationship went through some bumpy passages.

I said that this was simply not realistic and that the TUC would walk out of the meeting if there were no discussion of the possibility of a return to voluntary collective bargaining. I said that my guess was that the TUC might not die in the last ditch for an immediate return to collective bargaining but that they would not be prepared to talk seriously at NEDC if they thought that Phase 3 in its present form (or tighter) would last for the whole of 1974.

Campbell said that he had been told by the Minister for Industry, Tom Boardman, that the government might impose drastic controls on the use of oil by industry (for production as well as space heating) later this week.

We talked about the lack of leadership shown by the government and the possibility that overwork and fatigue were sapping the Prime Minister's energies.* I asked Campbell what the CBI would do if it looked as though the drift was going to continue till after Christmas. He said that he hoped in that case they might make a joint approach with the TUC to the government for changes in policy.

Finally, we talked about the miners' overtime ban. I said that I thought the statesmanlike thing would be to settle the dispute before Christmas. Campbell disagreed. He thought that the right course was for changes in economic and social policy to be made as a result of discussions in Neddy and elsewhere which would maximise the

---

* I believed then – and still believe – that fatigue played an important part in the events of winter 1973–4. With the Sunningdale conference on Northern Ireland and an EEC summit in Copenhagen occurring within days of each other in early December, the Prime Minister's work load was unusually heavy, even by the standards of his office. In *An End to Promises* Douglas Hurd has a revealing passage: 'Historians sometimes lose sight of the pell mell of politics. Problems crowd in on top of each other, competing for scarce time. The principal actors thrive for a time on the excitement of this way of life. They do not notice the onset of fatigue. But if they allow themselves no respite their pace slows, they increasingly miss their stroke, then begin without realising it to move through a fog of tiredness. This happened to Ministers in the winter of 1973.' See also the entry for 21 January 1976.

chances of the miners voting to end industrial action when the issue finally went to the ballot.

I had lunch with Basnett immediately after this morning's meeting of the TUC economic committee. I started off as I had with Hugh Scanlon by telling him that I did not regard my appointment to NEDO as simply another move in my career; that I thought that the problems that Neddy was set up to deal with were and would remain at the centre of our affairs; and that I would be happy to spend the rest of my working life trying to improve the relationship between the trade unions and the rest of society and generally to reduce industrial tensions. Whether because of this or not, we got straight on to the same wavelength and he talked very much more freely to me than he had done before.

Basnett was very critical of Heath and made it clear (as others have done to me) that his view was generally held in the TUC. He said that at the beginning of the last round of Downing Street talks in 1972 Heath had been very well regarded by the trade union leaders because of his willingness to talk freely and frankly about the real problems. But about half way through the last talks, Heath's attitude seemed to have changed. He appeared to have written off the chances of reaching any agreement with the trade unions and to have lost interest in the proceedings. As a result, the general view of the TUC leaders was that there was little to be gained by talking seriously to him. Basnett gave the impression that this attitude had to some extent changed because of the present national emergency. He personally regarded the Neddy meeting on 21 December as very important and he thought that the Prime Minister ought to take the chair. He also said that in order to ram home to people the importance of the problem the council should meet on Christmas Day!

Basnett said that the meeting on 21 December would probably be a rough one although it would be a mistake to try to avoid controversy. The TUC ought to say plainly to the government that they recognised the seriousness of the situation, that it called for a joint effort and that the government had better change its policies quickly. He said that although he and his own union did not regard it as especially important, he thought that the government would have to suspend the Industrial Relations Act if they wanted TUC co-operation.

He was less emphatic about a return to voluntary collective bargaining and I had the impression that he personally would not necessarily regard this as a TUC sticking point. I suggested that the government might put a time limit on the operation of Phase 3. Basnett said that if the government had done this a couple of months ago, they might have got the TUC's agreement on Phase 3 (though I personally do not believe this) but that it was now too late.

One other interesting point that Basnett made was that the trade union movement was drifting and the TUC were determined to put a stop to this before Christmas. He also made a strong point about the need for the government to involve the TUC in discussions about rationing, oil allocation, priorities etc.

Thursday 13 December 1973

I spent about an hour and a half with Douglas Allen this morning while the Cabinet was still sitting and the result of the NUM meeting was not known.* He told me that the Prime Minister would be making a strong statement about energy supplies today but that he was not clear when the economic measures would be announced or what their content would be.

He took a very gloomy line about the future and said that the Treasury predicted that GDP would fall next year. This would lead

---

* The miners decided at this meeting to continue their overtime ban.

to high unemployment (perhaps a million at the end of 1974) and hence a drop in the standard of living. He talked about the possibility of our moving into a siege economy with rationing on the wartime model.

I got the impression that the government, having under-reacted at the start, were now going to overreact.

I told Allen that from my conversations with trade union leaders I thought that there was some willingness on their part to try to reach agreement with the government and that if ministers were skilful and statesmanlike they could use the meeting on 21 December to take things a bit further forward. I said that I could not believe that the TUC would press to the very limit for a return to voluntary wage bargaining, provided they had some assurance that statutory controls would not be kept in being for the whole of this Parliament. I urged him to do everything he could to persuade ministers that it was worth taking the meeting on 21 December seriously and trying to get a constructive result from it. He said that a number of ministers had written off the TUC on the grounds that they could not deliver anything. I said that I thought this was a mistaken view – the thing to do was to isolate the miners and ASLEF* and make some arrangement with the other unions which would deter them from industrial action and that this applied particularly to the AUEW.

I asked George Smith, the general secretary of UCATT, to look in for a few minutes after the Building EDC meeting† for a word about the general situation.

He spoke bitterly and obscurely about some of the troublemakers

---

* The train drivers' union, dominated by a militant and unpredictable group of left-wingers, had introduced an overtime ban the previous day.

† There were upwards of fifteen economic development committees (or 'little Neddies'), which were tripartite bodies with independent chairmen. They were concerned with individual industries or sectors and reported as necessary to the NEDC.

in the General Council of the TUC and said he thought that as a result of the energy crisis there might have to be some kind of showdown within the TUC. He was very critical of ASLEF but not of the NUM, because he thought that miners were genuinely under-paid compared with people in offices and shops and bricklaying and because of the need to mine a lot more coal now.

Smith seemed to be saying that the TUC would have to face up to the need to evolve a common policy, stick to it and see that the membership by and large observed it. He said that there was great antagonism to Heath but that he (and by implication most of his colleagues) did not want the present situation used as a means of overthrowing the government.

He wished us luck at the meeting on 21 December and said that the TUC team would be coming with a reasonably positive brief and with a free hand to play things as they thought best.

Friday 14 December 1973

Group of 4 meeting* at 11.45 a.m. – Len Murray, Douglas Allen, Campbell Adamson and myself. I flew up to Edinburgh immediately after the meeting.

Bill Gregson of Ferranti met me and said that everyone thought it very good of me to come up in all the circumstances. The dinner consisted of about twenty-five people, all quite substantial industrialists plus one or two professional men, including the president of the Scottish Law Society. The CBI's Scottish chairman

---

* The group consisted of the permanent secretary of the Treasury, the general secretary of the TUC and the directors general of the CBI and NEDO. It met about four or five times a year in the NEDO offices. The members of the group, who were not allowed to send substitutes to its meetings, exchanged views on common problems with complete freedom, in the certain knowledge that what they said would not be reported to anyone else. No record of the meetings was circulated.

was host. I spoke for about twenty minutes after dinner. I said we were facing four crises. First, an acute emergency based on coal shortage. Second, a difficult year for oil supplies. Third, a permanent increase in oil prices and a changed balance between the Western world and oil producers. Fourth, fundamental changes going on in our own society. Among other things I said that employers had a heavy responsibility because of the evident inability of either ministers or the TUC to show leadership.

My remarks seemed to go down well. I was struck by the difference between the Scottish industrialists' views and what one hears in London. There was no talk of 'seeing it through' with the miners or of the need to 'stand firm', 'avoid appeasement', etc. Instead there seemed to be great concern about the social and industrial effects of the three-day week,* and several people questioned whether this was not too heavy a price for holding on to Phase 3. From what was said in discussion I realised belatedly how much Phase 3 would come under strain on the prices side as output fell and unit costs rose. There was some discussion of North Sea oil which confirmed my hunch that it is all going on rather haphazardly and that there is no vigorous planning or oversight from the centre.

Saturday 15 December 1973

I phoned Roy† to find out what he made of the situation. I tried out on him my theory that next week will provide a short-lived opportunity to reintroduce some sanity into our national life. I said that public awareness of the prospect before us could be expected to

---

* Severe restrictions on the use of electricity and the introduction of a three-day week for industry and commerce had been announced by the Prime Minister the day before.
† Roy Jenkins and I had met at Oxford in 1938. We remained close friends until his death in 2003.

grow rapidly, that Barber's statement on Monday would presumably have a sobering effect and that I was sure the front benches on both sides would try to cool things in the debate on Tuesday and Wednesday. In the circumstances I thought there would be a welling up of moderate feeling among people in all walks of life who saw the dangers and wanted to avoid them. But if nothing constructive happened, people would go off for Christmas in a fatalistic mood and attitudes would harden.

Roy agreed that the debate should be a moderate one and said that he would be winding up for Labour before Willie Whitelaw. I said this was good news; they both had a great opportunity to be constructive.

We then spoke of the miners. Roy said he did not see how we could 'give way' to them. If we did we should soon have domestic inflation of 25 per cent or more. I said I thought we needed to stop using terms like 'give way'. I understood the dangers of inflation but I was convinced that the disruption we were going to suffer was too high a price to pay. With the world situation so fragile and our position so weak it was just not on to have a three-day week.

Roy asked about Len Murray, who had obviously not impressed him on radio and TV. I said he was trying hard to work for sensible solutions but had not yet established his authority within the TUC.

Sunday 16 December 1973

Piers Dixon* looked in for a drink at home at my suggestion. He said that the Tory Party was much more united behind Heath than ever before. Piers and the other Finance Committee officers saw Tony

---

* Conservative MP for Truro. He was my next-door neighbour in Westminster. Two other Conservative MPs, Roger Moate and George Sinclair, lived in the same street. Among them they covered more or less the whole spectrum of party opinion, which was very useful to me.

Barber (whom he greatly admires) just before the PM's statement last Thursday to express their disquiet at the government's handling of affairs. Barber was very tense and touchy. He evidently mentioned the episode of my press statement – without rancour but the matter had clearly got under his skin. Piers said that the incident had strengthened my position because it had made me in a few months better known nationally than my predecessors had ever been.

He said that the Tories were unanimous in refusing to give in to the miners. I said I thought the miners could hold out longer than the government. But Piers thought that Harold Wilson would get them back to work by persuading them that otherwise Heath would call an election and win handsomely. I said HW would have no influence with the miners. Piers said that if the government gave way the Tory Party would disintegrate and Enoch Powell* would take over. He guessed that if Powell came in he would 'do a de Gaulle', i.e. ditch his own supporters and follow less right-wing policies.

Piers' own position is that the threat to democracy posed by the miners outweighs the dislocation which the three-day week will cause. He wants severe cuts in public expenditure and would accept higher taxation but is afraid Barber may go in for overkill in his Budget tomorrow. I said he underrated the dangers to democracy of the three-day week. This would create great social tensions as, for example, fathers went on three days' pay in factories while their daughters in offices got normal weekly pay even if they only worked three days. The best way to protect democracy was to recognise the willingness of those who had industrial power to use it and to avoid outright conflict.

---

* Conservative MP for Wolverhampton South West. The most prominent figure on the right wing of the Conservative Party, whom Heath had sacked from his shadow Cabinet in 1968 for his overtly racist 'rivers of blood' speech.

Monday 17 December 1973

Lunched with Fredy Fisher, editor of the *Financial Times*. He thinks there is a real risk of a right-wing authoritarian government next year. He doubts whether the unions have any wish to reach an accommodation with the government but thinks that, if there were to be one, it could now only be achieved with Whitelaw as PM. He said that although Heath had clearly hardened, there was a body of opinion in the Cabinet in favour of a conciliatory line: but when I tackled him about them he could only produce the names of Keith Joseph, Geoffrey Rippon, Margaret Thatcher and Joe Godber.* He said that at present he was against giving in to the miners because it would result in an inflation rate of anywhere between 20 and 25 per cent. I queried this, saying that I was not sure that any other groups would have the industrial strength to get increases comparable with the miners. The car workers and dockers no longer have power and the electricians would probably not want to press theirs too far in present circumstances.†

Fisher said that in any case he might well prefer inflation to the lasting damage to our industrial capacity which a prolonged inter-ruption of coal supplies would produce. On leaving, he urged me to see that the Neddy meeting ended with a positive agreed statement.

Harold Watkinson‡ telephoned to say he was making a speech in the Lords tomorrow and would like to suggest that Neddy at its

---

* Respectively Secretaries of State for Social Services, the Environment and Education, and Minister of Agriculture.

† The electricians' union was led by Frank Chapple, who was fanatically anti-communist and would take no action which was likely to strengthen the influence of the left.

‡ Lord Watkinson was chairman of Cadbury Schweppes. He had been a Conservative MP for fourteen years and a Cabinet minister (under Harold Macmillan) for five. This combination of political and industrial experience gave him a breadth of view which was none too common in the business community.

meeting on 21 December should review the place of the coal industry in the new situation, provided the miners accepted a settlement under Phase 3 and went back to work.

I said I thought there was no chance of the miners doing this and that it might prove counter-productive to bring Neddy in. Our job was to try to find a way through our present difficulties which might enable negotiations with the miners to take place successfully elsewhere.

Vic Feather,* who is coming to work as a consultant to NEDO in the new year, looked in. He said he thought Ted was suffering from overwork and strain. He described Barber as a consistent hard liner. He said the miners would not give in – they had no need to and would soon be the only people working a five-day week. He also said that Jack Jones and Hugh Scanlon would be very difficult – unless they could shuffle the responsibility off onto someone else, for example by being outvoted in the General Council.

Vic thought that the tensions set up by the three-day week would be very great because of the different impact it would have on different people's earnings. He thought that the Neddy meeting might be the last hope and shared my view that attitudes would harden after Christmas if no solution seemed in sight.

Tuesday 18 December 1973

In the afternoon I went to the House of Commons to hear Whitelaw. He spoke very well and although the House was nearly as noisy as it had been for Heath the previous day it was all very good tempered. The contrast was very striking.

Roger Moate† told me he was mystified by Barber's Budget but

---

* Len Murray's predecessor as general secretary of the TUC.
† Conservative MP for Faversham.

that the mood at the 1922 Committee meeting after it was euphoric. The hard-liners thought Barber had done too little but his answer was that he could always do more next month if need be.* He said that Denis Healey had done very badly in the House.

Wednesday 19 December 1973

I went to see Gordon Richardson† at 9.30a.m. Dick Lloyd,‡ as the City member of Neddy, was there. Richardson was very friendly and talked more than I had known him do before. He said he thought Ted Heath was suffering from acute fatigue – the clear implication being that he thought his judgment was impaired. He said the Bank was spending a great deal of time on the liquidity problems which were likely to arise as a result of the energy crisis and that these might well be very much bigger than most people realised.

John Burgh telephoned to ask if there was anything the CPRS could do to help us to restore a little sanity to the nation's affairs. We agreed to meet after the Neddy meeting on Friday.

I lunched with Sidney Greene§ at Inigo Jones. The more I see him, the more I like him. He said that the General Council meeting that morning had been a good one. Everything he said bore out my belief that the trade unions are not looking for a new confrontation just now. I think he regards the miners' case as a pretty good one and he is not optimistic about an early return to normal working. He pointed out that if there were a ballot the question asked would

---

* The mini-Budget introduced on 17 December aimed to reduce demand by some £1.2 billion in the ensuing year.
† Governor of the Bank of England.
‡ Chief executive of Williams and Glyn's Bank.
§ Sidney Greene was general secretary of the NUR. He had been a member of the TUC General Council since 1957 and was a founder member of NEDC. He was a responsible and constructive leader of the TUC team on NEDC for whom I had a very high regard.

not be 'Do you want to return to work?' but 'Do you want to work overtime again?'. Sidney said that he fully realised that Ted would need help to climb down from the exposed position to which he had committed himself. The unions would do their best to 'build a ladder for him' if he would postpone or drop the three-day week.

Hyde Park Hotel: the CBI annual dinner for Whitehall. I arrived feeling pretty tired and stayed that way all evening. I talked to the chairman of the NCB, Derek Ezra, who said the important thing was to get a settlement with the miners which would last for more than a year. The NUM had already decided what their claim would be next year. The industry must have stability to develop the huge new mines we should now need.

Sat next to Alex Jarratt at dinner. He takes over as chairman of IPC Newspapers next month and will have to give up his CBI work. The editorial staff of the *Mirror* have told him he can't combine CBI work and his new job.

Arthur Peterson[*] chatted after dinner. He asked if I was aware how much the NUM campaign was controlled by the Communist Party and whether I had access to secret reports now. I said I had not but that my previous jobs had given me a pretty thorough knowledge of that side of things. I added that I had recently asked Conrad Heron[†] if there was any change I ought to be aware of in CP activity in industry and he had said 'no'. Peterson was astonished and tackled Heron about it. Later I had a talk with Heron about things generally.

---

[*] Sir Arthur Peterson was permanent secretary of the Home Office.

[†] Conrad Heron was permanent secretary of the Department of Employment. He had spent virtually his whole career dealing with industrial relations, on which he was an acknowledged expert. Normally we got on well together and, although I thought then – and still do – that the line he took on the miners' dispute was mistaken, there was no need for me to have so fierce an argument with him. Feelings were running high at the time.

This depressed me beyond measure. Heron showed all the anti-union venom which I had so disliked in many people in the Department of Employment. He said the miners were panicking and on the run and that we must now stand firm and 'see it through'. He has absolutely no idea of the damage which the three-day week will do to industry or to industrial relations. No wonder Heath goes wrong if he gets advice from someone who sees relations with the miners in terms of tactics and game plans.

Tuesday 20 December 1973

Lunched with William Rees Mogg.* I had not met him before and liked him more than I expected. A bit pompous and serious-minded but not at all conceited or show-off. He regards the present gloomy mood as rather exaggerated and said that so far as the medium term is concerned he is an optimist. That is all very well, as I pointed out, provided we get as far as the medium term. He showed some interest in tomorrow's Neddy meeting but is not really interested, I think, in trade unions or industrial relations. For a man in his position he seems curiously detached.

At 4.30 I went across to the Treasury to see Douglas Allen. He was at his best and wisest, I thought. He repeated that nothing on earth would induce Ted to give the miners anything over and above Phase 3. He didn't let on whether he agreed with this policy or not but he did say that if the government intended to stand firm there might be a long struggle and it would be best if ministers tried to lower the temperature rather than raise it in public statements after the Neddy meeting.

Frank Figgures was waiting in my room when I got back from the Treasury. He was clear that the miners would not settle within Phase

---

* Editor of the *Times*.

3 – the only question therefore was whether the government should amend the pay code to accommodate them or use the escape clause in the Counter-Inflation Act (for which I was largely responsible) which allows the secretary of state to override the pay code in exceptional cases.*

Frank's view of the situation is more or less identical to mine. He thinks that in any trial of strength with the government the miners will win and that we need to settle their claim as soon as possible, so that we can deal as a reasonably united country with the problems arising from the oil price rise.

Just after Frank had left Len Murray came. He seemed to want to unburden himself. He said that one of four things could happen tomorrow. The government could agree to drop the three-day week; they could refuse to listen to the TUC; they could postpone the introduction of the three-day week; or they could say, 'All right, what's the deal?' The TUC delegation would be listening hard to see whether the PM slammed the door on any of these options.

Murray said that opinion in the TUC had swung violently in the last few days in favour of action to defer or get rid of the three-day week. Murray said we should try to keep the Neddy meeting going through the day; he would like it to go on after dinner. I deduced from this that he is very anxious to do some kind of deal with the government. I don't think he knows what sort of deal is possible but he made it clear that the TUC leaders understand the problems created by the oil price rise and will 'try to find a formula' if the government shows any sign that this would interest them.

---

* As a senior official in the Treasury I was closely concerned with preparing the counter-inflation legislation introduced in 1972. I advised ministers not to make it so inflexible that, in the event of a serious industrial dispute, they could find themselves caught up in a situation from which there was no practicable exit. This advice was not welcome but in the end it was accepted, and the legislation was drafted accordingly.

At about 7 p.m. Murray and I went on to the NIESR party. Virtually everyone I spoke to wished me luck at tomorrow's Neddy meeting. Everyone wants it to succeed.

Friday 21 December 1973

An unbelievably depressing day.

It began badly for me because the lifts were out of action due to power cuts and I had to run down fifteen flights of stairs to welcome the PM at the door of the building. He was preceded by Tony Barber who greeted me very warmly – perhaps to show photographers that the incident at the last council meeting had left no ill will between us. There was a small crowd in the street demonstrating in support of the Shrewsbury builders who have been prosecuted for illegal picketing. Inside there was a group of office workers who clapped Heath as he walked through the lobby.

The meeting began promptly. Heath said a few words of introduction in which he referred to the fact that we were facing a number of different problems, partly due to industrial action and partly to the Arabs. He then gave me a very half-hearted invitation to introduce my paper which he clearly expected me to decline.

I decided not to be put off by this and spoke as I had planned for about five minutes. I stressed the need for us to get down urgently to the difficult job of analysing the changes which the new oil prospects would give rise to here, so that we could maximise the undoubted advantages we had over our main competitors through our coal and oil reserves. As far as I could tell this went down quite well and even Heath grunted approvingly.

We then had a couple of hours or so on the three-day week. The unions pressed the CBI on their attitude and for a long time the discussion consisted of a dialogue between the TUC and the CBI, with the government remaining silent. As a result the NEDC came to life in a way it hasn't often done and for the second meeting running one felt it was doing the job for which it was really created. About 11.30 or so Ted Heath intervened. He spoke too long and too forcefully, dominating the meeting in a way which seemed to me counter-productive. He took a fairly hard line, making it clear that the three-day week was all the miners' fault and that the government had a responsibility to see that industry did not grind to a halt for lack of power, as happened in 1972.

The discussion lasted until lunch and remained amicable. About 12.15 I was handed a note, which I read out, saying that the NCB–NUM meeting had ended five minutes ago and that they were making a joint approach to the Pay Board.

The PM had to go back briefly to No. 10. So we had half an hour or so for drinks in my room, in the course of which most people agreed that after lunch we should get on to the longer-term problems posed by the oil crisis. Ted got back just before 1.30 and we all went down for lunch, except for Conrad Heron, who left to keep in touch with the miners' negotiations. I had reserved a table for eight to which I asked the PM, Tony Barber, Sidney Greene and Len Murray, Michael Clapham and Campbell Adamson and Eric Roll. The PM, Murray, Roll and I talked together for most of the meal – with Eric working hard to keep the conversation light and interesting. In fact it was all quite enjoyable and though Murray was a bit tense, Ted was agreeable and (for him) easy. Over coffee he had a long talk with Sidney Greene.

After lunch I took Ted into my room (with Nick Stuart, his private secretary) and said I would like a couple of minutes' talk alone. I said I didn't know what he wanted to get out of today's meeting but in my view he had a chance to pull off the accommodation with the unions which he had tried so hard to get a couple of years ago. I reminded him of a conversation we had shortly after I took over as DG in which I said that I wholeheartedly supported his attempt to reach an accommodation and that, though I should guard Neddy's independence jealously, he could count on me to help in this.

Heath asked me why I thought he had this opportunity today. I said that I had talked to all the union people on Neddy recently and that they were more willing than I had ever known them to reach an agreement with the government. No doubt some of his advisers would say that this showed that the miners were panicking and would urge him to stand firm but I thought the opportunity was too good to lose. Heath asked what the 'agreement' would cover. I said that it would not include an undertaking that other unions would hold back if the miners got special treatment (since this would not be worth anything) but that I thought, if he showed his old patience, he could get from the TUC a worthwhile statement publicly recognising that the oil crisis made the need to control wage inflation even greater than before.

At this point Barber walked in, closely followed by Whitelaw. I didn't think it worth pursuing the conversation as Heath had clearly registered it – so I left them together. They stayed closeted together for the next twenty minutes or more while the others waited in the council room. About 3 p.m. they came out. Whitelaw went back to the Department of Employment and the others came back to the council. In the interval Murray and I agreed we should aim for an adjournment about 5 p.m.

The afternoon session was a very depressing experience. We had a desultory discussion of the long term for an hour or so, with myself and others trying hard to keep it going against the obvious lack of interest of ministers and most of the trade union people. Eventually Hugh Scanlon asked the PM when he expected to get news of the miners' negotiations. Heath said he would find out and shortly afterwards he read out a note I had received saying that negotiations had been suspended and would be renewed next Thursday.

Discussion then returned to the three-day week. Sidney Greene argued strongly for a postponement – if only until after Thursday's meeting between the NCB and NUM. But Heath was resolutely opposed to this and so were the CBI. It was clear that Heath had put the shutters up.

At my prompting we then adjourned for a drink in my room (about 5.15 p.m.) to meet the unions' request for more information about the coal negotiations. As we left the room I said my office would check up on the state of play but the PM snapped at me that he would do the checking up. 'Neddy should not get involved in industrial disputes,' he said. 'I always said it was a mistake to have this meeting.' From then on he was very tense and irritable. During the adjournment everyone hung around feeling miserable and trying to think of some way to avert the breakdown.

Eric Roll spoke to the PM, urging him to make some conciliatory statement which would enable the meeting to issue some kind of agreed communiqué on the lines that 'members of the council would hold themselves on call to meet as soon as the outcome of the miners' negotiations was known'. But Heath went back into his room for a further talk with Barber and Peter Walker.

Eventually Heath re-emerged and the council resumed. He reported briefly that the NCB–NUM negotiations had been adjourned so that both sides could consider a letter from the Pay Board. He then looked at the TUC and CBI, who both agreed we should end the meeting.

There followed a longish talk about the next meeting and what should be said to the Press. I tried to get the council to meet on 2 January but no one would have this and Hugh Scanlon said that if the three-day week were put into effect the trade union members might not be willing to attend the regular Neddy meeting on 9 January. As to the Press, I said there were three alternatives: I could report the proceedings in the normal way; or the three parties could give press briefings together or separately on our premises; or they could do this on their own premises. I said that of the three the last was much the worst.

The PM said (as I knew he would) that he wanted to see the Press himself and it was agreed that he should do it in our building and that Len and Campbell would give separate briefings immediately after he had finished.

I took him down and introduced him to the Press. He spoke quietly though still tensely. At one point he was asked whether the government and NEDO now took the same view about our economic prospects and if so what that view was. (The journalist who asked the question was the *Daily Telegraph* man who had caused all the stir after the last Neddy meeting.) Heath gave a long and somewhat involved answer in which he made no attempt to criticise the NEDO view or me, even by implication.

I saw Heath out and introduced Murray and Adamson in turn. I then went back to my room and had a drink with Lucas* and others who were left. I felt very tired and unutterably depressed. It is a dreadful thing to sit and watch a country slide into chaos, through the obstinacy of a few individuals, and be powerless to stop it even in a central position like mine.

I cannot believe that the miners will settle next Thursday and I am sure that the three-day week will bring greater chaos more quickly than ministers realise. It will also cause great bitterness and will mean that we face the tremendous problems which the oil crisis will bring as a deeply divided country. I have been forced today to revise my opinion of Heath, whom I have hitherto greatly admired despite his obvious faults. I now think that he is behaving irresponsibly – the

---

* Chris Lucas was an unorthodox Treasury official who had been seconded to NEDO as secretary of the council. He was wholly committed to Neddy and seemed to share my ambivalent feelings about his parent department.

miners will get a settlement outside Phase 3 in the end and even if they don't, the damage done by the three-day week will outweigh the temporary victory over the militants. Heath thinks he is fighting for a great principle – but the fact is he can't see the wood (i.e. the enormous national problem created by the oil crisis) for the trees (i.e. Mick McGahey* and co. in the NUM).

Once again, on a bad day, Sidney Greene is the man who stands out in retrospect as the best.

Sunday 23 December 1973

A long article in the *Sunday Times* on 'how Heath was forced to order the three-day week'. It is critical of Walker and Barber and has a piece about me. 'Barber', it says, 'took the exceptional step of in effect rebuking McIntosh' after the Neddy meeting on 5 December. The effect, as with most of these stories, is to make Barber look foolish.

Monday 24 December 1973

The *Times* has a leader called 'How deep goes the crisis?' It ends with these words: 'In the years immediately ahead society in Great Britain may well be subjected to strains more structural than those with which the nation has been preoccupied in the recent past. The response of the government will have to be one that pays close attention to those institutions and policies which serve to give the nation cohesion and which help to contain within a framework of civil peace and economic order the conflicting interests and assertions that all societies always exhibit.' Perhaps my lunch with Rees-Mogg had some effect after all.

---

* The Communist vice-president of the NUM.

Thursday 27 December 1973

Stayed down at Throwley.* Heard on the radio that the NCB–NUM talks have been adjourned till 2 January. Ken Johnson was evidently called in to elucidate the Pay Board's interpretation of the code relating to wash-and-brush-up time.[†]

We shall now have to wait and see – and I don't think we shall be able to judge until after 2 January whether our Neddy meeting on 9 January will go ahead or not.

I may be overpessimistic but I still do not rate the chances of an agreement within Phase 3 very high. Frank Figgures's message to me on 21 December was that it was going to be very difficult to get much money out of the wash-and-brush-up business; and in any case I would guess that the militants are going to stick to their earlier line – 'You can have Phase 3 and no coal, or coal and no Phase 3, but you can't have both Phase 3 and coal.' The news we heard at Christmas of the doubling of the price of oil will have strengthened the miners' hand considerably and I am sure they realise this. But of course there may be something going on behind the scenes which I don't know about yet.

Friday 28 December 1973

Motored to London. Heard on the radio that the NCB and NUM were to meet today 'to clarify certain matters'. There was criticism in this morning's papers of the decision to adjourn the talks until 2 January. I imagine that Heath blew up and pressurised the Coal

---

* Our country house, near Canterbury.

† A suggestion had been made that, in order to increase miners' pay without breaking the Pay Code, they should be paid for time spent cleaning up after their shifts and not simply for time spent underground. This was known as 'wash-and-brush-up time'. Johnson was deputy chairman of the Pay Board.

Board into getting the talks going again earlier. But Mick McGahey had already gone to Scotland and when Gormley and Daly* spoke after today's talks they did not sound optimistic.

I read today the speech which Roy made in the House at the end of the economic debate on 19 December. It is a very powerful speech, one of the best he has ever made, I should think. Roy referred to the fact that the Chancellor had 'petulantly and publicly rebuked the DG of NEDO for daring to suggest that the 3½ per cent growth target for next year was no longer valid'. He also said, 'What is required is neither an imposed solution nor an open hand at the till. One alternative to reaching a settlement with the miners is paralysis. The task of statesmanship is to reach a settlement but to do it in a way which opens no floodgates.' These last words are almost exactly the ones I used when I spoke to Roy on 16 December. Perhaps my talk had some influence on him!

Monday 31 December 1973

Throwley. Len Murray telephoned to ask what I thought about the prospects for the Neddy meeting on 9 January. He said he had been greatly surprised to hear Sidney Greene suggest that the TUC members might not necessarily attend the next meeting. (Actually, I believe that Greene said something to this effect only to stop Hugh Scanlon or Jack Jones saying something more definite from which it would have been difficult to climb back.) I said that I thought it particularly important to hold the meeting on 9 January as planned – one of Neddy's principal advantages had always been that the three parties came to meetings as a matter of course, however bad their relations in public might be at the time. After some discussion we

---

* Joe Gormley and Lawrence Daly, respectively president and general secretary of the NUM.

agreed on a suggestion of mine that the agenda should be in three parts: the current situation, latest developments on the oil front and a paper from the office on the Posner exercise (this is a study, which I have asked Michael Posner* to take charge of, on the implications for British industry of the permanent increase in the price of oil and its reduced availability). Murray agreed with me that the prospects of an early settlement with the miners did not look good. He said it was difficult to get much out of Gormley – he was right up at one moment and right down at the next.

I later spoke to Lucien Wigdor at the CBI, who said they would certainly want the meeting on 9 January to take place and agreed with my suggested agenda. Let us hope that I get an equally helpful reaction from the government. Radio reports of speeches by Jim Prior† and Peter Walker suggest that the government are seeking to inflame public opinion against the miners and to a lesser extent against the unions generally. To my mind ministers are behaving with a frightening lack of responsibility.

One of yesterday's papers had a report that there had been strong disagreement in the Cabinet on the day before the PM announced the three-day week. It would be surprising if the cracks did not begin to show more sharply from now on. My guess is that within the next couple of weeks Enoch Powell will come out publicly in favour of a negotiated settlement with the miners outside the limits of Phase 3.

Wednesday 2 January 1974

I phoned Douglas Allen and told him of my talks with Murray and Wigdor about the meeting on 9 January. Len Murray then phoned to say that, though his own side might not be entirely happy with my

---

* A Fellow of Pembroke College, Cambridge.
† Lord President and leader of the House of Commons.

suggestions, he was and he hoped I would go ahead.

I then phoned Tony Barber, who asked me to go over to the Treasury to see him and Douglas Allen at about 5.30. I told him that the others all seemed keen that the meeting on 9 January should take place and that I had agreed a three-item agenda with them: first, the current situation; secondly, the latest developments on the oil front; and thirdly, our proposed longer-term study. Barber wanted to cut out the first item. He said it would simply provide the TUC with a platform and in any case the only developments since the previous meeting were the new decisions about the supply and price of oil. I said that the TUC would not agree with this and I didn't think the CBI would either. For them the most important new development was the introduction of the three-day week and the TUC would certainly want to discuss its operation. Barber accepted this but said he didn't want Neddy to become too mixed up with short-term developments – the discussions at the last meeting had been very difficult, partly because it was too much concerned with the TUC's complaints about the three-day week. The decision to maintain the three-day week was now 'policy' and there was no point in Neddy discussing it. I said that the discussion on 21 December had been difficult because the situation was difficult and serious. While I agreed that Neddy should not normally concentrate on the short term, I thought it was quite right in our present state of national emergency that the council should discuss the immediate situation. I added that I had tried on 21 December to get the council to consider some longer-term issues but that I had got no support from any of the three parties. I had found the meeting infinitely depressing.

After some more talk I agreed to lump the first two items under one umbrella heading. We shall do one paper instead of two but it will cover both the first two items on my suggested agenda. Barber seemed happy with this.

For the first time I found myself quite out of sympathy with Tony Barber. The vindictive way in which he spoke of the trade unions – the miners and the TUC – belonged to a different world from the one which I, and I would think most moderate people, inhabit.

Friday 4 January 1974

Peter Parker* telephoned. He is appearing with David Basnett on the *Money Programme* and asked if I would also be on it. I said I had been asked but had ducked it because I had to keep my lines reasonably clear with all my members if I was to be of any use and I should find it difficult to appear on TV and not criticise the government just now. Peter agreed and said that clearly anything I could do would have to be done behind the scenes. He himself was in great difficulty as he doesn't agree with the CBI line – he thinks the consequences of the three-day week will be quite intolerable for industry. He believes that the miners' claim should be settled and followed by a Phase 4, which should be worked out by some Council of Industry-type body which should sit continuously.

Later I spoke to Len Murray, who said he could see no possibility of movement and couldn't at present see what Neddy or the TUC could do to improve matters. It had just been announced that Willie Whitelaw was to see the miners' executive next Wednesday. Murray said that he hoped Whitelaw would have something to offer them – if he simply appealed to them to settle within Phase 3 in the national interest he would not get very far. He added that this had been the trouble at the Neddy meeting on 21 December. The PM should not have agreed to chair the meeting if he had nothing to give.

Finally I rang Roger Dawe, Whitelaw's private secretary. He said

---

* A lively, left-leaning businessman who was chairman of the Rockware group and of the Clothing EDC. In 1976 he succeeded Richard Marsh as chairman of British Rail.

that Whitelaw's discussions with the miners would unfortunately clash with our next Neddy meeting. He did not expect anything to come from the discussions – it was a matter of going through the motions.

Sunday 6 January 1974

Roy and Jennifer came to spend the weekend with us. We had some long talks about the industrial and political situation. I outlined my views of the industrial situation, which were briefly:

- that the miners would not settle within Phase 3;
- that they would continue the overtime ban and perhaps tighten it up but would not go on strike;
- that other unions would not be particularly militant but that the mood would become more and more sullen as the three-day week continued;
- that within a couple of weeks or so management opinion would begin to move strongly in favour of a miners' settlement to end the three-day week.

Roy said he found the political situation very difficult to predict. He agreed with my guess, which is that criticism of Heath within the Conservative Party will grow and the divisions in the Cabinet will increase; and that if Heath thinks this might lead to pressure to replace him as leader he will call a general election. He may in any case be forced to do this if he gets into a completely blind alley over the miners. Roy thought that if Heath called an election now the press would be solidly anti-Labour but that this would change if an election were delayed.

I predicted that Enoch Powell would make a strong speech within the next ten days advocating a settlement with the miners outside Phase 3.

Monday 7 January 1974

Douglas Allen spoke to me about the Neddy meeting. He said that ministers were not happy about the idea of holding it but he thought he had persuaded them to do so. He then said in a menacing tone that 'if the TUC used the meeting for political purposes it would be the last NEDC meeting to be held'. This is, of course, rubbish. Both the tone and content of Douglas's remarks were uncharacteristic of him – it looks as thought the strain is beginning to tell on him too.

Tuesday 8 January 1974

In the evening I phoned Len Murray. I said that somebody had to introduce some mobility into the situation – otherwise the various parties would go on glowering at one another from their trenches until the country came to a stop. It seemed clear that neither the CBI nor the government would move, so the TUC would have to. My objective was to find a way in which the three-day week (which would do very serious damage to the country if it lasted for any length of time) could be brought to an end honourably and without stoking up inflation unduly. Len listened carefully and said he didn't know how the meeting of his Economic Committee would go tomorrow – but couldn't the CBI join the TUC in asking for the miners to be made an exception?

I said that he couldn't expect Campbell Adamson to say anything which would imply a willingness on the part of the CBI to see Phase 3 breached but that short of that I thought Campbell would be willing (as I was) to say anything he could at NEDC which would make it easier for the TUC to react positively.

I had incidentally had a talk with Campbell Adamson on 7 January. At this he had told me that he wanted the CBI to keep absolutely quiet about the miners' dispute for the next two weeks and added that they would in no circumstances encourage a breach of Phase 3 'at this stage'. I accepted this but said that I had been disappointed at the way in which the CBI had almost instantaneously closed ranks with the government against the TUC at the meeting on 21 December under the PM's chairmanship. This had contrasted sharply with the CBI's approach at the earlier meeting where Campbell had taken a very constructive line and by this had helped the TUC to do the same.

Campbell accepted this a little ruefully and said he was very conscious of what was happening at the time. But the CBI had felt they had no alternative as they had been urging the government to introduce the three-day week to conserve supplies of power.

This evening Enoch Powell made a speech in which he violently attacked the government's incomes policy.

Wednesday 9 January 1974

I spent all morning preparing my notes for introducing our paper at the council meeting. The great thing is to get the ending right so that if the CBI or TUC are ready to make a move they can pick up naturally something I have referred to in my opening remarks.

I went home for lunch and in the middle of it Len Murray rang. He told me – strictly for my own information – that the TUC would be making a statement at the Neddy meeting to the effect that if the miners were given an increase outside Phase 3, other unions would not pray it in aid in their negotiations. I said this sounded excellent. Len said it wasn't exactly excellent but it might provide a piece of cotton for people to pull and that, if they did, it might turn out to have a three-inch rope on the end of it. He said it would be particularly helpful if the CBI could say something which would enable the TUC to make their statement naturally. Len added that the decision to make it was unanimous and that Jones and Scanlon were completely committed to it.

I tracked down Campbell Adamson at the London Chamber of Commerce and left a message asking him to look in on me before the council meeting. When he did so I told him that Len had been in touch with me since his Economic Committee meeting and that it looked as though there might be some possibility of movement by the TUC. I didn't tell him what form it would take but suggested that it might help if he were to say something, before the TUC came in, about the CBI's worries that high settlements in one industry could lead to a burst of inflationary settlements in other industries. In passing Campbell congratulated me on the close relationship which I had built up with Len Murray. He thought this was very helpful.

I thought seriously whether I should phone Douglas Allen to let him know of the new development but came to the conclusion it was too big a risk to take. I suspect the government are so dug in that they would try to stifle any TUC initiative at birth if they heard of it in advance. When Douglas spoke to me yesterday on the telephone he said that if the TUC used today's meeting for political propaganda it would be Neddy's last meeting. I do not believe this for a moment – the government is in no position to do without Neddy in this time of national crisis and strife. But the conversation worried me because it seemed to indicate that Douglas has become infected with the neurotic attitude which Barber and others are now showing towards the TUC.

After I had seen Campbell and the others started to arrive for the council meeting, Basnett looked in. He said he hoped the meeting would go on for at least 2½ hours.

When the council began I gave a longish introduction to our paper on the effect of the three-day week. The gist of it was that if three-day working lasted only until the end of January the consequences would be manageable and recovery reasonably quick; but that if it continued into February we should run into problems of an altogether different order and that the effects on output, exports and eventual recovery would get quickly and cumulatively worse.

Len Murray and Campbell Adamson both agreed with our analysis. Campbell broadened the discussion out a bit with a reference to the miners and Phase 3. Sidney Greene then came in with the TUC statement which Len Murray had told me about. He said that if the government made a settlement with the miners possible (i.e. outside Phase 3) the TUC *and the trade union movement* would not use this in other negotiations or quote it as an excuse for other exceptional settlements. He said they were willing to make this offer in order to get the miners' dispute out of the way and so bring three-day working to an end. After a pause in which most of us held our breath, Barber said, 'Does this mean that the TUC is ready to agree to a tripartite incomes policy with statutory back-up powers for groups which don't conform?' I could hardly believe my ears when I heard this tendentious question and the hostile tone in which it was asked. But Sidney, imperturbable as ever, simply repeated the TUC assurance.

There then followed a lively discussion in which all the TUC team spoke up in favour of their offer. In the course of it Sidney said two things which seemed significant to me. One was that the TUC were 'against inflation and wanted to control it'; the other was that unions would 'instruct their negotiators to abide by the TUC assurance'. Barber intervened three or four times – each time in a negative and hostile tone. He said several times that HMG could not in any circumstances contemplate any settlement outside Phase 3. The CBI team mostly sat silent – except for Dick Marsh, who tried to probe the TUC offer to see what it really meant, their interventions were unconstructive.

I imagine that most people round the table – and in the back row* – were as startled as I was at the Chancellor's brusque rejection of the offer. One would have expected him to be more adroit, however much he disliked it. Sidney Greene pressed him to consider it seriously. Barber said he would report it to Willie Whitelaw, to which Greene said, 'That's not good enough; you should report it to yourself and to Ted because I reckon if you two don't agree it then it won't be agreed and if you do it will.' Barber simply repeated that it would be wrong to think that the government would be prepared to settle any individual case outside Phase 3. Hugh Scanlon said that in that case the TUC might well decide to withdraw their offer.

At this stage I came to the conclusion that if someone didn't try to rescue it the TUC offer might founder. So I intervened as follows. I said the DG of NEDO was the last person to want to get involved in an individual dispute. However, the afternoon's discussion had flowed from a statement by myself about the three-day week which showed how serious the consequences for the economy would be if it were prolonged. We must also bear in mind that the brunt would be borne not by people like ourselves but by weekly paid manual workers. The TUC had made a statement which seemed to me to be very important – like all such statements it was no doubt imperfect but it might provide a basis on which people could build. It was important to record accurately what the TUC had said and subject to correction now I would record that:

- the TUC team had given an assurance (in the terms used by Sidney) on behalf of the General Council and the trade union movement and had said that negotiators would be instructed to abide by it;

---

* Senior officials from the Treasury and other government departments, and from the CBI and TUC, attended NEDC meetings, though they did not take part in the discussions.

- the TUC had recognised the need to check inflation;
- they had made no request that the government should repeal the Counter-Inflation Act or amend the pay code.

Silence followed, so after a moment I raised the question of what should be said to the Press. After some discussion we adjourned.

In the event I held a press conference in the council chamber in the normal way. I made a full introductory statement and then said that in view of the nature of the TUC assurance and the discussion on it I thought the press should hear from the three parties about it. Murray, Adamson and Barber then spoke in that order. We then took questions, addressed to all or any of them, together. A much better way of proceeding than the entirely separate statements to the press on 21 December.

Thursday 10 January 1974

I spoke to Monty Finniston by telephone. He said that Barber should not have rejected the TUC's offer outright – it was a great mistake to be so flat footed about it even if he had no intention of taking it seriously. Monty said that after the meeting Hugh Scanlon had told him that, although he could never say this publicly, it was clear that in the present economic climate trade unions other than the miners would have to settle within Phase 3. I am sure this is right – none of them will have the industrial power this winter to do anything else.

I then spoke to John Partridge. He said that he didn't think the TUC offer meant much and that the Chancellor had no real alternative yesterday to rejecting it as he did. John said he had met Barber at dinner after the council and that Barber had said that he thought the TUC had put both himself and me in a very difficult position at the council meeting, through their failure to give any advance warning of their offer. I said it was clear that there had been very little pre-planning and that the proposal to make the offer had emerged for the first time during the TUC Economic Committee yesterday morning.

John sees no alternative to 'sticking it out' with the miners. He evidently had hoped that the TUC would 'lean on' the miners but he agreed with me that perhaps this was never really on (as I am sure it was not).

I gave Frank Figgures an account of the meeting. He said the offer was a very important one which should not have been rejected and that I ought to go and see the PM and Whitelaw right away. I said this could do more harm than good – I was clearly suspect in government quarters because they knew or guessed that I disagreed with Heath's strategy. Frank demurred and rang back later to say I ought to circulate to ministers or permanent secretaries the expanded version of the TUC offer which I had given at the end of the meeting.

I had lunch at the BBC with the team who produce and run the *Money Programme*. They were very keen that I should appear this week and subsequently but I said that I was sure this would destroy any usefulness I might have just now, since it would be almost impossible to discuss the present situation without fouling up my relationship with one or other of the parties on Neddy. They accepted this quite readily.

I then went down to the House of Commons, expecting to hear Willie Whitelaw and Reg Prentice.* As I arrived the PM was answering a question from Harold Wilson about the TUC suggestion at Neddy and Barber's rejection of it. In the course of this he said he had invited the TUC to see him at No 10 tonight. So I hurried back to the office and made sure that we finished the

---

* Labour MP for East Ham North and opposition spokesman on employment.

minutes of the Neddy meeting in time for those concerned to have them before this evening's meeting at No 10.

In the course of the afternoon I spoke to Dick Marsh. He took the same view of yesterday's proceedings as Monty Finniston. He also said that in conversation with Farrimond, the British Rail negotiator, Sidney Greene had expressed himself as deeply disturbed and rather bitter about Barber's rejection of the TUC offer. Marsh thought that this was a genuine expression of opinion and not simply said for passing on to ministers. I thanked Marsh for being the first person at the Neddy meeting to acknowledge the fact that the TUC offer was new and important. He said the offer was partly a public relations exercise but also reflected a genuine fear of what might happen if the three-day week went on too long.

The Bond-Williams came to dinner. Noel said that the board of the Delta Metal Company, of which he is a member, had met that day to consider the situation. They thought that the outlook was unacceptable; while they themselves were financially strong and liquid, their customers were beginning to feel the strain and would be in real trouble if the three-day week did not end soon.

Friday 11 January 1974

I rang Norman Willis, who has just been appointed assistant general secretary of the TUC,* to ask him how the talk at No 10 had gone. He said that the mood had been sombre. Ministers seemed prepared to listen and there was no atmosphere of confrontation. The TUC team spoke of what they could do as general secretaries of their own unions and Barber was led to say that he accepted that they could deliver the goods on the promise they had made. After some time an adjournment was proposed and the government team stayed out for

---

* Willis would go on to succeed Len Murray as general secretary in 1984.

30–40 minutes. When they came back they suggested that the talks should be resumed on Monday and that there might be some unpublicised conversations in between.

Willis added that the TUC people were getting bitter about the CBI attitude and there was consequently no prospect of tripartite talks at the present time. The bitterness was such that it might leave a 'scar' on TUC–CBI relations.

I spoke to a number of other people during the day. David Basnett said that he sees a chink of light as a result of the meeting at No 10. He said he thought the TUC had the government over a barrel.

Douglas Allen, who was much less tense than when I last spoke to him, said he was a little more optimistic after last night's meeting than he had been after NEDC. The TUC would not be drawn last night to offer anything very firm and refused to commit themselves not to claim increases outside Phase 3. But they had implied that they would use their influence to prevent settlements being made outside Phase 3. The government line was still that the TUC offer was no good. Ministers were clearly afraid that if the miners smelled the possibility of a settlement outside Phase 3 the next move might be a meeting between the PM and the TUC plus the NUM executive.

William Armstrong was very delphic. I gave him some account of the Neddy meeting. I said I thought the TUC's offer was important, even though their motives were undoubtedly mixed, and that I had found Sidney's use of the word 'instruct' most interesting. It is not a word you often hear from trade union mouths these days. I also thought the fact that the TUC meeting of presidents and general secretaries of trade unions was to take place next Wednesday provided an important opportunity to get the leaders of the trade union movement to enter into some collective commitment. I doubted if they could publicly agree to abide by Phase 3 but I thought they could 'take note' of a statement by the government that the miners were the only group whom ministers might be willing to exempt from the provisions of Phase 3.

Sidney Greene had told Armstrong that the meeting had not gone too badly last night. Sidney thought the government would be silly not to take up the TUC offer – if it didn't work they could blame the TUC and call an election, if it did work they could take the credit for extracting it from the TUC. He added that he hoped it would be possible to stave off a special congress, which would be bound to include a lot of left-wingers and wild men.

I lunched with Geoffrey Gilbertson* at the Cavalry Club. He told me that the Pay Board (of which he is a member) had considered a draft of their report on wage relativities earlier in the week.† The newspapers are all saying – I would guess on briefing from ministers – that it may provide the way out of the impasse with the miners. Geoffrey said they are hoping to let Whitelaw have it about the end of next week.

Anthony Rawlinson, our Treasury representative in Washington, called. We had a long talk by candlelight about the situation. He told me that everyone he had spoken to in the (British) Treasury was very gloomy and expected the three-day week to go on for another six weeks or so.

Saturday 12 January 1974

The *Observer* wanted me to comment on a report they have commissioned on the three-day week. The report is good and I agreed to comment provided they kept me out of political

---

* General manager of ICI and later chairman of the Shipbuilding EDC.
† The Pay Board had been asked to produce a report analysing the relative positions held by different groups of workers in the league table of wages over recent years. It was expected to show that the miners had consistently held a position at or very near the top.

controversy. I spoke to Patrick Jenkin, who had also been asked to comment. I congratulated him on his appointment as Minister for Energy* and said that I hoped that despite the present troubles and my bruised relations with Barber, we could co-operate. He thanked me for this. He thinks the country is behind the government in their stand against the miners. He said Heath believes that if the miners can be convinced that they have no chance of getting an increase beyond Phase 3 they will cut their losses and agree to talk about pensions, a long-term review of the coal industry etc. I said I thought this was a gamble but time would show whether he was right. I also said that I thought it would be very helpful if he could avoid saying or doing anything just now which would make it more difficult for the TUC to co-operate with the new Energy Department after the present shambles was over (especially bearing in mind that Peter Carrington, the new secretary of state, was also chairman of the Tory Party). Patrick fully accepted this.

Sunday 13 January 1974

The newspapers are full of talk about an election on 7 February – pretty clearly inspired by ministers.

Geoffrey Howe† made a very hard-line speech about the TUC offer but has softened it a bit today after an attack by Wilson. Even if ministers have no intention of moving on Phase 3 why don't they welcome the TUC offer, point out unaggressively that it would need a good deal of tightening up before it could be accepted and say that they will be working with the TUC to see how far this can be done when they meet tomorrow? The fact that they all adopt this rather

---

* He was the minister who encouraged us to clean our teeth in the dark in order to save electricity.
† Sir Geoffrey Howe was Minister for Trade and Consumer Affairs.

strident approach confirms my opinion that their minds are closed and that the TUC initiative was simply an embarrassment to them.

The only man in public life I have spoken to today is Roger Moate, who had to come back from a skiing holiday in Davos because of the recall of Parliament. He says it would look like a cheat to hold the election before the new register comes into force on 16 February. He also said that the 1922 Committee was divided 50-50 on whether there should be an early election or not.

Hugh Scanlon is reported on the radio as having said in public that the AUEW will not press its claim beyond the limits of Phase 3 – that should put the cat among the pigeons.

Tuesday 15 January 1974

Len Murray told me that he had found last night's (5½-hour) meeting at No. 10 a puzzling occasion. The TUC team had expected to hear a high moral tone from ministers about the iniquity of the miners and so on but it hadn't been like that. Whitelaw had been actively exploring the possibility of a deal, the PM had shown some interest in one and Barber, while not questioning the TUC's good faith, had taken a thoroughly negative line.

The discussion had turned on the TUC's capacity to deliver and the level at which the miners might agree to settle. On the first point the TUC had given an assurance that they would regard the miners not just as exceptional but as unique – in other words they would not ask the government to treat any other groups as special cases. On the second point, the TUC had hinted that they would be prepared to talk to the miners and take a view on what would be a reasonable level for them to settle at – but only if they had an assurance from the government that they would be prepared to use their powers under the Counter-Inflation Act to authorise a settlement with the miners outside Phase 3. Murray said that the TUC were not working any more on their offer – they would not try to find ways of strengthening it, though they would leave it on the table for the government to pick up if they wanted to. He said Heath had not given him the impression of a man who had finally closed the door on the TUC offer, though some of the TUC team thought he had. Meanwhile the TUC would hold their meeting with presidents and general secretaries of unions tomorrow. I got the impression that the TUC leaders would not try to hot things up at this meeting.

In the late afternoon I saw Douglas Allen. He said that he didn't think that Heath had yet finally made up his mind about an election. Jim Prior obviously wanted one as soon as possible because he thought the Tories had a better chance of winning one now than they would have later on – and it was said that Carrington took the same view. Barber seemed undecided – perhaps because he was worried about what might happen to sterling during an election campaign.

Douglas said that at one point during yesterday's discussion there had been an adjournment during which Heath and Armstrong had had a private talk with Len Murray and Sidney Greene. During this the government had expressed concern that the miners, if allowed to settle above Phase 3, might insist on getting their claim met in full. As Murray had told me earlier, he and Greene had suggested that they might sound the miners out on this but only if they got an assurance that ministers would be willing to settle outside Phase 3. Heath had not been willing to give this assurance and the talks had accordingly broken down on this point.

Douglas also said that, while ministers were prepared to accept that all the TUC team were sincere in saying they would deliver what they had promised, they noted that neither Jones nor Scanlon had said they would settle within Phase 3.*

---

* But see entry for 13 January 1974.

I said I thought that the TUC would not be willing to talk to the NUM about a settlement if ministers were not prepared to contemplate a settlement outside Phase 3: but that they would talk to them if they knew that a settlement outside Phase 3 was not ruled out. I also said that I thought that the TGWU and the AEUW would in practice settle their various negotiations within Phase 3, with the possible exception of the TGWU's tanker drivers. Ministers could talk to Frank Chapple to ascertain his intentions – my guess would be that the electricians would not want to press their power to the limit this year. This left ASLEF – and we both agreed that no one could tell what they would do. Douglas was inclined to think – as I am – that if the political will was there, there could probably be a settlement with the TUC: but even if his mind was not already closed to it, it would be very difficult for Heath to contemplate a breach of Phase 3 even for the miners.

I said I couldn't see how any government could successfully deal with the economic situation which would face us in the next few years against the background of the tensions caused by the miners' strike and the three-day week. If Heath were returned I didn't think he would last more than six to nine months as leader of the Conservative Party. Douglas said that there was no one other than Heath who could effectively lead the Conservative Party and the only effective politician on the other side (presumably Roy) would not be allowed to lead the Labour party. Ergo, we should have authoritarian rule.

Enoch Powell has made a speech saying that for Heath to call an election now would be fraudulent because he knows he would have to settle the miners' claim outside Phase 3 as soon as it was over.

Wednesday 16 January 1974

I gave a lunch for Geoffrey Gilbertson to meet Tom McIver and other shipbuilders for a discussion about the Shipbuilding EDC which I want Geoffrey to chair. As we were leaving I mentioned the suggestion Roy Mason* made yesterday that miners should be paid for all the time they were on coal board premises. Mason said this could be done within Phase 3 and might give the miners an extra £3.50 a week. Contrary to my expectations Gilbertson said that Mason's proposal would be within Phase 3 and that the Pay Board had put him on to it.

The TUC meeting of presidents and general secretaries seems to have gone off well. As expected, it gave the Economic Committee's proposals an overwhelming endorsement – quite a feather in Murray's cap.

I learned that Murray told Dominic Harrod, the BBC economics correspondent, that the way I introduced our paper at the last Neddy meeting (that is the one at which the TUC first made their 'offer') had been very helpful from his point of view. Good.

Thursday 17 and Friday 18 January 1974

I flew to Brussels in the morning. I went to the Economic and Social Committee of the EEC for a talk with Delfini, the director general. Then on to Michael Palliser's,† where I was staying the night. Michael is very gloomy about Europe, where almost everything seems to be at a standstill. He was very scathing about the performance of British ministers at EEC meetings. It appears that Alec Douglas-Home‡ is listened to with respect and that Joe Godber has earned a reputation as a tough negotiator who knows his subject. But the rest compare very unfavourably with their counterparts

---

* Labour MP for Barnsley. A former miner, he had been Minister of Power in 1968–69.
† Sir Michael Palliser was ambassador to the European Communities.
‡ Sir Alec Douglas-Home was Foreign Secretary.

from other countries. According to Michael, French ministers are much the best and streets ahead of ours.

He shared my gloom about the political situation at home. I told him about our last three Neddy meetings and how depressed I was when Heath 'put the shutters up' at the afternoon session of our pre-Christmas meeting. He said he could picture it exactly – he had more than once seen Heath (for whom he had great respect and even affection) do the same at meetings with foreign statesmen.

In the morning, Michael and I spent an hour with George Thomson.* George has had a very frustrating time recently trying to get his regional proposals through the Council of Ministers against strong German opposition. He is resolutely optimistic about the outcome. He maintained that there was no reason why other countries' attitudes should be influenced by the possibility of a general election in Britain – elections, he said, were held so often in a community of nine that one couldn't afford to hold up business until they were over. This overlooks the fact that one of the two main parties in Britain is committed to renegotiate the terms of our membership and Michael clearly thought George was being over-optimistic. George confirmed that the community was at present in poor shape. He said that it was not generally realised that the enlargement of the community, so far from being the end of a chapter, had meant that it must begin a whole series of long and difficult negotiations on such things as regional policy. This was bound to hold back progress for a time. He added that one could now see that enlargement had coincided with a watershed in German attitudes to the community and that this had made things much more difficult. Michael commented that our failure to build a solid

---

* One of the two British Commissioners of the EEC. He had been Commonwealth secretary and Chancellor of the Duchy of Lancaster in the second Wilson administration.

relationship with Germany in the last ten years had been a major mistake in our foreign policy and that we were now paying the price.

We then talked of home affairs. I said that the tragedy of the present situation was that the Labour Party was in such a parlous state that it didn't really offer a credible alternative government. George agreed with this. He thought that if Labour won the next election the internal strains would be so great as more or less to paralyse it. If the Labour Party lost he thought it would split, giving rise to a new Social Democratic Party. I said I couldn't see that this would help matters. The experience of the last ten years had shown that for Britain to be run successfully a measure of trade union co-operation was essential; but if the Labour Party split, the trade union movement would almost certainly side with the leftist part of it. George did not disagree.

Saturday 19 January 1974

I got back to find that the political and industrial situation had changed remarkably in the thirty-six hours I was away. After starting the week with the most gloomy forecasts – including a ridiculous story that restrictions on the domestic use of electricity would be enforced by spot checks by the police to see how many lights were on in private houses – the government is now talking of getting back to four- or five-day working almost immediately. The prospects of an early election, which seemed almost certain when I left for Brussels, have also receded and there is quite a lot of talk in the Sunday papers about Heath doing a deal with the TUC.

Roy told me he didn't think there would be an election now; Heath was like a pilot who reversed engines at the end of the runway – the passengers would take some persuading now that they should take off.

Monday 21 January 1974

The French government have decided to let the franc float. This has put the EEC in further disarray and it now seems to be in a really severe crisis.

I lunched with Anthony Frodsham of United Dominions Trust. He is concerned with financing North Sea oil and says people in the City have still not woken up to the amount of money which will be needed. UDT alone should be providing about £100 million a year – but his authority so far is for only £20 million.

In the evening I had my first meeting with the EDC chairmen. Twelve turned up, out of fifteen, and they stayed two hours, which is longer than usual, I am told. I opened with a longish bit about the national crisis and an account of our last three council meetings. I spoke very gloomily about the prospects and said the real question was whether we had the capacity and leadership to cope with the economic situation now facing us. I spoke of the need for activities which united rather than divided and of the need to reconstruct our economic policy. There was no disagreement – indeed a number of chairmen were even more pessimistic than me.

After the meeting we heard that the PM's talks with the TUC had come to nothing and the TUC's offer now seems to be dead.

I had a letter from David Howell – newly appointed Minister of State for Energy – saying he wants to keep in close touch with Neddy on the problems ahead.

Tuesday 22 January 1974

I spent the morning at the Peckham headquarters of the AUEW, where Hugh Scanlon had arranged for four of us from NEDO to meet his executive council. I had a private talk with Scanlon to begin with. He said that at the Downing Street meeting the previous day ministers had made it clear that they were not prepared to contemplate a settlement for the miners outside Phase 3. There had therefore been no discussion of how the TUC might improve their offer or make it more effective. Scanlon believes that ministers have never had any intention of making an exception for the miners outside Phase 3 and that they have simply been stringing the TUC along. He says that from his point of view this is very unfortunate. He has gone out on a limb to support the TUC initiative and his critics in the AUEW will be quick to say 'I told you so'. Scanlon said he saw no prospect whatsoever of the miners settling within Phase 3.

We went on to lunch at a restaurant in Dulwich. The whole executive was present and the occasion was very friendly and convivial. They are a varied lot with political opinions which cut right across one another. In this company Scanlon seems – and perhaps is – a middle-of-the-road character.

In the evening I went to the CBI, where John Davies* delivered a memorial lecture for Douglas Taylor on the future of industrial society. Articulate but not very profound – it was largely a hymn of praise to the professional manager and didn't seem to me to show much appreciation of the underlying forces at work in society now. Clapham, Partridge and others to whom I spoke were glum about the country's prospects.

Wednesday 23 January 1974

I lunched with Harold Watkinson at Cadbury Schweppes. He said he thought the government and management should now be prepared to take a positive and forward-looking line on worker

---

* Conservative MP for Knutsford. He had been Secretary of State for Trade and Industry in 1970–72 and before that director general of the CBI, with Douglas Taylor as his deputy.

participation as a means of helping us through what looks like being a very difficult industrial situation in the next few years. I think this is right.

At lunch Dominic Cadbury* was mildly critical of Heath but Watkinson defended him. He said he was playing for very high stakes. His aim was to isolate the miners in the hopes that this would lead them to settle within Phase 3. If on the other hand the NUM called a strike there would be an election and the Tories would get back for another five years.

Ken Clucas of the DTI, who was in the back row at our last council meeting, told me he admired my courage for summing up as I did at the meeting 'and so rescuing the TUC initiative'.

Thursday 24 January 1974

Had two good meetings in the office. The first was with Professor McGregor,† our new sociological adviser, who thinks there is now a real risk that political democracy will not survive in Britain. The second was with a group of economists and businessmen who are advising us on our study on the effects on industry of the changed energy prospects. They were extremely helpful – I think people are so sickened by what is happening to the country just now that they are only too delighted to be asked to play a constructive part for an independent outfit like ours.

At 6 p.m. I went to Congress House for a talk with Len Murray. It had been announced shortly before that the NUM had decided to ballot their members on strike action. Len was outwardly cheerful but thought the prospects were terrible. He said he was racking his brains to see if there was anything the TUC could now do, directly

---

* Chief executive of Cadbury Schweppes.
† Oliver McGregor, Professor of Social Institutions at the University of London.

or indirectly, to get us out of our present jam – but he could think of nothing. I said it was now clear that the PM was not prepared to contemplate a miners' settlement outside Phase 3 and that the NUM would not accept one within Phase 3. In these circumstances there was nothing anyone could do and as far as I could see there would have to be an election.

Friday 25 January 1974

I went to see Douglas Allen at the Treasury. His attitude to the crisis has changed. He is out of sympathy with government policy and says he is persona non grata with ministers because he has been telling them that if three-day working continues for any length of time the country may face collapse. According to Allen, ministers have no plan for getting out of the situation the country will be in if the miners vote in favour of a strike – unless, that is, they have already decided that they would have an election. He thinks the trouble is that none of them have any real understanding of economic matters, except perhaps Ted. Barber has no judgment and Whitelaw has not been getting good advice from his department, which doesn't know anything about economics and is emotionally committed to the Phase 3 rules on pay which are its own creation. He said that William Armstrong was taking a more active part again but that he is a tactician and not a strategist. John Hunt,* he says, tends to think, like all Cabinet Secretaries, that if the Cabinet are in favour of something it must, by definition, be right.

I said that his being persona non grata with ministers was the best news I had heard for a long time – up to now I had been afraid he

---

* Sir John Hunt had become Cabinet Secretary (in succession to Sir Burke Trend) the previous year. He went on to become one of the most respected holders of the post.

agreed with them. I said I thought the country really would begin to fall apart if we had a miners' strike now and if I could help Allen in any way to influence the government towards a more sensible policy I should be more than glad to do so. He said it was a great pity that Murray had sprung his initiative on everyone without warning at NEDC – if he (Allen) had known about it in advance he might have been able to persuade Barber to react more helpfully. I am afraid I doubt this, so I said nothing.

I went on to lunch with Dick Marsh, who was in good form. He told me a lot about his early life – apparently he had never intended to go into politics but had set his sights on the general secretaryship of NUPE of which he was an official. He said he was not really surprised about what was happening. He had thought for some time that the system would collapse before many years were out. He was totally disenchanted with politicians and the political system.

Marsh said that the current ASLEF dispute was entirely political. The union executive was in the hands of the communists, who were simply using industrial action to create chaos and bring down the system. But outside Southern Region they did not have much support. He also said that the government seemed to be in a state of chaos. Up to now he had always thought that however bad ministers were, the civil service machine could keep things from getting out of hand – but this was no longer true.

In the afternoon Kenneth Adams[*] came to see me about a conference at Windsor which he wants me to speak at. He said he could see no way out of the present situation except a change of leadership in the Conservative Party.

---

[*] Director of studies at St George's House, Windsor Castle.

Saturday 26 and Sunday 27 January 1974

Radio and press reports seem to bear out my belief that more than 55% of the miners will vote in favour of a strike. This means that next week will be crucial if we are to draw back from what I think would be a national disaster. Carrington spoke on the news of the possibility of a two-day or even a one-day week.

I have been racking my brains to think of some solution. If the crisis is to be solved without a complete capitulation by one side or the other it would have to be on the basis that the government agreed to settle the miners' claim outside Phase 3 in return for an undertaking by the TUC on behalf of its constituent member unions that they would not seek to reopen Phase 3 settlements already made or to negotiate new ones outside Phase 3. I don't know whether Heath would accept the first part of this formula but I think that some influential members of the Cabinet would. Up to now the TUC have not been willing to go as far as the second part of the formula but one or two things said by union leaders, in public, in the last few days make me think that they might be brought to agree. I shall explore possibilities with Murray tomorrow – the present course is leading straight to disaster and is playing the militants' game.

Monday 28 January 1974

Geoffrey Gilbertson telephoned first thing in the morning to say he had been brooding over the weekend on what might be done to save us from disaster. Like me he had been impressed by Frank Chapple's statement that the electricians had settled within Phase 3 'in order to help the miners'. Geoffrey asked whether I thought it would help if companies such as ICI negotiated Phase 3 settlements now, even though the operative dates might be some way ahead. I said I thought

this was worth exploring. I mentioned I was in touch with the TUC
– he said he was hoping to see Jack Jones later that day.

I chaired a NEDO committee meeting in the morning at which
Peter Linklater of Shell was present. I took him up to my room
afterwards and asked him what he, as an old pro in the industrial
relations field, thought of the present situation. He said what
worried him was that the government seemed to have got themselves
into a fix without having planned an emergency exit: he would never
allow this to happen in his own dealings with the unions. He and
other members of the CBI Employment Committee were getting
very worried at the lack of movement on the part of the government
or the CBI. This view had been expressed quite strongly at the CBI
Grand Council last week. The 'platform' had, however, taken a hard
line about the need to stand firm against militants, though one or two
influential people, including Harold Watkinson, had urged a more
conciliatory approach.

Lunch with Lord Donaldson* at the Travellers. He was very
anxious to know whether there was anything helpful he could say –
e.g. in a debate in the House of Lords. I told him how I saw the
situation – especially that I thought the miners were bound to come
off best from a straight trial of strength and that one must fashion
policy accordingly. He said this fitted closely with his ideas.

In the afternoon I telephoned Richard O'Brien, the chairman of
the CBI Employment Policy Committee. He said the CBI was
deeply divided and he personally was strongly urging the need for it
to get into direct contact with the TUC. He also told me that the CBI
had more or less (though not explicitly) told Heath yesterday that he
would have to settle the miners' claim outside Phase 3 if the ballot
went in favour of a strike.

---

* Lord Donaldson of Kingsbridge was chairman of the Hotel and Catering Industry
EDC.

At 6pm I went to see Len Murray at Congress House. I told him about my talk with O'Brien and also (in strict confidence) about Douglas Allen's change of attitude. I said that while I had no doctrinal objection to revolutionary change, I didn't think the situation we were heading for was a good way of bringing it about and that the only people who could be pleased about what was going on were the Communists. It was clear that the miners' claim must be settled before a strike took place and that it must be done on a basis which did not involve capitulation on anyone's part. Murray agreed. I then said that the only formula I could think of was the simple one that the government should agree to settle the miners outside Phase 3 and the TUC should agree that affiliated unions would not seek to reopen settlements already made or to negotiate new ones outside Phase 3. I added that I assumed that the TUC would not want to take any initiative themselves but that they might be willing to react to one. Murray thought for quite a while. He then said it might not be impossible but having got his chaps united he wouldn't want to go in for anything new unless he was sure of a good majority on the General Council. Hugh Scanlon would as usual be the key figure. Murray said he himself had been trying to think of a completely new approach, rather than building on the existing TUC offer, but confessed he hadn't so far been able to think of anything. He made it clear he was scared stiff of seeming to be dealing with the government from a position of weakness, to which I said that I was sure the government felt exactly the same vis-à-vis the TUC.

Tuesday 29 January 1974

Richard O'Brien told me that Campbell Adamson and Michael Clapham were consulting various influential CBI tycoons to see if they could get a new mandate. Their idea was that the time had come for the CBI to take a new initiative.

Later in the day Richard telephoned to give me an account of the morning's meeting. He said the tycoons had agreed that we couldn't afford to sit out a miners' strike; that the worst thing to do would be to allow chaos to begin and then settle; and that some new initiative had better be taken soon. They thought this should come from the government, not the CBI, and despatched Campbell and Clapham to give Whitelaw their views. Whitelaw had been receptive and had left them with the impression that Heath would be willing to authorise some approach to the TUC. One of the complicating factors, however, is that Len Murray is in the doghouse with ministers for springing his offer on them at NEDC without warning and for the line he took in public after the meeting at Downing Street.

Wednesday 30 January 1974

Three interesting things in the papers this morning. John Elliot[*] has a pretty accurate account of yesterday's CBI meeting in the *Financial Times*. David Wood has a piece on the front page of the *Times* saying that Conservative MPs, though still overtly supporting Heath, are getting increasingly uneasy about the outcome of a confrontation with the miners. And Reggie Maudling[†] has a letter in the *Times* referring to the electricians' recent settlement and saying in effect that if the engineers would settle within Phase 3, it would have achieved its object and this could open the way to an exceptional settlement for the miners. The letter is very well written to appeal to Conservatives who want the government to get out of the present jam without too much loss of face. The idea behind it is precisely the same as the one I put to Len Murray on Monday.

---

[*] Industrial editor of the *Financial Times*. A well-informed and perceptive journalist.
[†] Chancellor of the Exchequer 1962–4 and Home Secretary 1970–72.

I had a long lunch with Derek Mitchell.* He is utterly opposed to the government's attitude, which he thinks will lead us to economic and social disaster. He said the Treasury was finding it very difficult to get the reality of our economic situation and prospects across to ministers, partly because so much was filtered through William Armstrong. He said Armstrong was playing an extraordinary role. He was clearly unbalanced and took a high moral line about the miners' dispute and their challenge to the government.

In the afternoon I rang Reggie Maudling, who used to be chairman of Neddy, and told him I thought the suggestion in his letter to the *Times* was a very helpful one. I did this in the hopes that it might encourage him to pursue this idea in the Conservative Party. He was pleased to have this support. He said he had consulted Reg Prentice before sending the letter but not Len Murray, whom he didn't know well enough. He asked me if I would tell Len that he would have liked to consult him but didn't want to bother him when he must be so busy. I said that I was clear that the only way to settle the dispute was for the government to use its powers under the Counter-Inflation Act to give the miners exceptional treatment but that I didn't think ministers accepted this. Reggie said that he was sure the realistic members of the Cabinet understood this all right.

Later John Elliot and Peter Jenkins† rang to find out what I thought of the situation. I told them that I didn't think one could tell what the next move would be until one knew the way in which the majority mood in the Conservative Party was going to settle down. I

---

* Second permanent secretary of the Treasury. He had previously been economic minister at the embassy in Washington. A good man to take with one on a tiger shoot.

† An influential *Guardian* columnist. Author of *The Battle of Downing Street* (London: Charles Knight, 1970), a riveting account of the events surrounding the Labour government's White Paper *In Place of Strife* which led Harold Wilson to ask Hugh Scanlon to 'get your tanks off my lawn'.

added that the right thing would be to settle the dispute behind the scenes without capitulation on either side between now and Sunday night: but that I didn't think this would happen and therefore the only way out might be a settlement followed immediately by an election – or a change of leadership in the Conservative Party.

When I got home I heard on the news that after a long meeting of ministers the PM had invited the TUC and the CBI to meet him to discuss the relativities report. Hugh Scanlon has made a statement saying that if the government could use the report to settle the miners' dispute the TUC would do all they could to help. This is in line with Harold Wilson's views, expressed in a letter to Heath yesterday. What worries me is that the government should have made public their invitation to the TUC without (so far as I know) having done the preliminary groundwork behind the scenes, which is essential if a thing like this is to succeed. My guess is that the Cabinet have not yet accepted the need for a settlement outside Phase 3 and that if the new initiative fails they will call an election.

Thursday 31 January 1974

I went over to ICI to see Geoffrey Gilbertson. He had been pursuing the idea he put to me earlier in the week that it might help if as many companies as possible negotiated settlements under Phase 3 now, even if the operative date was some distance away. He said he had got promises of support from Ford, ICI, the British Steel Corporation, the oil companies and GEC. He had discussed the idea with Jack Jones and David Basnett, both of whom were ready to co-operate.

Geoffrey said that it was the unanimous view of the members of the Pay Board that the miners' dispute could not be settled within Phase 3 and that the government would have to use its special powers to override the Pay Code. They had told the government that, provided the extra payments were tied to underground working or something similar, the repercussions could be contained.

After lunch David Basnett rang – ostensibly to talk about a TV programme about Neddy which he wants me to appear on but really, I think, to have a chat about the crisis. I said I assumed that the TUC would accept the PM's invitation but I didn't see that the relativities report would provide the way out; in my view it was essential to settle the dispute – or agree a basis for settling it – secretly before the ballot result was declared on Sunday or Monday. Basnett agreed. He said his information was that all except one member of the Cabinet now favoured a settlement.

Campbell telephoned to ask if the Group of 4 meeting was still on for tomorrow afternoon. I said it was and that it seemed to me very desirable to stick to it as it would provide a useful opportunity for him and Len to talk. I said I was seeing William Armstrong tomorrow and Campbell told me that he and Michael Clapham had seen Armstrong this morning and had been shocked by his condition. He seemed to be under great strain and almost mentally ill. This unexpected news chimes with what Derek Mitchell told me yesterday.

Finally I went to see Frank Figgures. He said he understood that the PM realised as clearly as he and I did the need for a settlement outside Phase 3 but that he couldn't carry a majority of the Cabinet. He mentioned Howe and Prior as particular opponents of conciliation. He said that he didn't think that Armstrong was against a settlement though he had strong views about the political (i.e. social) consequences of a capitulation which he thinks would create a right wing backlash. He said Armstrong was emotionally committed to the present policy but didn't say anything to suggest he had gone off his head.

Friday 1 February 1974

The day began badly with telephone calls in quick succession cancelling my appointment with William Armstrong; telling me John Hunt was ill and couldn't have lunch; and warning me that Douglas Allen might not be able to join the Group of 4 meeting.

After lunch Campbell Adamson and Len Murray came for the Group of 4 meeting. I strongly urged on them the need to establish by secret discussions whether a basis for settling the miners' strike existed. I was sure this ought to be done by Sunday evening at latest – i.e. before the result of the miners' ballot (or rather the size of the majority) was known. Len said he wasn't really ready for this and Campbell said Sunday was too early. Campbell stayed behind for a few minutes after Len had left. He spoke about this being the first occasion for years when the TUC had not been able to call the tune and said that as a result they were bewildered. If Heath won his way through the present struggle the industrial relations scene would be transformed for five years. I am afraid this is nonsense and that Campbell's judgment in the present situation is not all that good. Later in the afternoon I went over to see Douglas at the Treasury. He told me that they had packed William Armstrong off home for a rest. He had been under strain for some time and had become 'elated' and was consequently giving bad advice. This, I gathered, had happened once or twice in the past but Armstrong had recovered quite quickly.

Saturday 2 February 1974

After speaking to several of those involved, I ended the day feeling that an honourable agreement between the TUC and government could be reached without too much difficulty, but that it was hard to see the miners accepting any settlement which didn't give them money now, especially bearing in mind that the warmer weather will soon be here and their power will be correspondingly reduced.

Sunday 3 February 1974

We drove over to the Seligmans' for lunch. Madron* and I had a long talk about the crisis. He is, of course, completely loyal to Heath but thinks that the government have played straight into the militants' hands. Madron is all for an accommodation. He said that one can't let the miners challenge Parliamentary rule but that the government should never have got into a fight which it had no chance of winning. I told him of my conversation with Heath at Neddy on 21 December. We talked of the sycophancy round Heath and his tendency to bully. I said that I admired Heath's radicalism and his 'one nation' approach, but that I was afraid that through fatigue or party pressures he was losing some of the latter.

Monday 4 February 1974

At 9 p.m. we heard that the PM's talks with the TUC, which had begun at 4.30, had ended (in Murray's words) in deadlock. Whitelaw is evidently inviting the NUM negotiators to see him before their executive meets but this looks like a piece of political window-dressing and one can only assume that the government are set on having an election.

---

* Madron Seligman was an industrialist who later became an MEP. His close friendship with Edward Heath went back, like mine with Roy Jenkins, to pre-war Oxford.

Tuesday 5 February 1974

Len Murray telephoned and gave me a full account of last night's meeting with the PM. He said that what really mystified him was that throughout the discussions in the last few weeks the government had made no attempt to build on the TUC offer or to extract improvements on it from the TUC. Similarly, on Monday evening the TUC had made a number of suggestions and these had not provoked any questioning, let alone probing, by ministers.

Len said that the TUC were prepared to respond in some way to the government's attitude on relativities. They had also told the government that they would try to help to prevent the miners from escalating their demands if a settlement were offered to them but the government had shown no interest in this. Throughout, the TUC had the impression that Whitelaw was trying to be helpful and was unhappy at his colleagues' attitude. After a while there was an adjournment – during which the government decided to invite the NUM leaders to see them before the union's executive meeting tomorrow morning. The TUC had advised strongly against this.

Len said that the statement issued after the CBI Grand Council had been given to the meeting about half way through. The TUC had not considered it helpful. He ended by saying, 'Thanks for your help.'

I passed this reference to the CBI on to Campbell Adamson, whom I have been urging to get away from the CBI's apparent subservience to the government line. I pointed out that the CBI and TUC would have to live with one another when all this was over and it would be a great pity if their relationship had been permanently damaged by the position taken by the CBI in the current dispute.

Richard O'Brien telephoned. He said that the CBI Grand Council had agreed that the Relativities Board should be set up quickly, that the miners should be the first case to be referred to it and that any award should be backdated to 1 March. He said there was massive support for the view that a way must be found to settle the miners' dispute now. John Whitehorn* had accurately summed up the mood as one of 'stand firm but settle quickly'.

In the evening, while I was preparing for tomorrow's Neddy meeting, John Elliott telephoned to ask if it was still on. Fredy Fisher, who was in the room with Elliot, came on the line. He said his position was that if the government gave the miners more money now it would destroy its authority and might nearly destroy the Conservative Party. The miners would have to get their money but, in his view, it was better that they should get it from a new government even though this meant that there would have to be a three week strike which would be very damaging to industry. He was full of foreboding about the effect of televised clashes between pickets and the police during an election campaign.

I said none of this would have happened if the government had settled before Christmas. It was all the result of their gross misjudgment of the industrial relations situation.

Wednesday 6 February 1974

The papers are full of a new CBI initiative. I phoned Campbell Adamson to ask him if he was planning a move at the Neddy meeting. He said that the feeling was growing strongly in the CBI that the miners' dispute must be settled now. They had told the PM this last evening.

The TUC came to Neddy at 10 a.m. for their normal pre-Council briefing meeting. Tony Barber came in, fussing endlessly about who was to take the press briefing. At about 10.35, five minutes after the scheduled start of the council meeting, Len Murray emerged and

---

* A deputy director general of the CBI.

told me the TUC would like the meeting to finish by 11.30 so that they could have a private talk with the CBI. We spoke to Campbell Adamson and Barber, who both agreed to this.

We then had an amicable council meeting in which we got through the agenda in record time. The main item was our report on the effect of the three-day week. This was bleak but none of the other parties challenged it.

At about 11.45 the CBI and the TUC started their private talk in our council room. Donald MacDougall told me that he had been pressing my line in the CBI for some time but that until recently it had had no effect. He said the tycoons in the CBI seemed out of touch with reality – people lower down in the big companies (i.e. managing directors and other executives) had all along seen the need for a settlement with the miners.

Jim Netherthorpe* stayed on after the others had left. He showed me a letter he had written to Michael Clapham suggesting a formula under which the miners could be given a payment on account. The letter began, 'I had spent a sleepless night wondering if I could make a useful contribution towards settling this dispute.' I reckon a good many people have spent similar sleepless nights recently – all to no avail.

About 1.45 the TUC–CBI meeting broke up and they all came and had a cold lunch in my room. They were subdued and reflective – though their talk had obviously been amicable I gathered that no real progress had been made. There had been some plain speaking about their respective sticking points and the government's – and they had agreed to think things over. I had the impression that some further meeting might take place this evening.

At 3.15 I took my press conference, which was full to overflowing.

---

* Lord Netherthorpe was a former president of the National Farmers' Union and former chairman of Fisons who served on NEDC from 1971 to 1975.

I answered all questions about the TUC–CBI talks by saying that they had been private and that I understood the TUC and the CBI had 'brought one another up to date on their recent talks with the government' (this was the agreed line). I stressed that I thought it was a very good thing that these talks were taking place and that I was glad that they were taking place on Neddy ground.

I was questioned a lot about our assessment of the effect of the three-day week. I was asked how many people we thought would be unemployed or on short time at the end of February if there was a miners' strike. I said four million. I was then asked how many I thought would be affected if the strike went on until the end of March (when there would be no steel left). I said we had made no estimate. The reporter who was doing most of the questioning said, 'Ten million?' I said I didn't know. 'Would it be astronomical?' I said we hadn't tried to calculate the number; the situation would be too serious to contemplate and it was probably better to use adjectives than numbers to describe it.

Thursday 7 February 1974

The papers are full of the impending election. The general view is that it will be announced about 5 p.m. today, though Peregrine Worsthorne* said on the BBC that he wasn't sure that there would be an election after all. Almost all the papers, including the *Financial Times*, which ought to know better, quote me as forecasting 'astro-nomical levels of unemployment'. They also report that Campbell Adamson and Len Murray met again last night.

I rang Campbell. Michael Clapham answered. He said that they had not really made any progress last night – not enough to justify enlarging the discussions. I said I supposed there was nothing for it

---

* Deputy editor of the *Sunday Telegraph*.

but to let events – the strike and an election – unfold.

I then spoke to Len Murray. He confirmed what Michael had said. He complained about the stories in the press but said he would keep trying.

I decided to phone Roy Jenkins and Reggie Maudling, as former chairmen of Neddy, to see if they could suggest anything. Roy said he thought an election was certain and that he didn't think anyone who was outside it could sensibly suggest a basis for solving the dispute. Maudling said he thought the gap was now too wide to bridge. The government would have to stand firm on the issue of 'brute force'. He had advised Heath that if an election was unavoidable he should get it over as quickly as possible.

I then phoned Harold Watkinson, a former Cabinet minister and pillar of the CBI. He said he couldn't see anything that could be done now. Campbell couldn't move much without a further mandate from the CBI Council. The real difference with the TUC was that they would not agree to anything which would involve their accepting a continuing incomes policy, whereas the government couldn't agree to pay more to the miners except in the context of a coherent incomes policy. Watkinson said that all any of us could do now was to keep in contact with the unions so that we could rebuild things later on.

At 12.45 we heard that Heath had called an election for 28 February. One can't help feeling he has announced it early in the day for fear that if he left it longer the TUC and CBI might make some joint approach to him which could make it more difficult for him to call an election. On the other hand, looking back it seems clear that he and his principal colleagues decided on an election last Sunday.

I lunched at the American embassy with Bob Brand, the economic minister. Donald MacDougall was there and we drove back together. He told me he thought I had done a magnificent job at NEDO. I was pleased about this because I am always afraid the CBI will think I am too trade union orientated.

Friday 8 February 1974

Lunched at the Park Royal brewery with various Guinness directors. They were all very scathing about the government's inept handling of the dispute and their disregard of the most elementary principles of industrial relations.

I decided that we could reasonably stick to our holiday plans and leave for Courchevel this weekend. A DG of NEDO is better out of the way during an election campaign and it will be a good thing if somebody is fresh after the election!

Saturday 9 February 1974

Richard O'Brien telephoned. He was very depressed about everything, especially the failure of the CBI–TUC talks to produce any result – probably, as he acknowledged, because they were started too late.

He said that although the prevailing view in the CBI had moved strongly in favour of a settlement during the last week or so, the CBI line had been greatly influenced by political considerations. There had been a widespread feeling among the tycoons that they could not let the Conservative government down altogether. This was why the talks had foundered. The TUC were quite prepared to tighten their undertaking that the miners would be regarded as a unique case and Richard said the formula Len Murray had produced for this was quite satisfactory. But they were adamant that the miners must have more money now and the CBI could not agree to this because it would completely undermine the government's position.

He also said that he had spent some time with ministers at No. 10 after the civil servants 'had been sent away' – presumably on Tuesday. There had been a good deal of talk of the Munich spirit, men of appeasement etc. Richard had not liked this. I suspected this was the mood among some ministers. It really is nauseating; whatever one may think of Mick McGahey, the 81 per cent of miners who voted to support their executive are our fellow citizens not foreign enemies.

PART TWO

MARKING TIME

25 February 1974 to 14 October 1974

The general election ended in stalemate, with neither of the main parties securing an overall majority in the Commons. The main conclusion to be drawn from this election was that there would have to be another one very soon.

This prospect dominated the political scene throughout the summer. Harold Wilson, who had begun his first term as Prime Minister in 1964 with a majority of four, was a master of parliamentary tactics and devoted all his energies to ensuring that the next election would give him a workable majority.

The dispute in the coal industry, which had caused the Heath government so much trouble in the winter, was immediately settled on terms which even the miners probably considered generous. The government and the TUC then reached a loosely formulated agreement under which ministers undertook to repeal the Conservatives' hated Industrial Relations Act, increase old age pensions and make other policy changes the unions wanted, while in return the unions agreed to limit wage increases to the amount needed to compensate for price increases in the previous year. This 'social contract', of which the transport workers' leader, Jack Jones, was a principal architect, became the centrepiece of the government's counter-inflation strategy.

Their poor showing in the election, coming after the traumatic events of the previous winter, left the Conservatives feeling somewhat demoralised. Mutterings about the need for a change of party leadership soon began to be heard but as there was no obvious successor to Edward Heath in sight they did not come to anything very much. Among the Tories as well as Labour, all eyes were directed at the second election, which, as the diary makes clear, everyone knew must come before the end of the year.

Monday 25 February 1974

I had a meeting with Dan Pettit,* Alf Allen and a couple of management people about the work of the Distributive Trades EDC. Alf Allen stayed behind for a short talk about the election. Like most people he thinks it is still open but that a Heath victory is probable. This seems to be the general impression in the office too.

Tuesday 26 February 1974

I called on Douglas Allen. He doesn't think that either of the two main parties will be able to handle the economic problems we shall face after the election. He would like to see Roy Jenkins as PM, leading some sort of centre party, but knows this isn't practical politics at present.

Douglas is pretty sure that the Conservatives will get back and that Barber will remain Chancellor until the summer recess. He said this was certainly what Barber himself was expecting and was more or less unavoidable in view of the need to introduce a Budget before the end of March and of the complexity of this year's Finance Bill (which will incorporate a number of tax changes relating, for example, to property and North Sea oil, to which the Conservatives are already publicly committed). I said that I thought this would be a disaster – my opinion of Barber had plummeted as a result of his attitude in the last three to four months and he had clearly lost the confidence of Neddy. Douglas said he would like to see William Whitelaw at the Treasury; Keith Joseph was said to be very indecisive and this would not do for a Chancellor just now.

---

* Chairman of the National Freight Corporation and of the EDC in question.

Wednesday 27 February 1974

Campbell Adamson is reported in the press as having said at a conference yesterday that any new government would do well to repeal the Industrial Relations Act, which had 'sullied relationships between management and unions'. Coming on the day before the election this has caused a great stir. I wonder whether Campbell has done this deliberately to stress his own independence?

Lunch at the Savoy with the managing director of Urwick Orr and Ivor Young, who used to be an industrial adviser at the DEA. They said that wherever they went they heard tales of the gains in productivity which had been achieved during the three-day week. The idea emerged that we might commission a survey to find out how this was done while it was all fresh in people's minds. I think I shall follow this up – because one thing that is becoming clear above all else is that if we don't manage to get really substantial gains in productivity during the next few years we shall not be able to meet our balance of payments problems and may face some kind of economic collapse.

I spoke to Campbell after lunch. He told me he was in real trouble over yesterday's statement and might well have to resign. He put the chances at 60–40 on his staying. He said that he had believed that his remarks were off the record and would not be published.

Thursday 28 February 1974

Doreen and I went down to Throwley last night so that we could vote in Faversham rather than in Westminster, where the result is a foregone conclusion. We have both decided to vote Liberal. I have never even contemplated doing this before. But one can't vote for the Conservatives after their behaviour in the last few months – if Heath gets back he will draw the moral that he was right all along and that would be quite disastrous. Equally, one can't vote Labour this time – they simply aren't a credible alternative government. The Liberals have a good manifesto, they are sound on Europe and they are preaching moderation so they seem to us to be well worth voting for.

Having returned to London, we started to watch the results come in on television. Shortly after 11 p.m. Campbell and Gilvray Adamson came in. They were very depressed about his position at the CBI and Gilvray said she thought Campbell was determined to go. I told him that he certainly ought not to resign but should wait to be dismissed, if that was what the members wanted – which they almost certainly don't. We stayed up till after 4 a.m., by which time it was clear that neither Labour nor Conservatives could get an overall majority.

Friday 1 March 1974

It looks as if the electorate have produced a stalemate. The election is clearly a resounding defeat for Heath, who is certain to end up with fewer seats than Labour. But it doesn't look like a win for Labour in any real sense of the word. Despite a large popular vote the Liberals have won disappointingly few seats.*

I took Reg Bottini, the general secretary of the farm workers' union, to lunch at Inigo Jones. He is a very likeable man – cultivated and moderate in his views. He has been on the TUC General Council for four years. We talked about a possible realignment of the political parties. I said that many people hoped for a social democratic party under Roy Jenkins which would combine the Gaitskellite wing of the Labour Party with the Liberals – such a

---

* The final figures were: Labour 301 seats, Conservatives 296, Liberals 14, others 24.

party would stand for policies which I personally could wholeheartedly support but I didn't think it would be a good development.
It seemed to me that it would lead to the isolation of the Labour left,
which would accordingly move closer to the Communists, with most
of the trade union movement following suit. Bottini entirely agreed
about the trade unions, which in his view would have no option but
to join up with the left. He attributes most of our current troubles to
our failure to reduce class divisions. He agrees with me that the real
gulf is between those who leave school at fifteen to take manual jobs
and all the rest of the community.

I spoke to Len Murray after lunch. I said it looked as though the
electorate had given a resounding vote of confidence for the things
that Neddy stands for. They had also put the politicians in baulk,
which meant that the rest of us would have to help them to get the
country moving forward again. Murray agreed that we should aim
for a Neddy meeting as soon as was reasonably convenient. I told
him about my plans for getting trade union chairmen for EDCs and
said I would count on him for help, which he readily agreed to give.

When I got home in the evening Roy Jenkins rang up. He was very
depressed and said he felt a prisoner. I said that his position was now
very strong and the electors had clearly voted for the things he stood
for. If Wilson had any sense he would make Roy Chancellor of the
Exchequer if Labour came to power. Roy considered it unlikely; he
thought the commitment to Healey was too strong. We both thought
it probable that Heath would resign this weekend. I said I thought
the Labour shadow Cabinet had been silly to issue a statement saying
they would be willing to form a government – far better to sit on
their hands and say nothing while Heath makes up his mind.

Later on Michael Clapham telephoned. He said that feeling
against Campbell was running very high among CBI members,
about twenty of whom had already resigned. Clapham said that he
had decided – when he saw the election results this morning – that

Campbell would have to go but the staff had persuaded him that this would be very bad for the CBI in the longer run. He added that Campbell had done a very good job and that if he went in these circumstances the CBI would be unlikely to get anyone of his calibre to replace him. He would make up his mind what to do after a meeting on Monday at which he is to consult various CBI bigwigs.

Monday 4 March 1974

A Group of 4 meeting at 11.15 a.m. but without Campbell Adamson. A useful meeting from my point of view. The most interesting point was when Len Murray talked about the 'social contract'. He was honest enough to say that he didn't believe that any agreement by the unions to exercise wage restraint would last very long. He implied that in 1975 it would be honoured more in the breach than the observance but that it might hold until the next election.

Chatting with Douglas Allen afterwards I said that one good feature of the present political impasse was that however it was resolved we seemed certain to get a new chairman of Neddy. He agreed and said he reckoned that Barber must have cost the Tories a lot of votes by his behaviour before and during the campaign.

I wrote a note to Campbell this morning saying that however things turned out he could be proud of what he had done at the CBI. In the evening Lucien Wigdor telephoned to say that the group of members whom Clapham had consulted had all agreed that Campbell should be asked to stay on. At 7 p.m. the news came through that Heath had gone to the Palace to hand in his resignation – I don't understand why he didn't do this on Friday. He is a proud man and ought to have sensed that the country has lost confidence in him. I'm afraid that in the last four or five months his judgment has gone sadly awry.

Jennifer Jenkins told us that Roy had been offered the Home

Office plus Northern Ireland; he had accepted the former and declined the latter. In general posts were going to their 'shadows' except for Employment, which Michael Foot would have. So I shall have Denis Healey as chairman and Benn and Foot as members.* Not what one would call a heavyweight economic team.

After dinner Campbell rang to say that he was going to stay on at the CBI – he gathered that he had got the support of 'forty-eight out of fifty' at the CBI meeting. He seemed pleased with my letter.

About midnight Roy rang. He is not enthusiastic about his new job. He said that in the last few days (in which there have been a lot of suggestions in the press that he should go to the Treasury) he had become quite nostalgic for his old job as Chancellor of the Exchequer.

Wednesday 6 March 1974

I took Danny McGarvey, the president of the boiler makers' union, to lunch at the Stafford. Like almost all the powerful trade union leaders he is genial and easy to get on with on a purely social occasion. We talked about the social contract and the new government. He had just come from a meeting of the General Council, which had issued a statement suggesting that in the new circumstances unions would be willing to show a degree of restraint both in claims and in settlements. I asked McGarvey if he really thought this would mean anything in practice. He said it would – the unions had learned in the last year or so just how bad a Tory government could be from their point of view and with the present balance in the House of Commons, they would be very keen not to do anything which would increase the prospects of a Conservative victory at the

---

* Denis Healey became Chancellor of the Exchequer and Tony Benn Secretary of State for Industry.

next election. He was ecstatic about Michael Foot's appointment. He said that Foot was so clever that when the General Council went to see him he would run rings round them. I wonder!

In the evening we heard that the coal strike had been settled. The coal board and the NUM were given freedom to negotiate and they agreed on a settlement which will give the unions £5 million more than they would have got under the Pay Board's Relativities Report. I wonder how many people will consider, in retrospect, that the troubles of the last three months have been worthwhile?

Thursday 7 March 1974

Geoffrey Gilbertson telephoned. He said the members of the Pay Board were feeling somewhat disenchanted. They had put a tremendous effort into their report on the miners and he himself had never worked so hard as he had in the last three weeks. Now it looks as though the Pay Board will be abolished.

Friday 8 March 1974

I called on Denis Healey at the Treasury at 10 a.m. Douglas Allen was there as well. We had a friendly talk about Neddy. Denis said that at the meeting on Monday he would make a positive statement about the need for full consultation and tripartite discussion. I had sent him a note on the previous evening in which I had said that my predecessors and I from time to time ran into trouble with the Chancellor of the day over the post-NEDC press conferences and that I supposed this was bound to happen occasionally. Denis said he hoped it wouldn't happen now – but no doubt it will sometime or other.

I said that one of the characteristics of Neddy was that the TUC and CBI met ministers as of right and on neutral territory. This meant that the atmosphere was different from what it was at other meetings, which almost always took place in a minister's office with the TUC or CBI making representations or being summoned to be told of some change in policy. I said that the chairman of Neddy had to take account of this in handling meetings. Tony Barber had understood this but Ted had not and consequently had played too dominant a role. Denis said that his instinct would be the same as Ted's but he would do his best to suppress it.

Saturday 9 March 1974

Tommy Balogh* is to be Minister of State at the Department of Energy – not a bad appointment; I would guess he is sounder on the subject of North Sea oil than on other things. I am very glad to see that Bill Rodgers has got a job too – minister of State at Defence. It's a pity he hasn't been given his own department but given his relations with Wilson he is lucky to get anything at all.

The papers say that on TV last night Heath blamed Campbell for losing the Conservatives the election – the *Daily Mail* makes it the lead story. What a vindictive thing to say, especially as he is also reported to have said that Enoch Powell's intervention made no difference at all.†

Monday 11 March 1974

Neddy meeting in the afternoon. A full house except for Ralph Bateman,‡ who is abroad. We had no fewer than seven ministers:

---

* Dr Balogh was a Hungarian-born economist who was close to Harold Wilson and had been economic adviser to the Cabinet in the 1960s.

† Powell resigned his seat on the day the election was called, describing it as 'essentially fraudulent', and later advised the public to follow him in voting Labour.

‡ Chairman of Turner and Newall, Bateman succeeded Michael Clapham as president of the CBI.

Healey, Foot, Varley, Shirley Williams, Benn, Shore and Lever.*
This must be a record. I must say that I was very pleased that Neddy
has so much pulling power.

Harold Lever told me at the beginning that he was very busy and
thought he could reasonably leave after the first item but he stayed
until the end and took an active part in the discussion. He is a bit frail
physically but says he has quite recovered mentally from his stroke
and certainly that seems to be the case. We had also heard that
Michael Foot would have to leave as soon as the meeting was over
but I am glad to say he stayed for drinks afterwards.

Denis Healey opened the meeting with a short speech about
Neddy's unique role and the importance which he and the government generally attached to it and then asked me to speak. I was a bit
taken aback as I had expected to come in after the others had spoken
but I adapted what I had prepared and it went off all right. In the
discussion which followed both the TUC and CBI put great
emphasis on the need to communicate our conclusions to people in
industry more – it was no good simply sitting around the NEDC
table thinking beautiful thoughts and saying wise things if nothing
resulted from them. I very much agree.

All the ministers took part except – oddly – Michael Foot. Benn
said some sensible things about economic planning and Neddy's
possible role in it but was critical of our papers. Peter Shore
intervened at one stage to make an obviously party political point
and was picked up sharply for it by – of all people – Hugh Scanlon.
Eric Varley, whom I have never met before, spoke sensibly about
energy. Campbell was, not unnaturally, very subdued. In the
discussion about the work of the council Monty Finniston urged
that Neddy should pay more attention to the problems of

---

* Eric Varley, Shirley Williams and Peter Shore were Secretaries of State for
Energy, Prices and Trade respectively. Harold Lever was Chancellor of the Duchy
of Lancaster.

nationalised industries and was strongly supported by Dick Marsh.

Denis seemed quite happy with the meeting afterwards. I think he will be a good chairman – let's hope he is a good Chancellor too.

All in all I thought it was a good meeting and got us off to a good start in the new Parliament.

Tuesday 12 March 1974

Monty Finniston telephoned to say he thought it was the best Neddy meeting he had attended. I said that potentially the most important part of it was that there seemed to have been general agreement with his own proposal that Neddy should involve itself in the problems of nationalised industries. This, as I imagine he intended, could be a first step towards taking the nationalised industries' problems out of politics.

Piers Dixon came in for a drink – he said he had done badly at the election and his majority was well down. He would like to see a change of leadership in the Conservative Party but only if Heath was replaced by someone further to the right. He is strongly opposed to the idea of a consensus man – e.g. Whitelaw or Carr[*] – taking over.

Wednesday 13 March 1974

George Sinclair[†] told me that this evening's meeting of the 1922 Committee had been very *mouvementé*. The Conservatives have put down an amendment to the Queen's speech about incomes policy on which they could possibly bring down the government.

---

[*] Robert Carr had been Home Secretary from 1972 to 1974.
[†] Sir George Sinclair was Conservative MP for Dorking.

Thursday 14 March 1974

I lunched with Michael Clark in the Plessey office upstairs in Millbank Tower. We talked of Campbell Adamson and it emerged that he thought Campbell had deliberately intervened in the campaign to help Labour – 'after all he was an adviser to Harold Wilson when he was last in power'. I hope I was able to persuade him that this was nonsense but it shows what Campbell is up against.

Clark is well disposed to Neddy but when I talked of my desire to get trade union chairmen for some of the EDCs he plainly thought it a very bizarre idea.

Friday 15 March 1974

In the evening Doreen and I went to the Dorchester as guests of honour at the annual dinner dance of the Chartered Institute of Transport. There were 750 people there.

I had taken a lot of trouble over my speech and was relieved to find it went down well. I said that during the miners' strike I had felt surrounded by men who knew precisely where they were going but hadn't always stopped to think whether their choice of destination was a wise one. We stayed till 'Auld Lang Syne' at 1 a.m. and came home exhausted. But we are both pleased because it went off all right.

Doreen sat next to Dick Marsh at dinner. He agreed with her that in the past Neddy had flourished more under Conservative than Labour governments but said that this would not now be the case and that the Labour government would in fact make good use of Neddy.

Sunday 17 March 1974

Throwley. I have been thinking for some time that I would like to write to Ted Heath. I have after all known him for a long time and worked quite closely with him and although I parted company completely with him over the miners' strike I greatly admire a lot of what he did and in particular his honesty.

In the last few days I have mentioned this to Madron Seligman and Piers Dixon and they both said I ought to write. So I have just sent him a letter in the following terms.

Dear Ted

While I won't pretend that I took the same view as you of the miners' strike and its surrounding context I wanted to let you know that I very much enjoyed working with you and greatly admired what you did as Prime Minister – not just on specific issues like Europe and Ulster but also for raising the standard of intellectual honesty brought to bear on all our problems and policies.

I hope that however events may develop things will go well with you personally.

Yours ever

Monday 18 March 1974

Lunched at Inigo Jones with Tom Jackson of the Post Office workers' union and Cyril Plant of the Inland Revenue Staff Association. Plant told me that the press stories about the TUC's agreement with Foot are correct. The 'Neddy Six'* told him last Monday that the TUC's priorities were to repeal the Industrial

---

* The TUC had six seats on NEDC, held by the chairman of its Economic Committee (Sidney Greene), the general secretary (Len Murray) and four influential union leaders (Alfred Allen, David Basnett, Jack Jones and Hugh Scanlon). This group, which was known as the 'Neddy Six', usually represented the TUC in talks with the government.

Relations Act and the Housing Finance Act – they realised that if the government tried to repeal the Counter-Inflation Act and abolish the Pay Board now (which I gathered Foot had offered to do) it could easily be brought down so they hadn't asked for it. They are quite happy to settle within Phase 3 because they know they couldn't expect to get more in the present economic climate. Plant said that when the result of their meeting with Foot was reported to the TUC Economic Committee last Wednesday, it was endorsed with only one dissentient, Danny McGarvey (Scanlon was not present). McGarvey felt that the line taken by the Six implied agreement with the statutory pay policy.

We had an agreeable lunch talking about Neddy, incomes policy etc. Jackson is an old-fashioned, idealistic sort of socialist – Plant is more of a realist. I like them both. They were both, on the whole, in favour of a statutory incomes policy; they were sure their members would do better with this than with a free-for-all.

In the afternoon I had a visit from John Grigg, who is doing a long piece for the *Observer* on the election and the events leading up to it. He gave me an explicit undertaking that he would not quote me or say anything which could damage NEDO's usefulness or involve us in party political crossfire and I spoke to him pretty freely about my own views on the mishandling of the miners' dispute. He had obviously been pretty well schooled by ex-ministers and made a particular point of the fact that the TUC had not told anyone in advance that they were planning to make their offer (to treat the miners as a special case) at the January meeting of Neddy. He asked me if I had known about it in advance but I side-stepped the question – I don't propose to have that come out in the newspapers. I did, however, tell him that Campbell Adamson and Len Murray met in my room on the Friday before the election was called and that so far as I knew this was the first time they had talked intimately together during the whole of the miners' dispute.

Dined at George Dobry's,* where we learned that the much-heralded constitutional crisis had fizzled out. The Conservatives withdrew their amendment to the Queen's speech before the end of the debate.† The general feeling at dinner was that Heath would not last long as leader of his party after this turn about – he was an ass to put down the amendment in the first place.

Tuesday 19 March 1974

Lunch with Ralph Bateman at the Royal Thames Yacht Club. On the miners' strike he said that the government had broken every rule in the industrial relations book with the inevitable consequences. He was scathing about ministers taking over negotiations which ought to be handled by experts and thought that for the NCB to offer the full amount allowed by Phase 3 at their first meeting with the NUM had made a strike almost inevitable.

He said that Campbell had made a very bad error of judgment but that the CBI were right to keep him on and that he would re-establish his authority before very long. I'm afraid I rather doubt this. Bateman seems intelligent and humane, though rather old fashioned in his outlook. From what he said I gather he will run the CBI rather as Jack Jones claims to run the TGWU – in other words he will seek to reflect the members' views rather than to shape them.

---

* A leading QC who advised the government on planning matters.

† The government had faced the real prospect of defeat on a Conservative amendment, backed by the Liberals, which called for effective measures to prevent high wage settlements from giving rise to uncontrolled inflation. The Conservatives' explanation for withdrawing their amendment was that Foot, in his opening speech, had announced action on pay which largely satisfied their demands.

Thursday 21 March 1974

The phone rang at 8 a.m. It was Sam Brittan,* who had just got my letter telling him I couldn't after all offer him the post of economic director at NEDO. He was clearly upset – much more so than I expected – and angry with Len Murray, having guessed rightly that the opposition had come from him. Poor Sam said he had now been blocked for two jobs – once by the leader of the Conservative Party and once by the general secretary of the TUC. I fear we shall see some waspish articles in the *Financial Times* in the weeks to come.

In the evening I went with Pat Fisher† to see Len. We discussed possible trade union names for chairmen of the little Neddies. It will be difficult to get good people but I am determined to redress the balance – at present all our EDC chairmen except two are management men. (The exceptions are a duke and a professor.)

Friday 22 March 1974

Lunched with Ian Bancroft‡ at the Oxford and Cambridge. He has been very much concerned with the recent changes in Whitehall organisation. He said that when Wilson came in he let it be known that he was not going to propose any changes in the machinery of government. But on his first full day in office he had told William Armstrong that he intended to break up the DTI. Ian shares my view that Wilson did not want anyone – and especially Tony Benn – to have such a strong power base as the old DTI could provide. He

---

* An influential and highly respected economic commentator on the *Financial Times*.
† Pat Fisher had recently joined NEDO as manpower director, having previously been a senior official at the TUC.
‡ Second permanent secretary of the Civil Service Department. He subsequently became Head of the Civil Service and was said to be the model for his fictional counterpart in the TV series *Yes, Minister*.

said that Wilson had clearly taken great pleasure in plucking feathers from Wedgie's backside – i.e. taking away from him responsibility for newspapers, prices and various other things.

Ian said that William had since the election confined his activities to looking after the Civil Service Department. He confirmed that William had lost his balance during the miners' strike and that he had become too closely identified with Heath's policies to be very acceptable to the Labour government. Ian said that he himself would now have to look elsewhere for a job – i.e. go to another department. I asked him whether he couldn't just hang on where he was for another year and then slip into Armstrong's place. But he said that the succession* would have to go to 'a grey beard' and confirmed that it would be Douglas Allen.

Saturday 23 March 1974

I got a very nice letter from Heath in reply to the one I sent him last Sunday.

Monday 25 March 1974

We got back about 9 p.m. after a fabulous three days in Italy as guests of David Nicolson, the chairman of British Airways. We and the rest of the party – a mixture of business people and politicians – assembled at Heathrow at 9.30 on Saturday morning. The whole thing was splendidly organised and although we were rushed off our feet – largely because so many Italian hoteliers and restaurateurs wanted to do honour to the chairman of British Airways – the party remained happy and relaxed throughout and everyone got on well with everyone else.

---

* As Head of the Civil Service.

After an early flight out with copious champagne etc. en route we arrived at Naples – after the most perfect landing we had ever experienced – in time for lunch. We lunched with John Boyd-Carpenter* and his wife, whom we liked. Inevitably we discussed the recent industrial and political turmoil and John clearly felt much as we did about it. He said that at least three ministers had discussed the pros and cons of an election with him and that he had told them all that he didn't think the Conservatives would win an election and that even if they did they would gain nothing from it.

After lunch we drove to Sorrento, where we were installed in a charming old hotel which was built in the days before air-conditioning and well adapted to the climate. Our room was at the back of the hotel – and therefore very quiet – and had a balcony with an enchanting view over the Bay of Naples. On Sunday we sat at lunch with David and Margaret Crouch, who live near us in Kent. They know Ted Heath well and like him but David, who is MP for Canterbury, spoke out in favour of a settlement of the miners' strike well before the election and incurred Ted's displeasure as a result.

Tuesday 26 March 1974

I went to the House of Commons to hear Denis Healey's Budget speech. On the way in I ran into Maurice Macmillan.† He said that he missed the Department of Employment – he had enjoyed his time as secretary of state more than anything else he had done in government or opposition. Healey did his speech well – it lasted for

---

* Lord Boyd-Carpenter was chairman of the Civil Aviation Authority and of Rugby Portland Cement. He had held a number of Cabinet posts under the Conservative governments of the 1950s and 1960s.
† Conservative MP for Farnham. He had been Chief Secretary to the Treasury from 1970 to 1972 and Secretary of State for Employment in 1972–3.

two hours and twenty minutes and he threaded his way through the complexities very skilfully. But it somehow missed being an occasion and I thought the enthusiasm of his backbenchers was muted. I ran into Tom Boardman on the way out – he said he thought the Budget would go down quite well with the Tories.

At 6 p.m. Tommy Balogh came in for a drink and a brief chat. He said that whether the Budget was good or bad would depend entirely on whether it induced the trade unions to moderate their wage demands. He wasn't very optimistic that it would and inveighed against Hugh Scanlon, whom he described (quite wrongly in my view) as a Maoist who wanted to overthrow the present system, even if this could only be done by violent means.

Wednesday 27 March 1974

This evening BBC2 devoted fifty minutes to a programme about William Armstrong. It began with snippets from various prominent people, including Vic Feather, who said that during the last parliament many people regarded Armstrong as a kind of deputy Prime Minister. (This statement, which was evidently pre-recorded, was prominently reported in this morning's papers.) When questioned about it by the interviewer Armstrong admitted that his relationship with the Prime Minister had gone 'slightly askew' in the sense that he had sat alongside him at press conferences during the talks with the TUC and the CBI on counter-inflation and in some other respects played a role which might be considered more appropriate to a politician than a civil servant. This caused me a wry smile as some years ago Armstrong told me that some permanent secretaries were opposed to my being promoted on the grounds that I was too political.

Armstrong, though in many ways a likeable chap, is not a big man and his whole attitude during the interview brought out the essentially subordinate nature of the civil service as a career. As I watched, I felt how lucky I was to be out of it.

Thursday 28 March 1974

We had a Group of 4 meeting in the morning. As Chris Lucas* said afterwards, it was in some ways a depressing meeting. He and I had both – as I now realise rather naïvely – felt that, in view of all the recent ministerial activity and the comings and goings between the TUC and the new administration, we should learn a lot about what had been decided and what was planned for the future. But it became clear from the discussion that very little had in fact been planned or decided and listening to Len Murray and Douglas Allen we realised the extent to which the nation's affairs are still drifting.

Len said that the previous evening's meeting between the TUC Economic Committee and the PM had been a non-event. A large number of ministers, even including the new Foreign Secretary,† had been present but not, as I understand it, any officials. The meeting had consisted of 'desultory chat' and a lot of time had been spent in explaining to Hugh Scanlon (who was evidently in a very suspicious mood) why the Industrial Relations Act couldn't simply be repealed by a one-clause Bill.

It seemed clear from what Len said that the unions are resolutely opposed to any idea of constructing an incomes policy, even though they can be expected to moderate their wage settlements as a result of the Budget. Len himself spoke strongly against the retention or creation of any institutions for implementing an incomes policy.

---

* As secretary of NEDC he attended meetings of the Group of 4.
† James Callaghan.

Douglas stayed on for a bit. He said that no one expected this Parliament to last beyond October.

I went on to lunch with Frank Figgures at the Pay Board. He was very relaxed and we drank a bottle and a half of Aloxe-Corton. Frank mentioned that Michael Foot, who had never held any ministerial office, however junior, until he was sixty, had handled his brief very ineptly at his first meeting to discuss the future of the Pay Board. I gathered that Frank did not expect him to last very long as secretary of state. He also talked of William Armstrong, who he thought had done very well on TV last night. He said that at the Treasury Armstrong had never committed himself to any view and that it was impossible to tell what his own opinions were. It was therefore all the more surprising that when he began to work directly for Heath on regional and industrial policy (before the counter-inflation talks began) he immediately became committed to a set of policies and from then on abandoned his previous detachment. I have always been in favour of civil servants who took sufficient interest in the substance of their work to become *engagé*, but since he started giving positive advice Armstrong has been consistently wrong – just as much on the Industry Act* as on counter-inflation.

Back at the office I learned that Harold Wilson has decreed that all Treasury ministers should attend our Neddy meeting next week. This is splendid and should help to ensure that the government generally takes us seriously – but I fear that at least two of the Treasury ministers will have to sit in the back row because our council table can't accommodate them and this may prejudice them against us!

---

* Armstrong played a crucial role in Edward Heath's famous U-turn in 1972, when he decided to embark on an interventionist industrial policy, in direct contravention of his party's previous doctrine.

Friday 29 March 1974

I took Dai Davies, the general secretary of the ISTC, to lunch at the Savoy. He is a friendly, voluble Welshman. Like most of the moderates he resents the influence of the big unions and especially Jack Jones and the TGWU.

He mentioned two points of interest in connection with the miners' dispute. The first was that he claimed the credit – with Frank Chapple – for getting the TUC offer made at the January meeting of Neddy. He said that at the meeting of the TUC's Economic Committee on the morning of 9 January Hugh Scanlon had been going on about the Industrial Relations Act and Jones about the need to restore voluntary collective bargaining, when he and Chapple had urged the need for the TUC to come out clearly in favour of making the miners a special case. Sidney Greene had come out strongly in their support and in the end the decision to take the initiative at the Neddy meeting was taken unanimously.

Monday 1 April 1974

I took Tommy Balogh to lunch at Romeo and Juliet. He is tickled pink at being a member of the government and says that he is the oldest man ever to be appointed a minister for the first time. He looks much less than his sixty-eight years and attributes this to 'aggression and sex'. He doesn't think anything of the civil servants around him and says they try to keep things from him but he says the Treasury has never been stronger than now since Warren Fisher's day.* He expects an election in June.

---

* Sir Warren Fisher was permanent secretary of the Treasury from 1919 to 1939.

Tuesday 2 April 1974

In the afternoon I had an hour's talk with Tony Benn about British industry's troubles and what the Department of Industry and NEDO might do to help to solve them. He was subdued and quite sensible and didn't bring out any of his wilder ideas. He gave the impression of feeling caged in – both by the fact that the government is in a minority position in the House and because his departmental responsibilities are so restricted.

Wednesday 3 April 1974

We had a very full attendance at Council – of the regular members only Sidney Greene and Eric Roll were absent and there were ten ministers present. Harold Wilson arrived half an hour late having been detained at No. 10 as a result of the stories in the *Daily Mail* and *Daily Express* that some of his close associates, including Marcia Williams* and her brother, have been mixed up in some not altogether respectable property deal in Lancashire.

We had what was by general consent a good meeting. Denis Healey opened up with a fluent and sensible account of the thinking behind his Budget. There then followed a discussion about the prospects for investment in which, I fear, the CBI team showed up badly, although I think they had a stronger case than their critics. At one point I got depressed because whereas in the last Parliament we had the Conservative government and the employers ranged against the TUC, we now have Labour ministers and the TUC lined up against the CBI. I must try to get the council back to a genuinely three-sided discussion. However, matters improved when we got on to a discussion about the 'social contract'. Jack Jones made a very

---

* Harold Wilson's political secretary.

forthcoming statement about the trade unions' determination to make it work. He said the Budget had made it possible for the union leaders to press their members to put in 'realistic' wage claims by which he evidently meant claims which would do no more than keep pace with the rise in the cost of living. He also spoke of the need to reduce lightning strikes and invited the CBI to have talks with the TUC about this.

All the other trade union leaders spoke on similar lines. The CBI welcomed the suggestion for joint talks. In summing up, I made a particular point of the need to get a degree of consensus on basic policies affecting investment, exports etc. which would survive a general election and a change of government.

When we went in for drinks the PM was very affable. He was clearly pleased with the meeting and said Neddy seemed in much better shape than when he had last attended it in 1970. Denis Healey stayed for lunch and was in very good form. He implied that there was likely to be an election in June. I had a long talk over lunch with Edmund Dell, whom I knew at DEA. I should think he will make a very good Treasury minister.*

Thursday 4 April 1974

Dick Marsh and Monty Finniston came in at ten for a talk about the possibility of Neddy discussing nationalised industries' affairs. They were vitriolic – as all nationalised industry chairmen are – about the way in which ministers and civil servants interfere in their affairs. They were also critical of the CBI performance at Neddy and generally.

I had lunch with Frank Kearton† at Hanover Square. He was very

* He was Paymaster General.
† Lord Kearton was chairman of Courtaulds and formerly chairman of the IRC.

critical of the CBI leadership and said that a large number of members shared his views. He said that during the coal strike Don Ryder* had tried to organise a mass walkout from a Grand Council meeting but it hadn't come off. Kearton spoke interestingly about the efforts Courtaulds have been making to involve their workers in decisions about their working arrangements. They are decentralising to the maximum. They try not to have any unit which employs more than 250 people and they do all they can to create feelings of loyalty to the individual unit rather than to Courtaulds as a whole. They also take infinite pains to 'cool' things before they can break out into industrial disputes. I thought Frank much more impressive than he used to be.

I am very glad to have got yesterday's council meeting behind me. I feel now that we have really established ourselves as an effective body which can do good work under either administration.

Friday 5 April 1974

I had a nice letter from Bill Rodgers, to whom I had written when he got appointed as Minister of State for Defence. He said Wilson 'seemed very pleased with the Neddy meeting'.

Wilson now looks as though he might be in serious trouble over the land transactions in which Marcia Williams and her brother are involved. Michael Posner, who spent an hour with me going over the work on energy on which he is helping us, said he thought the affair could do Wilson and the Labour Party great damage. I said I was inclined to agree but that both Piers Dixon and George Sinclair (two Conservative MPs of very different views) had told me that it would die down very quickly. Perhaps their judgment, as parliamentarians, is better than ours in a matter of this sort.

---

* Sir Don Ryder was chairman of Reed International and later of the NEB.

I took Douglas Wass to lunch at the Travellers. He said that relations between ministers and officials during the miners' strike had been rather similar to what they had been at the time of Suez. Wass and most people in the Treasury were completely out of sympathy with Tony Barber's line – but he confirmed that both William Armstrong and Conrad Heron had been hawkish in the extreme.

Wass was very scathing about the CBI, which he regards as quite unrepresentative of industry. He wants to have more direct contacts with industry and asked if I could help him in this. Like Douglas Allen he has always seen the value of Neddy as a non-governmental link with industrial opinion and is as anxious as I am to keep close contacts between NEDO and the Treasury.

Monday 8 April 1974

At lunch at the Travellers Arthur Peterson said that on coming back to Whitehall from the GLC in 1972 he noticed a big change in the relationships between ministers and civil servants. It seemed clear that ministers of both parties now looked on their permanent secretaries as superior establishment officers, whose job was to run administrative machines, not as policy advisers. He thought that in future ministers would get all their policy advice from a new breed of political advisers. I think Arthur may be unduly influenced by his experience with Roy Jenkins, who always – and in my view rightly – wanted to hear the opinions of people who were close to him, politically and personally, as well as those of his departmental officials.

But in so far as Arthur is right the civil service have only themselves to blame. They should have recognised years ago that a good minister wants two sources of advice – one tuned to Whitehall wavelengths and one to party feeling – and should have encouraged the formation of political 'cabinets',* working in parallel with the civil service. But the mandarins resisted this for fear that it would diminish their influence over their ministers. I think they made a great mistake and that their loss of influence will in fact be greater as a result.

Tuesday 9 April 1974

I went to a lunch which Trust House Forte gave at Grosvenor House after their annual general meeting. The AGM went on for longer than expected and while we were waiting for the directors to come out I chatted to Henry Grunfeld, the president of Warburgs. He said that the Budget would have a bad effect in the City because it would drive away a lot of foreigners who had come to work in American, Swiss and other foreign banks; this was because of the heavy extra personal taxation they would have to pay. I expect he is right but it is odd how people in the City are always obsessed by questions of personal remuneration.

At lunch, which was presided over very genially by Peter Thorneycroft, I sat between Charles Forte, whom I had never met before, and Alf Robens.† Forte, who came to Britain when he was four, told me about the ice-cream parlours which his father had built up all over southern Scotland – including one in Alva, where my grandfather was a Presbyterian minister for thirty years or so. He seems a likeable and vigorous man and I was glad to find him well disposed to Neddy and the work we do in the Hotels and Catering

---

* The term is used in Paris and Brussels to describe a minister's private office.
† Lord Thorneycroft had been Chancellor of the Exchequer from 1957 to 1958. He was now chairman of Trust House Forte and Charles Forte was chief executive. Lord Robens was chairman of Vickers and a respected elder statesman. He had been Minister of Labour under Clement Attlee and chairman of the NCB from 1961 to 1971 and was a founder member of NEDC.

EDC. He introduced me to his son Rocco, a shy young man who is taking over as personnel director and will probably join the EDC.

Robens, who was on good form, talked about the miners' strike. He said he was sure it could have been settled within Phase 3 before Christmas if the miners had been promised a further rise in November 1974 plus an undertaking that by March 1975 they would regain their place at the top of the manual workers' league and that they would hold this place in March 1976. Robens said that he had persuaded Whitelaw of this but that Whitelaw had failed to carry the Cabinet, 'who didn't understand these matters'.

Wednesday 17 April 1974

I took Victor Rothschild* to lunch at the Royal Thames, which he said was the only 'sympathetic' club he knew. His outfit is to carry on as before under the new government. He said it was now accepted 'as part of the furniture' by the mandarins of Whitehall. It hasn't, however, done much so far in this parliament, largely because, according to him, the government are not in the least interested in governing until they have had an election and been returned with a working majority. Victor was away for the first part of the miners' strike, having had a small heart attack, but he evidently disagreed with the government's handling of it. He spoke with respect and kindness of Heath despite his having given him (Rothschild) a quite unnecessary public dressing down about a speech he made last autumn.

Tuesday 30 April 1974

I did some lobbying today. At tomorrow's meeting of NEDC we are

---

* Lord Rothschild was the first head of the Central Policy Review Staff, set up by Edward Heath in 1971, where he did an outstanding job.

to discuss a paper on profits and their relationship to investment. It would be idle to seek agreement round that table on the merits of profits as a motivating force, on dividends versus wages or on the share of the national wealth which should go to profits. But I don't see why the various parties shouldn't agree on the narrow issue of the relationship of profits to investment. With management in a bruised and apprehensive mood just now I believe that if we could say after the meeting that all three parties on Neddy had agreed on the importance for investment of a reasonable rate of profits – even though this had to be expressed in somewhat platitudinous form – it might do disproportionate good. I had mentioned this to Campbell Adamson last Friday and yesterday I spoke to Len Murray, who reacted quite sympathetically. Today I called on Denis Healey first of all, who promised to try and pick out and emphasise any points on which the CBI and TUC seemed to be agreeing. I then spoke to Harold Lever* on the phone. He was enthusiastic and said he would do all he could to help to overcome the TUC's 'obscurantist views' on profits.

Wednesday 1 May 1974

The discussion at Council started very well. After I had introduced our paper Campbell Adamson spoke very well for the CBI. Len Murray was not on very good form but Harold Lever, who had taken the trouble to prepare notes, made a very effective intervention, as did Richard Lloyd. In the ensuing discussion almost everyone took part but the conclusion was less definite than I had hoped. Jack Jones

---

* Lever was one of the most colourful personalities in successive Wilson governments. He had an astute financial mind and lived in considerable style in Belgravia; but, having been a Manchester MP since 1945, his Labour Party credentials were impeccable and he enjoyed instructing his political associates in the realities of the market economy.

tried to get the whole discussion deferred – he probably regarded it as quite unsuitable for May Day! Fortunately Healey did as promised and summed up pretty well. In discussion about what I should say to the press Murray and Jones made it clear they did not want the subject highlighted so that I had a difficult course to steer at my press briefing afterwards.

Shirley Williams stayed to lunch and had it at my table with Murray and Adamson. She is a nice woman of sensible views.

In the evening (by which time I was pretty tired) we went to Covent Garden with Ronnie and Myrtle Edwards for a superb performance of *Otello*.

We went on to the Edwards' flat in Lowndes Square for supper. We talked – at his initiative – about the CBI and about contemporary Britain. Ronnie has very right-wing views and has no time at all for the trade unions. Evidently he was brought up in a working-class family and left school at fourteen – after which he became a don, a civil servant, the chairman of the Electricity Council and now chairman of Beechams. I like him and his wife very much but as usual his reactionary views brought out the radical in me and I argued with him strongly – much too strongly according to Doreen, who says, probably quite rightly, that I gave the impression I was a raging revolutionary. But we parted on the best of terms and Ronnie said he would like to discuss the CBI problem some more with me.

Thursday 2 May 1974

I went to Esher with Pat Fisher and three others from the office to meet the GMWU. They were friendly and welcoming and as different from their counterparts in the AUEW as one could imagine. The GMWU people are almost all young, well-educated professionals and David Basnett seems to lead them very well. I had a private word with him in which I pressed him hard to accept the chairmanship of the Chemicals EDC. This would be the first chairmanship in twelve years to go to a trade union man and I am very keen to get David to do it.

Despite the equivocal conclusions of yesterday's council meeting we did very well in the press. We got a second leader in the *FT* and Kenneth Fleet in the *Daily Telegraph* referred to Neddy as a 'uniquely worthwhile organisation'. So the effort was worth it.

Monday 6–Friday 10 May 1974

On Monday morning I began what turned out to be a most interesting visit to Scotland. I flew to Glasgow airport where I was met by Ross Belch, the managing director of Scott Lithgow and president elect of the SRNA. He showed me round the four or five shipyards which the group operate on the lower Clyde and on the whole I got a pretty favourable impression from the visit. It appears, however, that though things are improving and the group's capital investment is beginning to bear fruit, we still lag a long way behind our main competitors in terms of output per man hour.

I had asked to meet the convenors of shop stewards wherever I went. Relations between them and management seemed good. One Communist shop steward whom I met was very proud of the submarine the yard had built for Chile and didn't seem at all disturbed that we should be exporting it to the new Pinochet government.

The next day I drove to Aberdeen, where I was briefed by the Burmah oil people about the next day's visit to the oil rig.

On Wednesday morning we assembled at Dyce airport at seven and flew in a little Trislander aircraft to Sumburgh at the southern tip of Shetland. The flight took about an hour and we flew over Fair Isle, which looked a lovely spot. At Sumburgh we transferred to a two-engined helicopter to fly to the rig.

The rig *Ocean Kokne* is about 120 miles east of Shetland and the flight took just over an hour. The weather improved as we approached it and we could see four other rigs in the area. We landed safely and then went on a tour of inspection. The whole operation is tremendously impressive. There are about sixty men on board. They work twelve hours on and twelve off and spend alternate weeks ashore. They work hard and there is no drink on board. They eat well and say that they are so tired when they come off watch that they don't want to do much but sleep. We were lucky because they were replacing the drilling bit when we arrived and we saw the whole process of pulling up the pipe, fitting a new bit and then sending the pipe down again. This is all done by the 'roustabouts', who are rather like able seamen and work very hard for their money (roughly £3,000 a year). The man in charge was adamantly opposed to trade unions and said that if they got involved the operation would be impossible to carry out.

Next morning we drove to Kinloss RAF airfield and picked up a small helicopter for Nigg Bay. We flew low across the Cromarty Firth and circled over a colony of seals which went lumbering into the water when they saw us. The pilot told me he had recently retired from the navy and settled in the Highlands, where he had started his own business. But when he saw what opportunities there were for flying he joined the helicopter firm and left his wife to run the business. He said that if you were prepared to work hard, the opportunities in north-east Scotland were unlimited now. I can quite believe this – you get a most exhilarating feeling of growth and expansion wherever you go here.

After about twenty minutes we landed at Nigg Bay, which is at the seaward end of the Cromarty Firth. We were then shown the most impressive piece of ironmongery I have ever seen – the production platform they are building for BP for use in the Forties field. It is built on its side on the top of an enormous raft at the bottom of the biggest dry dock in the world. When it is finished they will fill the dock with water and float it out to the site, where they will fill one side with water until it is vertical. They will then fix it to the seabed and when in position it will stand a lot higher than Millbank Tower.* It is treated with special paints which are supposed to give it a life of twenty-five years.

Wednesday 15 May 1974

The press is full of reports of the speech which Denis Healey made at last night's CBI dinner. He spoke very reassuringly about profits and their importance for investment and said that a broad consensus had been reached at the last Neddy meeting. It is clear that the discussion we had then made it possible for him to speak as he did last night – which is just what I had hoped for.

In the evening we had a very enjoyable dinner party at home. Madron Seligman said that Heath had been very badly shaken by the election result but perhaps it had been a salutary lesson for him. He blamed Jim Prior and Peter Carrington, rather than Barber, for the bad advice Heath had received during the miners' strike.

Friday 17 May 1974

In the evening I went down to St George's House, Windsor for a 'consultation' on workers' participation. I had never been before and was much more favourably impressed than I had expected to be. It was founded by the previous Dean of Windsor and the Duke of Edinburgh as a place to hold conferences of two kinds – one for the education of the clergy, the other for improving industrial relations. This conference was chaired by the general secretary of NUPE, Alan

---

* The thirty-storey building in which the Neddy offices were located.

Fisher, and the people on it consisted of shop stewards (some with their wives) plus three or four industrial chaplains. There were about two dozen people in all.

After dinner David Lea, the head of the economic section of the TUC, gave a talk about the TUC report on industrial democracy. He spoke well and confidently. He had a lot to say about the Labour government's plans and is evidently quite certain that they will soon be returned with a large majority and will then govern the country for at least five years. The possibility that they may be forced by an economic crisis to modify their plans does not, I think, enter his head.

Saturday 18 May 1974

I gave my own speech in the evening. I took the line that the time was ripe for a big move in the direction of workers' participation but that it must take a form which could increase efficiency and not impede it. I argued for an extension of collective bargaining in matters affecting employment and suggested that the CBI and the TUC might together draw up a code defining the matters which ought to be subject to joint control through collective bargaining. But I said that I was opposed to the concept of worker directors, which would act as a brake on innovation and hold up decision-taking at a time when we had to meet fierce competition abroad.

My talk went down badly. They all thought I was a capitalist reactionary and a number said that if they had been doubtful about the merits of the TUC proposals my talk would have convinced them that the TUC was right. I was a bit shaken but stuck to my guns and after it was over a number of people who had not spoken told me they agreed with me. (This is of course typical of the trade union movement.) Then we all went out to a pub together and everyone was very nice to me. I had a long talk with a shop steward from Corby steel works who said that if he had a Trotskyite among his activists he appointed him his deputy and then went on holiday. This, he reckoned, subjected the Trot to the discipline of the shop floor!

Sunday 19 May 1974

The morning began with reports from the various discussion groups into which the participants were divided. After the coffee break Alan Fisher asked me to lead off. I said that if I had my talk to give again I wouldn't alter the substance but, having heard what had been said in the discussion, would have put more emphasis on participation and less on consultation. I added that I was afraid that if the trade unions pressed for worker directors on a 50-50 basis they would set back the move to greater participation because the employers would dig their toes in and if need be take to the barricades to preserve their power. Much better, I said, to follow my prescription, which pro-gressive employers might be brought to acquiesce in voluntarily. After some further discussion a shop steward from the paper industry, Frank Walsh, who is well known to be a left-winger, spoke. He said the group should be grateful to me for introducing a note of realism into discussions which had otherwise had a strong dose of wishful thinking about them. He agreed that the employers would take to the barricades rather than surrender their power. If the workers wanted joint control (which he admitted the majority probably didn't) they too would have to man the barricades – and no doubt Ronnie McIntosh would run up and down between the two sets of barricades blowing his whistle. Fisher then summed up well and included a graceful reference to my own contribution – and we all parted good friends. A curious experience – it shows how hard is the lot of someone who genuinely takes an independent line!

Tuesday 21 May 1974

I caught a four o'clock train to Leeds. In the evening Pat Fisher and I gave a dinner for four of the local trade union people – all prominent men in their region and all right-wing lay preacher-type moderates. People who prate about 'who governs the country' wouldn't believe that such trade unionists exist.

Wednesday 22 May 1974

I was shown round some textile mills by Roy Strand, the president of the Wool Textile Delegation. The first shed we went to was full of old-fashioned jacquard looms weaving fancy worsted cloths. It was dreadfully noisy and I expect it looked much the same eighty years ago. The second was clean and quiet and contained eight automatic knitting machines which operate twenty-four hours a day, seven days a week.

Thursday 27 June 1974

I had a message from No. 10 to say that Wilson had decided to take the chair at next week's Neddy meeting.

I took Peter Menzies, the chairman of the Electricity Council,* to lunch. He is a nice, unassuming sort – not a heavyweight, I should think. He told me that there was only a handful of good people among the senior management in the electricity industry and that until he arrived there had been no career planning of any kind. This confirms my own impression – I think people underrate the damage done by the mediocrity of the general run of managers in nationalised industries.

---

* Sir Peter Menzies had been deputy chairman of ICI before taking up his post at the Electricity Council.

Friday 28 June 1974

In the afternoon I looked in on Fredy Fisher. He was full of gloom. He said that if the election was held in October it would be too late – we should be in the middle of a raging crisis well before then. He attributes our problems primarily to our failure to work hard enough and expressed great anxiety about the position of middle management. He said Healey had been to lunch at the *FT* the day before and had admitted that he had underrated the danger of management backlash, just as the government had underrated the risk of Protestant backlash in Ulster. But Fisher said that it would take more than words to restore confidence – the government would have to do things as well.

Saturday 29 June 1974

After going to Dunsfold for the wedding of David Nicolson's daughter, we drove to Oxford in a great rush for the Balliol Gaudy, which began at 7.45. I arrived at the college at eight o'clock in morning dress and sat down in hall at ten past in a dinner jacket, having changed in the porter's lodge. Doreen drove back to East Hendred, where we were due to stay the weekend with the Jenkins.

After dinner Roy and I went off with Madron Seligman to have a word with Ted Heath, who was holding court in the old senior common room. I told him how much I liked his latest speech (in which he talked sensibly about trade union problems and undertook that the Tories would not try to reintroduce the Industrial Relations Act). Ronnie Grierson,* who was standing by, said that I seemed to imply that I hadn't liked his earlier speeches, to which I replied that that was quite true and that Ted already knew it. Ted acknowledged

---

* A director of GEC, he had been the first managing director of the IRC.

this and appeared pleased that I approved of his new conciliatory line.

Sunday 30 June 1974

We had a very pleasant day at East Hendred. Roy told me in strict confidence ('don't tell your trade union friends') that he had decided that if Labour won the next election he would tell Wilson he did not want office in the new government. He said this would give him some room for manoeuvre and get him free of 'people he didn't agree with'. This news came as a surprise to me but I said I thought he was very wise – he had nothing to lose and might have something to gain. We didn't discuss the matter deeply but later on in the day Roy said something about his 'thinking increasingly in terms of a government of national unity'.

His decision not to take office again if Labour wins is good news. It is fairly clear he won't ever be leader of the Labour Party as it is now but it is equally clear he has it in him to be a good Prime Minister and in certain circumstances he could be a great one. There is no doubt that a large number of people in all parties think that he would make a good leader of some kind of national government. Nevertheless I am not really in favour of splitting the Labour Party because I think the trade union leaders would be bound to go with the left – even those whose views would incline them much more to the social democratic wing of the party. I made this point to Roy, who said it was a risk he was very conscious of; but I don't think that in his heart of hearts he cares – or knows – much about the trade union movement.

Monday 1 July 1974

Our report on the effects of the oil situation on British industry was published today. I did TV interviews for BBC and ITN in the office but the BBC people forgot to put any film in the camera so I had to go to Wood Lane to do it again. We were well reported throughout the evening on radio and TV and in the evening papers. I decided in the dark days of January to launch the study, while everyone else was preoccupied with the three-day week etc., and I think industrialists and people generally are glad when independent bodies produce studies of this sort – especially when, as in this case, they do it quickly.

Tuesday 2 July 1974

A very good press this morning for our energy report, including a leader in the *FT*.

At 4 p.m. I went to the House to see the PM about tomorrow's meeting. He was affable, relaxed and chatty and didn't seem to want to get to the point quickly – but though he may have slowed down I got the impression that he was registering everything I said and had lost none of his professionalism. There were no signs of the ill health that is talked of so much nowadays – or of his having had too much brandy. He told me he hadn't had time to read the Neddy papers – though he said he would – and didn't seem to have given the meeting any great thought. I think his decision to take the chair was simply a reaction to Heath's conciliatory 'national unity' speech last week. I said I thought the meeting should be used to try to create more common ground among the parties about the way to handle our problems and that we should aim to rebuild confidence, which was now at a dangerously low point. This led on to a discussion of Tony Benn's proposals. Wilson said he had told Benn to belt up – he would see that he didn't make any more speeches about his proposals until the Cabinet had taken its decision.

In the evening I spoke to Campbell Adamson and to Len Murray,

who phoned me at home after he got back from the NUM conference at Llandudno. I congratulated Len on his success at the
NUM conference (where the moderates just defeated the left wing)
and on the new TUC document on the social contract, which I think
is very good – even though it may not work out in practice. I also told
him that I thought that it would be a good thing if he would give the
CBI a helping hand at tomorrow's meeting; and I told Campbell I
thought it would be helpful if the CBI would avoid making snide
remarks about the social contract. So I have now done all I can to try
to get a positive outcome from the meeting and we must hope for the
best.

Wednesday 3 July 1974

The Neddy meeting went off well. Wilson said at the end that he had
now chaired twenty such meetings and this was the best and I think
he probably meant it.

Ralph Bateman led off – very briefly and very badly. He has no
sense of occasion at all and in my view let industry down badly
through his failure to present their case properly. Campbell followed
him and spoke rather well about the reasons why confidence was so
low. He mentioned but did not press industry's worries about
'Bennery'. I spoke next, saying that there were certain factors which
should offset the gloom but that no one could blame industrialists
who in the face of the current uncertainties hesitated to invest.
Almost everyone on the council spoke but the PM made sure that
Tony Benn did not come in until the very end and then only very
briefly. Benn in fact spoke in very muted terms and one of the
strangest things about the meeting was that his proposals for
nationalisation etc. were hardly mentioned. Everyone was agreed
that while things were serious they were not quite so apocalyptic as
the stock market and some of the press were making out. Sidney

Greene, who really is excellent, said towards the end, 'Surely the purpose of this meeting is to see what we can do collectively to get out of our mess.'

Wilson asked me to speak last and I was able to say that I thought that in the light of the discussion I could tell the press that the council had agreed unanimously on a number of points which I spelled out without anyone raising any objection. We in fact achieved much more common ground than I had expected, though we shall have to wait and see whether it leads to action by the government – e.g. a relaxation of dividend control.

Friday 5 July 1974

At dinner with John and Madeleine Hunt, Barney Hayhoe* told Doreen that there was a lot of opposition in the Tory party to Heath continuing as leader. After dinner Peter Rawlinson† said the same to me – he was never, I think, a Heath man. He also told me that the middle-class backlash against the unions was now very noticeable in the suburban constituencies and that he thought the Conservatives had a real chance of winning the next election. He was quite clear that if they didn't, Heath would be finished as leader.

Tuesday 9 July 1974

I took Keith Joseph to lunch at the Royal Thames. He started off brisk, alert and suspicious. It was clear he hadn't much use for Neddy and thought the lunch would probably turn out to be a waste of time. But as lunch went on he relaxed and we found ourselves having a very good talk. His main worries about Neddy were that its

---

* Conservative MP for Heston & Isleworth.
† Conservative MP for Epsom. He had been Attorney General from 1970 to 1974.

composition encouraged appeasement of the big unions, that the voice of non-union people such as doctors was excluded and that any agreement reached round the table could only be a woolly compromise. I explained why I didn't agree and told him that I thought the Conservatives had missed a real chance of reaching a concordat with the TUC last December and January.

We went on to discuss industrial efficiency etc. He is setting up a little unit which he wants to produce published research on how to improve the workings of the free enterprise system. I told him we were working on the same thing – only we called it improving the performance of British industry.

Altogether it was a pleasant and successful lunch. I had never had a tête-à-tête with Joseph before and I must say I found him interesting and likeable. He said he would tell Heath and/or Prior what I had said about the unions and industrial relations.

Wednesday 10 July 1974

I lunched at the Ecu de France with Peter Wilsher, the editor of the *Sunday Times* Business News. He is an unassuming man with a good knowledge of history. He talked a lot – and well – about Germany in the 1920s and thinks that we may well be on the edge of some kind of collapse or revolutionary change. He seemed unperturbed by this.

Friday 12 July 1974

We had a Group of 4 meeting in the morning – the first to be attended by Douglas Wass.* I had phoned Wass before the meeting

---

* Sir Douglas Wass had become permanent secretary of the Treasury when Douglas Allen was appointed Head of the Civil Service on William Armstrong's retirement.

and found him a bit sceptical about its usefulness. This is because Len Murray has such open lines to the PM and Chancellor (with whom he had a long talk *à deux* this week) that Wass thinks he won't be much interested in spending time talking to officials. In the event I was glad to find that Murray was open and showed no signs of wanting to scrap the Group of 4 – rather the reverse. Campbell Adamson reminded us he was now the only surviving member of the original team (of which the others were Douglas Allen, Frank Figgures and Vic Feather).

I started off by suggesting we should think about the situation we might have to deal with in the last quarter of the year. The safest assumptions to make were that we should have an autumn election, that its result would not be decisive, and that the world situation would take a turn for the worse. I was clear that NEDO ought to do some work in preparation for this and would welcome their views on what this should be.

Wass then gave us a spine-chilling account of how easily things might go wrong on the international money front. He said that there were huge sums on seven-day deposit in London and that if their owners lost confidence in our ability to manage our affairs there was nothing we could do to stop them moving their money out. Murray said his main worries on the wages front concerned white-collar unions, which were coming increasingly under the influence of international socialists and other left-wing groups (this applied particularly to the civil service unions).

In general we had a good talk. I have clearly got a free hand to do whatever preparatory work seems best to me. At the suggestion of Murray and Adamson the group is to meet again in September after the Trades Union Congress.

I went on to lunch at the Cavalry Club, where Geoffrey Gilbertson had asked me to meet the ICI chairman, Jack Callard. He is a quiet man, not outgoing, thoughtful and apparently liberal. I asked him how pessimistic he was about our prospects. He said ICI were very busy at the present time and their export trade in particular was booming. Within the firm he had been saying for months that the boom would come to an end but so far there was no sign of it. He said Tony Benn's ideas were disastrous and were seriously damaging confidence, though he agreed that senior ministers were going out of their way to emphasise their disagreement with Benn. Callard would like to see a coalition government for the next five years. I said I agreed we should aim for much greater agreement about how to tackle our economic problems but that my time in the Cabinet Office (where I saw the strains which office imposed even with a one-party Cabinet) made me sceptical about the workability of a coalition. Callard and Gilbertson were both critical of the civil service, which, they claimed, gave industry far less help than it got in other countries. Callard was, however, very complimentary about the help ICI got from our commercial diplomats abroad. A useful and pleasant lunch, though Callard is clearly someone whom one would need a good deal of time to get to know well.

I have had a nice letter from Keith Joseph thanking me for 'a very civilised and worthwhile lunch'.

Tuesday 16 July 1974

Martin Redmayne* came in after lunch to discuss the possibility of the retailers being represented on Neddy. I said I thought the TUC would oppose it but that after an election, especially if it resulted in a Con–Lib government, there might be pressure to alter the membership of the council to admit a number of new groups – e.g.

---

* Lord Redmayne was chairman of the Retail Consortium. He had been government Chief Whip from 1959 to 1964.

professional people not affiliated to the TUC. I quoted the remark Keith Joseph had made to me over lunch – that the trouble with Neddy was that it didn't include the Royal College of Nursing. Redmayne said he wanted to see a stronger Liberal Party leading to a coalition; there ought to be more defections to the Liberals like Chris Mayhew's from the Labour Party* but also including some from the Conservatives. He surprised me by saying that he had always hoped Hugh Gaitskell would found a new Radical Party, implying that he (Redmayne) would have joined it.

Wednesday 17 July 1974

I had a real setback today. Ever since I came to NEDO I have been trying to get a trade union chairman for one of our EDCs. Up to now – in ten years – all the chairmen have come from management except for one or two academics and the Duke of Northumberland, who chairs the Agriculture EDC. With great tact and persistence (though I say it myself) I recently got David Basnett to agree to take on the chairmanship of the Chemicals EDC, having first ascertained that this would be acceptable to the employers and to Healey. This morning I phoned Jack Jones, whose union is strongly represented in chemicals, just to check that he wouldn't raise any objection. He exploded at the proposal and said it was quite unacceptable. The TGWU were the main union in chemicals and if the chairman was to be a union man he would have to come from the TGWU. He said that he was very annoyed that I should have sounded the employers before sounding him. I should know that the GMWU were not regarded in the movement as a 'real trade union' and that although Basnett was a nice enough chap he was much too academic and had

---

* Mayhew had been Minister for the Royal Navy in Harold Wilson's first administration but resigned and joined the Liberal Party in 1966.

never worked in a factory. I reacted sharply and said that if he took this line I should never get a trade union chairman of an EDC – an objective on which I had thought I could count on his support. Jack calmed down and after discussing it further we parted without any hard feelings; but it is extremely worrying for me and in my view very shortsighted on Jack's part. I now have the double problem of straightening things out with Basnett and finding a new chairman for Chemicals. The way of a DG is hard.

I discussed the incident later in the day with two ex-TUC members of NEDO. We all came to the conclusion that there was no point in going back to Jack to see if he would change his mind and no question of going ahead with Basnett's appointment in view of his reaction. The EDC system operates entirely by agreement and this means in effect that all interested parties (of which the general secretary of the TGWU is one in this case) have a right of veto.

Thursday 18 July 1974

In the evening we had a small dinner party at home. Neil Bruce* was staying the night having just flown in from Lisbon. He spoke interestingly about the revolution. He says that except for main-taining law and order there is no effective government in Portugal just now – in other words the government machine is not function-ing at all. Contrary to what I expected he said that the Communists were not a strong force at the centre though they are gaining control of the local authorities. He thought that a Communist take over was most unlikely because there is no proletariat and the army is so strong.

---

* An old friend who was a BBC foreign correspondent.

Tuesday 23 July 1974

We went to the Garden Party in the afternoon. It was a perfect day, which was just as well as there seemed far more people than usual. We met Robin Chichester-Clark,* who told us there would be a government of national unity by the autumn.

Thursday 25 July 1974

I took Frank Figgures to the Travellers for lunch. It is his last day as chairman of the Pay Board and he was very low key. He has been badly treated by politicians on both sides – a poor reward for disinterested public service. He thinks nothing of Whitelaw or Foot – the last two secretaries of state with whom he has dealt. He doesn't think Foot will last long – he wouldn't have the stomach for the problems we shall have this winter.

The Pay Board are issuing a valedictory report today with their reflections on incomes policies. So is John Donaldson, the able but wrongheaded judge at the National Industrial Relations Court, whose judgments seemed to me to show so little understanding of the contemporary trade union movement.

Saturday 27 July 1974

Yesterday evening Roy made a major speech, stressing the need for moderate policies if Labour is to win the election and by implication sharply criticising Benn's policies towards industry. As usual it is a very well-worded speech and I would guess that the ideas in it would be supported by at least sixty per cent of the British people.

---

* Sir Robin Chichester-Clark had been Minister of State in the Department of Employment from 1972 to 1974.

Monday 29 July 1974

After lunch I spoke to Denis Healey about the handling of Wednesday's council meeting. He seemed in low spirits. He was just off to a meeting of the Cabinet committee which is considering Benn's draft White Paper. Denis seemed fairly confident that his view – which is very close to the PM's – would prevail.

At 5 p.m. I went to the first meeting of a group which PEP* have set up to help them to write a report about the 'reconstruction of Britain'. Their idea is to have something ready immediately after the election containing the main elements of a programme for dealing with our present crisis. The papers were good though I thought they painted a somewhat exaggerated picture of our present troubles, bad though they potentially are. They have assembled an interesting group for the project.

In the evening Roy and Jennifer came to supper and we all went on to a film. Roy had suggested this earlier in the day wanting, I imagine, some relief from the publicity surrounding his recent speech. Because of this we didn't talk much about it but he did say that he was becoming an 'extreme moderate' and was thoroughly fed up with the party system, which he regarded as a conspiracy against the people.

Tuesday 30 July 1974

I spent most of the day getting ready for tomorrow's council meeting but in the afternoon I went to see Derek Mitchell to get some advice for my American trip. He said that the permanent secretaries were full of gloom about the prospects for this winter – they all thought the wages explosion would get out of hand.

---

* Political and Economic Planning, a well-regarded independent think tank.

Wednesday 31 July 1974

Another good council meeting. Our paper – mostly the work of David Stout* – on Britain's industrial performance was very well received on all sides. Campbell referred to it as the best paper he had seen from NEDO in five years and Sidney Greene pressed us to publish it (which we shall).

I spoke for longer than usual in introducing the paper. I said that we must now accept we couldn't hope to solve our problems by demand management policies. We had seen three attempts to break out onto a higher growth path by expansionary policies – under Reggie Maudling, George Brown and Tony Barber – and each time we had failed because we couldn't meet strong home and overseas demand at the same time. In summing up Denis Healey said that while he couldn't anticipate the contents of the White Paper on industrial policy, it might well lead to Neddy and the EDCs having a 'more operational role'. (No one seems to know what he meant by this, including Douglas Wass). I was asked to prepare papers for the October council meeting on the roles of Neddy and the EDCs, taking today's paper as a starting point. Michael Meacher, Parliamentary Secretary at the Department of Industry, came in place of Tony Benn. He spoke unprovocatively and well.

Thursday 1 August 1974

I had the first meeting of my new Advisory Group on Finance for Investment. This is a strong group of industrialists and City people, all of whom are showing great interest in the project. After the meeting was over a letter arrived from Gordon Richardson giving the project his blessing.

---

* An Oxford economist of high calibre who later became NEDO's economic director.

Sunday 4–Monday 26 August

On holiday in the Pyrenees and Majorca.

Wednesday 28 August 1974

I took Frank Chapple to lunch at Inigo Jones. He has a reputation for being aggressive and foul mouthed when you first meet him but on this occasion he was quiet and unassertive. He doesn't think much of Len Murray and says that he will have no real power in the movement so long as Jack Jones and Hugh Scanlon are on the General Council. He said Vic Feather was the only general secretary of the TUC who could have successfully given a lead to the movement over the heads of the General Council and that he (Chapple) had often urged him to do so – but Feather refused and wasn't interested.

Chapple sees everything in terms of the struggle against Communism. When I spoke of the need to create a consensus about economic policy after the election – meaning government, the TUC and CBI – he said, 'But there is a consensus already among those who want to see the system continue – it is only those who want to bring it down who are outside.' For this reason he thinks that General Walker and David Stirling, with their call for volunteers to help to prevent the destruction of the system, are right in their diagnosis. Chapple is a lonely figure – he is implacably opposed to the left, including Jones and Scanlon, but contemptuous of his colleagues on the right of the movement. In talking about Conservative politicians, lawyers and 'all the middle class people I meet nowadays' he said he was very much struck by how many of them had a guilt complex about their privileged upbringing. I assured him I had none.

Friday 30 August 1974

I had lunch with Derek Mitchell at Rules. He was uncharacter-
istically serious and we spent most of lunch talking about the
impending crisis. He said there was no systematic forward thinking
going on in Whitehall. All but a very few civil servants were
unwilling to do any contingency planning without ministerial
authority, with the result that such work as was done took the
prejudices and policies of the ministers of the day as its starting
point. He wants all the policy options to be examined – including
some which might be anathema to the present government. With an
election almost certainly coming this must be right but Mitchell
thought it would be virtually impossible to get done.

Monday 2 September 1974

I went down to Brighton for the Trades Union Congress. Alf Allen,
who is this year's president, made a strong opening speech about the
need for trade unions to face up to their responsibilities and not
simply pursue their own selfish ends. It was an outspoken speech
directed at the left wing and more courageous than I expected from
Alf, who is often criticised for not sticking up for his beliefs strongly
enough and so letting the left have things all their own way.

Tuesday 3 September 1974

Jim Callaghan, as chairman of the Labour Party, made a hard-hitting
and forthright speech stressing the need for the TUC to implement
their side of the social contract if we were to avoid heavy unemployment. He got a lot of applause and judging by conversations
afterwards it seems to have gone down well with most delegates.

Pat Fisher and I had a useful dinner with Richard O'Brien, the chairman of the CBI's Employment Policy Committee, and Alan Swinden, the deputy director general concerned with labour matters. Swinden was very depressed about the CBI and talked freely about his difficulties. In answer to his questions I said I thought that the CBI's performance at Neddy meetings compared badly with the TUC's and repeated my belief that the CBI should concentrate on representing effectively private-sector manu-facturing interests rather than trying to speak for the nationalised industries, the retailers and so on as well. Swinden said that although the CBI went to great trouble to brief its own team for talks in Neddy, its representatives had no idea how to conduct discussions with government and unions and seemed unwilling to take the trouble to prepare themselves properly. He said that the amateurish approach adopted by the CBI team in briefing talks before meetings with Harold Wilson 'would make your hair stand on end'.

Wednesday 4 September 1974

This morning there was an intensely interesting discussion on the social contract. I gather that the AUEW and the CPSA, who have sponsored a motion opposing the social contract unless certain preconditions are fulfilled, have been under heavy pressure from the General Council to withdraw it in the interests of pre-election unity. It seems clear that Hugh Scanlon tried to persuade his union to agree to this but they refused to do so; and Ken Gill, the general secretary of the AUEW's technical section (formerly TASS), moved the motion in a forceful speech this morning. He is a hard-line Communist and was elected to the General Council yesterday. The motion was seconded by Bill Kendall, the general secretary of the CPSA, who is personally a man of moderate views but is the prisoner of left-wing forces within his own union.

    Before Gill spoke, Len Murray gave the General Council's

reasons for supporting the social contract. It was his first major speech to Congress as general secretary – indeed probably the first time he had ever addressed a Congress at all. It was a closely argued and effective speech, though Pat Fisher and I thought the way he delivered it was somehow not quite right for Congress – he was, I think, quite naturally very tense and this resulted in a certain theatricality in his delivery. A number of well-known figures in the movement then spoke (including Lawrence Daly of the NUM) – all of them in support of the General Council and against Gill and Kendall. Harry Urwin of the TGWU in particular made an impassioned appeal to Congress to keep its side of the bargain with the Labour government, all argued in good old-fashioned emotional terms. Then there came a surprise intervention by Scanlon, who had not been expected to speak. He made two points: one, that the employers through their 'refusal to invest' were making the social contract unworkable; and the other, that the TUC ought not to confirm the social contract until after the election in case the Tories won.

Immediately after this Gill replied to the debate. He said his union were second to none in their desire to see a Labour government back but that they could not support wage restraint in any form and that they must press their motion to a vote.

Finally, Murray made a brilliant reply to the debate in which he stressed the need for unity – and called on the AUEW even now to withdraw their motion. If they did, he promised that the preconditions 'would be embodied in the TUC line in discussions with the government' – adding that he had not consulted the General Council on this and for all he knew they would impeach him for it afterwards.

Alf Allen then asked whether Congress would agree to a five-minute adjournment to let some delegations consider their position; but although the shouts of Yes and No seemed about equally balanced he said Congress was evidently against the idea and he would proceed to take a vote. After the voting had started Gill suddenly appeared on the rostrum and said that, while his union did not retract anything, they would in the interests of unity withdraw their motion and abstain in the vote on the General Council's proposals. This caused great excitement and Congress then adjourned.

This episode was a great personal triumph for Murray, who has now established his authority over Congress in a remarkable way. Reactions to it were, however, very mixed. Alan Sapper, the Communist general secretary of the film workers, told me he thought Gill would be in great trouble with his members for withdrawing the motion without consulting his delegation. (Apparently the decision to withdraw was taken in a hurried conversation between Scanlon, Gill and another Communist, Eddie Marsden.) Dick Briginshaw, another left-winger, said that Gill should never have allowed his union to become so exposed in the first place and that he would have been a fool not to withdraw. He said that although his own union, NATSOPA, was 'radical' – a euphemism for left-wing dominated – he had had no great difficulty in persuading them to support the General Council's line.

John Boyd of the CSEU was furious and Sidney Greene and Dai Davies were very unhappy that the left had been let off the hook. They are all right-wingers and would have much preferred the motion to go to the vote so as to isolate the only three unions which would have supported it – the AUEW, the CPSA and ASLEF. This was a spontaneous and unconcerted reaction because I spoke to them all, separately, within a few minutes of the adjournment. Alf Allen later told me he took the same view, which is presumably why he ruled against the five-minute adjournment.

Some people thought the whole thing had been hatched up in advance and stage-managed to produce a dramatic show of unity.

But I am quite clear from my various conversations – including one with George Doughty, who was Gill's predecessor and was sitting with the TASS delegation at the time – that this was not the case. Indeed, I think Murray may have been as surprised as the rest of us when Gill bowed to his pressure. Everyone says it was one of the most dramatic incidents to happen at Congress for many years. It is also clear that tactically it was a great achievement which will help the Labour Party considerably – and could even win the election for them.

In the evening I went to a General Council party and then gave a private dinner for the general secretaries of five public service unions with which NEDO does not have much contact – Geoffrey Drain of NALGO, Bill Kendall of the CPSA, Alan Fisher of NUPE, Gerry Gillman of the Society of Civil and Public Servants and Fred Jarvis of the NUT. They all confirmed the growing militancy among the public service unions, especially the white-collar ones. They attributed this to the slow growth of real earnings in the white-collar field, to envy of manual workers who used their industrial power to good effect, to resentment against government interference in public service wage negotiations and (in the case of the CPSA) to the growing influence of youngsters on the far left.

Thursday 5 September 1974

I spent the morning at Congress, which discussed international affairs. The EETPU and the GMWU had a motion down urging that, without prejudice to their position on British membership of the EEC, the TUC should co-operate with its institutions. This was moved by Derek Gladwyn of the GMWU, who made a very good speech and put forward what one would have thought was an unanswerable case. But nobody supported him – the trade union leaders' opposition to the EEC runs very deep.

At lunchtime Pat Fisher and I had a talk with Jimmy Jack, the secretary of the Scottish TUC. He is very concerned about the effect of the coming recession on employment in Scotland and thinks that a number of firms may concentrate production in their English factories to save transport costs, which have gone up a lot since the rise in the price of oil. He said that as yet there was very little support for the Scottish National Party among the working class of Scotland; its adherents were mostly professional people, shopkeepers and small businessmen – 'Poujadists' as he called them.

After lunch we went back to Congress to hear Harold Wilson's address. He looked bronzed and fit and I imagine hoped to give the lie to the widespread rumours that he is seriously ill. His speech was very long and lacked his old sparkle but I thought it was very good and followed very much a social democratic and not a Tribune line. He got a standing ovation but I found in conversation afterwards with a wide range of delegates that the general opinion was that his address was too long and uninspiring. I have also discovered this week that Tony Benn is neither liked nor respected by trade union leaders – indeed I have yet to find one who has a good word for him, which is remarkable considering all the trouble he has taken to woo them.

In the evening I gave my party for the General Council and the trade union members of the EDCs. I had asked Wilson, as chairman of Neddy, to come and there were two non-union chairmen of EDCs as well as half a dozen of the NEDO staff. Jim Callaghan also came.

The party was of course packed – about 100 in all. Everyone was very friendly and it seemed to be a great success. Wilson stayed for about an hour and seemed to get on all right, though somehow I got the impression that there was no real rapport between him and most of the TUC people, except for Jack Jones. Callaghan appears to have a much better relationship with them.

Shortly before the party I was asked by a team from the BBC

Millbank Tower: the Neddy offices were on the fifteenth floor, with a spectacular view downriver. (Crown copyright)

A typical NEDC meeting of 1976. The table was made specially for the council and was deliberately designed to be round so that no one block could be felt to have the upper hand. At this meeting James Callaghan is in the chair.

To his left are blocks of seven ministers and six union leaders; to his right are
he director general, two nationalised industry chairmen, a block of six from the
CBI and the independent Eric Roll. (*Financial Times*)

When told that his colleague George Brown was feeling out of sorts one morning, Harold Wilson said, 'He must be giving birth to another little Neddy.' In 1975 there were eighteen EDCs, whose chairmen are shown above with the director general. (*Times*)

Nationalised industry chairmen with Anthony Barber, the Chancellor of the Exchequer in 1973. Left to right: Derek Ezra (National Coal Board), A. F. Hetherington (British Gas), Sir Peter Menzies (Electricity Council), Lord Melchett (British Steel), Barber, Sir William Ryland (Post Office), David Nicolson (British Airways), Richard Marsh (British Rail). (Chris Ware/Keystone/Getty Images)

Hugh Scanlon: the president of the engineering worker union was not the left-wing firebrand popular belief. (Getty Images)

Jack Jones: the mo powerful trade unic leader of his day, though not always t most popular. (Getty Images)

Sidney Greene: 'once again, in retrospect, he stands out as the best'.

Len Murray putting a brave face on things as he went to see the Prime Ministe at the height of the miners' dispute in January 1974. (*Daily Telegraph*)

programme *Midweek* if I would mind their bringing the TV cameras and lights in to film the Prime Minister with trade union leaders. I refused, because of the risk that the film would be used in some election programmes and that the impression would get abroad that the director general of NEDO had given a 'political' party. The BBC people took this very badly. They said that the TUC and the PM's press officer had both agreed and exerted heavy pressure on me before and during the party to change my mind. I refused to budge – I am not willing to run any risk of Neddy getting caught in the election crossfire. I am not sure how pleased Wilson was but he made no objection to having the film made in a separate room. Len Murray entirely agreed with my decision and apologised for the pressure put on me to change my mind.

Friday 5 September 1974

I spent an hour at Congress and then motored back to London. It will take time to sort out one's impressions but my preliminary ones are these. The strength of the left has increased only marginally this year and the arrival of Ken Gill and Clive Jenkins on the General Council is not likely to change things much. Murray has increased his authority and will do his best to pursue moderate policies but probably wouldn't be able to assert his authority effectively on an issue on which Jack Jones opposed him. The country will be better off with the social contract than without it and the general run of union leaders will probably try to keep their side of the bargain at least for a while if Labour is re-elected. But the left will oppose any form of wage restraint and will try very hard to change our society and destroy capitalism. Until they succeed they will remain on the left of and in basic opposition to any government, even a Labour one.

I took Roy to lunch at Romeo and Juliet. He said he was feeling much more cheerful about the government and the election. This was partly due to Wilson's speech yesterday, all of which Roy could agree with. He also said that the manifesto would be all right from his point of view and would not contain any mention of a referendum on Europe. Roy was also cheered by the fact that Benn's influence in Cabinet seemed to have diminished. I asked him if this meant he would be willing to serve in a new Labour government after the election and he said 'yes'. He said he supposed there would be 'a great bust-up' after six months or so but he might as well wait till then before doing anything drastic. We spoke about Keith Joseph, who has made a major and in my view very high-quality speech about the need for a gradual return to 'sound money' policies if we are to get inflation under control. Roy said he entirely agreed with Joseph about the destructive effects of inflation and the need to give absolute priority to bringing it under control.

Monday 9 September 1974

I had a meeting with the chairmen of the little Neddies. We had a general discussion about Neddy and its satellite operations after the election. They all seem well disposed to using Neddy as a place to encourage or create a consensus about the economic strategy the country should follow over the next few years and to relating the work of the EDCs more closely to this strategy. Collectively the EDC chairmen, who are all able and reasonably prominent people, could be quite an influential force for sensible policies in industry if we can find ways of making them into a more coherent team.

Tuesday 10 September 1974

I went with two or three colleagues to BP to learn something of their problems in developing North Sea oil. They said inflation was putting a great strain on their resources. Up to now their programmes had been taking about eighteen months longer to complete than they had planned (because of design changes, labour shortages etc.) and these delays might increase. They were expecting the UK to be self-sufficient in oil by 1981.

I went on to a meeting with Peter Carey* and others at the Department of Industry to discuss the government's proposals for planning agreements.† They expect Neddy to play an active part in providing the economic background for their discussions with companies – assuming that Labour wins the election and the CBI don't boycott the whole idea of planning agreements. Carey's team is exceptionally able – but I thought that their ideas on what they could achieve through planning agreements were pretty naïve. I wonder very much whether the concept will come to anything.

I went to the Hilton for a lunch given by the US Conference Board. Denis Healey made a speech in which he said inflation in the UK would be down to single figures in 1976. No one in the audience, myself included, believed him.

Wednesday 11 September 1974

I went to see Douglas Allen at 9.30. He said that although he had been first of all head of the Treasury and latterly Head of the Civil Service, he had seen Harold Wilson only once since the election. Compared with past practice this is quite extraordinary. Allen thinks

---

* Second permanent secretary. Refreshingly iconoclastic in his approach, he was a highly effective civil servant.

† These envisaged that all large manufacturing companies would negotiate agreements with the DoI outlining their planned investment, exports etc. and any financial assistance to be provided by the government by way of grants for research and development or other purposes. The proposal, which was Tony Benn's brainchild, was to all intents and purposes stillborn.

Wilson is interested only in winning the election and will hand over as PM quite soon after it. We both agreed that if the change came quickly Callaghan was the most likely successor. Allen said he himself was not concerned with economic policy at all but that if Heath got back he would be. He thinks the pound will collapse before long – perhaps as a result of an expansionary budget in November. He thinks the US grip on money supply is too tight and that there is a real risk of a world slump.

David Basnett called at eleven to discuss the possibility of his being an EDC chairman. He knows about Jack Jones's 'black ball' and doesn't seem unduly resentful. He is to think the matter over and let me know what he thinks by the end of this month. Basnett said that this year's Congress marked some kind of landmark in TUC history. Unions had shown themselves willing to envisage giving the TUC a degree of influence or authority over their affairs which would have been inconceivable five years ago. This is Pat Fisher's view, too.

At twelve I went over to see Dundas Hamilton, the deputy chairman of the Stock Exchange. He put the collapse of confidence down to pressure on profits and uncertainty about the prospects for controlling inflation (and related political factors) in about equal parts. His own recipe for tackling the crisis is that all young men should be called up for two years' service of some kind! I asked him if the SE had any contact with the unions and to my surprise and pleasure he said that had very recently written to Len Murray offering to have a talk with him.

In the afternoon we had a good meeting of my advisory group on finance for investment. The general view was that no one in his senses would embark on new investment projects just now – retained profits were needed to provide working capital and long-term capital was not available. I spoke to David Nicolson about my trip to Toronto and he surprised me by saying he thought Roy

Jenkins should head the next government whatever its complexion. He said Roy's speech in July about inflation, industrial problems and so on was the most sensible thing he had heard for years. I was startled because I have never before heard David express views which contemplated a non-Conservative governing the country.

Thursday 12 September 1974

I went to the Bank of England to see Gordon Richardson. He had Kit MacMahon, an executive director of the bank, with him. Richardson said the pressure on profits and cash flow in industry was very severe. Ministers' approach to these matters (by implication Healey's in particular) was 'dotty' – they didn't understand the damage they were doing through the Price Code. He and MacMahon were both worried about the US authorities' refusal to take a serious interest in the problem of recycling oil funds, which they expect to flow in quantity to New York in the near future. They said that the German attitude to world economic problems was better than the American; Arthur Burns[*] was engaged in a crusade against inflation and didn't seem to be concerned if his tight money policy did all sorts of damage in the process.

I lunched with Douglas Wass at the Reform. He doesn't think the social contract will achieve anything at all. He thinks it is an open question whether the social contract will break or the pound collapse first – one way or the other he expects a real crisis some time next winter or spring. He said Healey didn't consult or warn the Treasury before saying that inflation would come down to single figures by 1976.

Peter Goldman, the director of the Consumers' Association, called in the afternoon to press for consumer representation on Neddy.

---

[*] Chairman of the board of governors of the US Federal Reserve System.

Friday 13 September 1974

A good Group of 4 meeting in the morning. Len Murray was much less sharp than he sometimes is – no doubt his success at Congress has relaxed him. He said that the TUC at Brighton had begun to inch its way to being 'a sensible trade union movement'. He expects something to come from the social contract but says that at the end of the day the individual unions are free to go their own way. The big problem was the attitude of the white-collar unions.

We had a useful discussion about the post-election situation. I urged the need for a return to some form of national economic planning in order to secure the maximum possible agreement about the way in which we should aim to use our resources over the next few years. Wass and Murray supported this – Campbell Adamson, who was just back from holiday, had less to say. I said I thought the first thing to do was to try and get some agreed analysis of the nature of the crisis we faced – one of the most striking things about the present situation was that people differed so widely, even within the same political party, on just what our real problems were. On this Murray said he noticed a big difference among working men between the attitude of under-35s and over-35s towards inflation. The younger men didn't regard it as a particularly worrying problem – the others did.

After lunch I had three-quarters of an hour's talk with Denis Healey. He accepts that profits have been squeezed too hard and would like to do something about it. He is aware that if he reflates in November it may lead to a run on the pound but says there is no chance of holding the social contract (from which he seems to expect a good deal) if unemployment rises sharply and he doesn't do anything about it. He does not think that the fabric of society is endangered by inflation – he thinks that inflation is causing some worrying economic problems but that much of the talk about its political and social effects is grossly overdone. He referred to the paper we put to the July NEDC as the best and most important he has received since he became Chancellor and he wants Neddy to concentrate on industrial policy and avoid getting bogged down in macro-economic discussions. When I said I thought Neddy ought to be used to get an agreed analysis of our economic crisis he said he thought this would be impossible because the theoretical apparatus on which such an analysis could be based no longer existed – the economists had to admit they simply didn't understand our present problems.

Denis said it was not so much that he was an optimist as that he was determined – to which I replied that no one who knew him would dispute this. He has a refreshingly independent mind but I think he wants to keep the strings of economic policy-making too much in his own hands – the post-election situation will, in my view, call for a real effort by the Chancellor to create a new consensus, involving both sides of industry, about at least the broad lines of economic strategy – and also about the assumptions on which it should be based. I was startled to find that Denis has been advised that we shall be self-sufficient in oil in 1978 – three years before the date BP gave me earlier this week.

Saturday 14 September 1974

Terence Higgins[*] telephoned about the reference in the Conservative Party manifesto to strengthening Neddy. He said they had nothing radical in mind – they wanted to build on something which existed and worked well rather than create anything new. I told him that I had received various approaches from people who wanted their group to be represented on Neddy – retailers, consumers, the

---

[*] Conservative MP for Worthing and an opposition spokesman on trade.

BIM etc. In principle I would have no objection to widening the scope of Neddy but practical considerations pointed the other way. The council as at present constituted was in good shape – its discussions over the last nine months, under both governments, had been realistic and serious, and no one on it seemed to grudge the time spent at meetings. I was very keen that the council should be used after the election to create some kind of consensus about medium-term economic and industrial strategy and I thought this process might be hampered if new members were brought in.

Higgins said that the Conservatives did not want to use unemployment as a deliberate weapon to restrain inflation – rather, they thought it essential to control inflation if mass unemployment was to be avoided. Higgins thinks that the wage explosion this winter and the accompanying shake out of labour will surpass those of 1971.

Sunday 15 September 1974

Roy rang just before I left for Washington. He said as of today his guess was for an overall Labour majority: but as the last two elections showed, big shifts of opinion could take place during the campaign.*

In Washington I stayed with Anthony and Mary Rawlinson. They were very kind and hospitable to me. Although the weather was hot and steamy the city was looking beautiful, with the leaves just turning.

Monday 16 September 1974

The people at the embassy, who were very helpful, had arranged a heavy programme for me and I spent most of the day seeing various people in the US administration. Peter Ramsbotham, the

---

* The date of the election (10 October) was announced on 18 September.

ambassador, gave a lunch for me at which one of the other guests was Lane Kirkland, the secretary of the AFL-CIO.* He is the closest they have in the States to an opposite number to Len Murray and I found him an experienced and impressive man.

Anthony Rawlinson and I were entertained to dinner by Henry Wallick, a governor of the Federal Reserve. He is central European by origin and perhaps because of this is very conscious of the social and political risks of prolonged inflation. He has a delightful sense of humour and we had a very enjoyable evening with him at the University Club. His views on how to reduce inflation are austere and make no concessions to the need to avoid unemployment and maintain growth in the economy: he regards these as dangerous western European aberrations, not to be treated as serious by any thinking person.

Wednesday 18 September 1974

More interviews – all interesting but I am still very short of sleep. At Eric Roll's suggestion Kermit Gordon had arranged a lunch for me at the Brookings Institution. About ten of their people were there plus Rawlinson and others from the embassy. They are a lively, independent-minded lot and we had a very good discussion about inflation, oil prices, Britain etc. They are critical of what the administration is doing both to reduce oil consumption and to check inflation and I am told they are the nearest thing to an official opposition in the USA just now. I wish we had some equivalent to it in Britain.

In the evening I caught the 9 p.m. shuttle to New York and checked in at the Waldorf Astoria just before midnight.

---

* American Federation of Labor and Congress of Industrial Organizations.

Thursday 19 September 1974

I spent the day at a conference on the business outlook for 1975 attended by about 950 people from industry, finance etc. The Treasury Secretary, Bill Simon, made an unbelievably reactionary speech about the capitalist ethic, of a kind which no western European politician could make nowadays. He got a standing ovation but even the stockbrokers at my table thought it was a bit right wing.

Friday 20 September 1974

I spent most of the day visiting bankers with Anthony Rawlinson. They are impressive people – more so than many of ours and than some of the people I saw in Washington.

Saturday 21 September 1974

I got up early to fly to Toronto, where Jane and Angus Smart* met me. We went out to their country place at Claremont – forty acres of wooded downland about forty-five miles from Toronto.

Monday 23 September 1974

I saw some bankers with Angus and then went to a lunch which his chairman, Bill Harris, had arranged for me at the Toronto Club. There were a dozen or so men there, all prominent people in banking or industry. I particularly liked Ken Thomson, the son of Roy Thomson and chairman of the company which owns the *Times*. He

---

* An old friend and former colleague who had emigrated to Toronto, where he was economic adviser to a leading finance house.

brought me two copies of the paper which had just arrived from England.

I spoke for between ten and fifteen minutes about conditions in Britain. I made no attempt to minimise our difficulties but emphasised that there were offsetting factors and that many of the reports one saw about the state of Britain were gross exaggerations. I then went on to describe the TUC conference at Brighton, which in my view represented a victory for the moderates. I also stressed the strength of the social democrats in the Labour Cabinet – for example in connection with the White Paper on Bennery. I could see the disbelief on the faces round the table – some may have accepted what I said but the majority clearly thought we were on the verge of a Marxist revolution and economic collapse.

Friday 27 September 1974

Back in London I had lunch with John Hunt. He said that if the Tories won his choice for Chancellor would be Margaret Thatcher. On the Labour side he said that two or three months ago he would have tipped Denis Healey to become Prime Minister if anything happened to Wilson but that he had since made himself so unpopular with his colleagues that this was no longer on. He also said that everyone hoped that Tony Benn would be moved if Labour won the election but that this could by no means be counted on.

John told me he was pretty sure he would succeed in suppressing the publication of Dick Crossman's diaries in book form, though the *Sunday Times* articles would go ahead. He clearly felt very pleased about this – what a pity that someone so nice and intelligent as John should regard it as a good thing to deprive us of such a potentially valuable contribution to both entertainment and history.

In the afternoon I wrote to Ted Heath, who has been telling the press that he will shortly make a speech about his ideas for strengthening Neddy, which he wants to use to forge a 'national contract'.

Tuesday 1 October 1974

I had lunch with Toby Aldington* at Grindlays Bank. He thinks that the Conservatives will have more seats in the new parliament than Labour. He doesn't know of any Conservative-held seat which Labour could expect to win and although he expects the Conservatives to lose some seats to the Liberals he thinks that Labour will lose more to the Scottish Nationalists. He assumes that the next government will be a Con–Lib coalition with Heath as Prime Minister. He said he had not discussed the future of Neddy with Heath (though I expect he has because he talks to him very regularly) but that it would obviously have a central role in future. He thought it would be a good idea to have some Cabinet minister other than the Chancellor in the chair – presumably someone who was dedicated to promoting a consensus approach to economic affairs. I argued against this. I said that in so far as Neddy had succeeded it had been because it represented different power blocs and in economic matters the only minister who had real power was the Chancellor. Toby thought the Chancellor could attend Neddy meetings without taking the chair but I said that in no time you would find that the Chancellor made excuses not to come and sent a junior minister in his place. Afterwards I wondered, from something Toby said, if Heath had suggested that he (Toby) might be chairman of Neddy

---

* Lord Aldington was chairman of Sun Alliance Insurance and Grindlays Bank. He had been a Conservative minister in the 1950s and was one of Edward Heath's closest friends.

with a seat in the Cabinet. This is unlikely but not far fetched in view of Toby's friendship with Jack Jones.* He said incidentally that he had dined with Jones a few days ago and that he had confirmed that the trade unions would work with Heath if he were returned to power.

We talked a bit about the affairs of last winter. Toby had been in favour of settling the miners' strike before Christmas. He thinks the February election was unnecessary and blames Tony Barber for it. He thought Barber's rejection of the TUC offer at the January Neddy meeting had been due to clumsiness – I told him I was sure it had been a deliberate, calculated act due to Barber's desire to have a 7 February election. Toby confirmed that Peter Carrington, of whom he has a high opinion, had been in favour of an election on 7 February. He doesn't think much of Keith Joseph, who, he says, is incapable of making up his mind.

Toby said that he and Carrington were with Heath from about 2 a.m. until 5.30 on 1 March. When the result became clear Heath said, with tears streaming down his face, that clearly 'he had got it all wrong'.

Wednesday 2 October 1974

Ronnie Grierson looked in about midday. He is just back from Japan, where everyone is – he says – astonishingly confident about their ability to overcome the problems created by the oil price rise.

In the afternoon I went with Chris Lucas and Dick Homan from NEDO to see Dick Marsh and Monty Finniston. We had a good talk

---

* They had become friends when conducting a joint inquiry, commissioned by the Prime Minister in 1972, into the intractable problems of dock labour. I was the Whitehall official most closely involved with their inquiry.

about the role of Neddy, the position of the CBI etc. Marsh said he had always been in favour of nationalised industries belonging to the CBI but he was beginning to wonder if this was right. He gave us a hilarious description of Monday's meeting of the CBI president's advisory group, which he said had become quite absurdly political in its approach. He thought Ralph Bateman was intelligent but liable to fall into the hands of the backwoodsmen who were beginning to dominate the CBI. Marsh and Finniston both made helpful comments about the role of Neddy after the election – they are very friendly and well disposed to it. We agreed that it won't really work until we get a government which is prepared to use it properly (as I suspect Heath might be). Up to now all governments have seen Neddy as a place where they can jolly the CBI and TUC along into agreeing with something they have already decided to do. We have not yet had a government which was prepared to change its mind as a result of discussion in Neddy – and we never will get one (again with the possible exception of Heath) until the non-government members of Neddy put real, and combined, pressure on. Marsh thinks that Labour will significantly increase their number of seats in the new Parliament although not to the point of having an overall majority.

Thursday 3 October 1974

I went to the Berkeley for lunch with Peter Seligman* and various other people from APV including Madron Seligman. There were a number of other guests there including Jake Warren, the Canadian high commissioner. Over lunch Peter Seligman and others were taking a very strong line about trade union militancy and about

* Madron Seligman's brother and chairman of APV, an international engineering company founded by their father in 1910, of which I later became chairman.

Wilson, whom they evidently regard as a near Communist. Warren spoke very sensibly about the influence of the moderates in the TUC and in the Labour movement but I don't think he convinced his listeners.

Madron Seligman said that Ted Heath was very relaxed, almost as if he didn't mind whether he won the election or not.

The press have reports today of speeches by Ralph Bateman and Harold Watkinson, both of which evidently advocated strengthening Neddy. I phoned Watkinson, who said that the proposal originated with a CBI working party of which he is chairman and the Conservatives had picked it up from them. He said that whatever government came in we should have to create a consensus about how to run the economy so that industry would have some assurance of continuity of policy. Neddy was the only place where this could be done and the meetings must take place at Millbank and not, as with Heath's talks with the TUC and CBI in 1972–3, at No. 10 or Chequers. Watkinson said he would like the proceedings to be made public, on some occasions at least, either by admitting the press or by having a Hansard-type record of the proceedings. He also said that the civil service didn't want to see any power given to Neddy and never had wanted it. There would therefore have to be an act of political will if his ideas were to work.

Later in the day we got reports of a statement Heath made in which he proposed to develop Neddy into a wider discussion forum with televised proceedings and meetings being held in Cardiff and Edinburgh as well as in London. He has clearly borrowed the idea from President Ford's economic summits but it hasn't come over well and I doubt if it will go down well with the unions.

Friday 4 October 1974

As I thought, Heath's proposal to televise Neddy meetings has not gone down well. If he was going to launch a proposal like this (which is not inherently absurd) he should have taken more trouble over it.

In the evening I went to Oxford for the Simon and Jude dinner at University College. It was a very pleasant occasion – excellent food and wine, no speeches and no undergraduates. I was there at David Stout's invitation. I had a long talk with Jack Diamond (who was Chief Secretary to the Treasury under both Jim Callaghan and Roy) about Europe. He said he had no doubt at all that we would stay in the EEC – Wilson and Callaghan were clearly playing things this way and Roy was helping. He also said he thought John Hunt was quite right to try to suppress the Crossman diaries.

Sunday 6 October 1974

The opinion polls in the Sunday papers all show Labour fairly comfortably in the lead – and yet everyone says the election result is still pretty open. There are said to be a lot of people who are still undecided about how to vote and also a lot who may not turn out on the day. My guess is that Labour will have a majority of about twenty over the Conservatives but not an overall majority in the House of Commons. Fortunately there is very little in the Sunday papers about Heath's ideas for televising NEDC etc.

Monday 7 October 1974

I took John Cole, the deputy editor of the *Guardian*, to lunch at Romeo and Juliet. He is a cheery and intelligent Ulsterman who was for many years a labour correspondent and knows the trade unions well. He said he wouldn't be surprised to see either the Labour or the Conservative Party get a large overall majority – with the extraordinary number of 'undecideds' swilling about in the bilges you simply couldn't forecast the result. I wonder if there has ever been an election before which was quite so open two days before the poll? Cole thought that if there were to be a Con–Lib alliance Jeremy Thorpe might well prefer to support it from outside rather than become a member of a coalition government.

In the evening I went to a dinner given by the Civil Engineers for permanent secretaries, of whom there were seventeen present. Douglas Allen told me he expects the Conservatives to get one or two more seats than Labour. John Hunt on the other hand expects Labour to get 350 seats, which would give them a large overall majority. My forecast is Labour 310, Conservatives 283, others 42 (compared with the February figures of 301, 297 and 37).

Tuesday 8 October 1974

I went to see Len Murray at Congress House in the afternoon. He was a bit subdued, I thought, and uncertain how the election would go. He said that relations between the CBI and TUC were very bad just now 'because the CBI had become so political'. In view of the TUC behaviour at Brighton this is a bit rich! Len said that if the Tories got back the TUC might perhaps be prepared to talk to them about wages but not with the CBI present and therefore not round the Neddy table.

Wednesday 9 October 1974

The *Times* has a feature article about Neddy by Maurice Corina. It is quite good and says that the DG earns every penny of his £17,000 salary! More important, Harold Wilson has made a statement saying that if Labour are returned they will make full use of the Neddy machinery. This is encouraging as it means that Heath's proposals for enlarging Neddy have not, as Murray feared, damaged the concept of Neddy. I called on Harold Watkinson this morning for a general talk at which Lord MacFadzean* joined us after a time. Watkinson thinks Heath may just scrape home but admits a Labour government is more likely.

We had a useful talk about Neddy, of which Watkinson is a strong supporter (he was in the Macmillan Cabinet† when it was formed). He thinks the main problem will be to get investment going next year – the pressure on companies' cash flow is such, he says, that no one can risk going ahead with investment plans except where it would cost more to cancel them. He thinks Neddy should discuss this problem at its first post-election meeting – he regards it as much more important than the prospective increase in wages.

I lunched with Tommy Balogh, who had just come from a talk with Harold Wilson. He told me that Wilson was cheerful but very apprehensive that over-confidence or bad weather would lead to a low turn out of Labour voters. He was pretty sure that Wilson would not form a government unless he got the overall majority for which he was asking at this election.

Tommy said that for the first time he felt quite at a loss about how to get the country out of its mess – we showed every sign of becoming a Caribbean-type country living on tourism alone. He does not know if he will be reappointed if Labour get back but hopes he will be allowed to finish his work on North Sea oil. I asked him if Jack Rampton, the permanent secretary of the Department of Energy, was obstructing his plans for the North Sea, to which he

---

* President of BICC Ltd and a former president of the CBI's predecessor organisation, the FBI.
† As Minister of Defence.

replied, 'I couldn't produce actual proof that he was.' Tommy has a burning patriotism for his adopted country and is depressed at the bleak outlook. He thinks an early wage freeze is essential but doubts if it will be introduced.

Thursday 10 October 1974

Doreen and I both voted Liberal.

We 'saw the election in' on TV with Campbell and Gilvray Adamson. Although most of his CBI members would disbelieve it, I would guess from Campbell's comments that he voted Conservative.

When we went to bed about 3.30 a.m. it looked as though Labour would have an overall majority of eight or nine.

Friday 11 October 1974

Labour's majority turns out to be three. The SNP has done very well in Scottish seats held by the Conservatives – less well in Labour-held seats and it is this which has given Wilson his majority. Piers Dixon is out to a Liberal at Truro but in general the results have been very disappointing for the Liberals.*

Monday 14 October 1974

Most people seem to think the result is a good one, including a lot of businessmen who would have been scared by a Conservative win or a large Labour majority.

Harold Wilson broadcast this evening. He was very much the father of the nation, appealing for unity and warning the trade

---

* The final figures were: Labour 319, Conservatives 277, Liberals 13, others 28.

unions not to use their power to achieve an undue share of the cake. He described inflation as the main enemy, for the first time in my hearing. Since he now has only the history books to think of he may do very well. After all, he can only go down to history as the man who pulled us back from the abyss or led us into it and there will be a strong incentive to follow policies which make the first of the two the more likely outcome.

PART THREE

DRIFTING TOWARDS
COLLAPSE

15 October 1974 to 19 March 1976

The Conservatives' second defeat in just over six months immediately led to pressure for a change of party leader and Edward Heath eventually accepted that he would have to submit himself for re-election. In the ensuing contest he was decisively beaten and – to the surprise of almost everyone outside the party and not a few within it – Margaret Thatcher was elected leader by a clear margin.

In the Labour Party, Harold Wilson's position as leader was not in question but it was generally known that he would not want to continue in office beyond the end of the current parliament. There were at least four highly talented members of his Cabinet who wanted to succeed him and thought they had a reasonable chance of doing so. In these circumstances Wilson (who was never one to miss an opportunity of suspecting his colleagues of plotting against him) was probably not displeased that his party would be subject to the strict discipline imposed by a small parliamentary majority.

Meanwhile, the underlying problems which had made life so difficult for the Heath government had not gone away. With the terms of trade still adverse, the balance of payments continued to weaken, productivity remained stubbornly below the levels of our main competitors and inflation showed no signs of abating. The social contract between the government and the unions, having achieved its purpose of helping to secure a Labour victory at the October election, had no discernible effect on wage settlements thereafter.

These were deep-seated and intractable problems which, in a world environment that was more than ordinarily full of uncertainty, called for strong, clear-minded government. But for the first six months of 1975 senior ministers' attention was focused almost entirely on the forthcoming referendum on Europe, on which the Cabinet was deeply divided. In addition, it seemed to me observing him from the sidelines, that the Prime Minister, though himself a former economics don, had by then lost all interest in economic problems – of which he had perhaps had his fill in the previous decade. These factors may go some way to explain the strong impression of drift conveyed by the diary.

Tuesday 15 October 1974

I went to the SMMT dinner in the evening. The president, Ray Brookes, made an emotional speech appealing to us all to unite behind Harold Wilson. I sat between Alexander Rhea of Vauxhall and Don Lander of Chrysler and had interesting conversations with them both about the condition of the motor industry. They both clearly regard the state of industrial relations in England as one of more or less complete anarchy.

I had a long talk with Ralph Bateman after dinner. He believes that Wilson will try to follow moderate policies but that he will in practice have to dance to the tune of left-wing trade union leaders. He said the CBI would have nothing to do with Tony Benn's system of planning agreements – they would tell the government that if they wanted to pursue the matter they would have to talk to individual firms direct.

Wednesday 16 October 1974

We had a dinner party at home. After dinner we talked politics. I said that Harold Wilson had only the history books to live for now. He could go down either as the man who took Britain over the edge into the abyss or as the man whose statesmanship avoided this; and it was pretty clear which he would prefer. I thought therefore that we could rely on him to follow reasonably sensible policies and to support the social democratic wing of the Labour Party (to which I thought that *au fond* he belonged) against the Marxists.

John Partridge said he doubted whether Wilson belonged to any wing – he was motivated only by expediency. He agreed that there might be something in the 'history books' theory but he didn't see how Wilson could stand out against the left-wingers in the trade union movement. I said that I thought the TUC would be dominated for some time by a coalition led by Jack Jones and Len Murray but excluding Hugh Scanlon. I surmised that Jones was still a full-blooded Marxist – but that he was very independent minded and would not take orders from the Communist Party or anyone else. He had only three years of power in the movement left and he wanted to make sure that during this period we had a government which he could influence to further the things he believed in. I thought he would do everything possible to keep Labour in power, including pursuing restraint on wages. Partridge agreed but mentioned Jones's implacable hostility to the Common Market. I said this derived from his Marxism; our membership of EEC would make it more difficult for us to work with the countries of eastern Europe. Jones believed in the 'Europe of Donegal to the Black Sea'.

After the others had gone, just after midnight, Piers Dixon looked in. He said that Margaret Thatcher was now front runner for the leadership of the Tory Party if Heath resigned. I asked whether she or Keith Joseph would win if the choice were between them. His answer was that Joseph would win hands down but that there would never be a contest simply between them. The left of the party would put up 'Whitelaw or somebody', and there would be only one candidate from the right.

Thursday 17 October 1974

Jack Jones has made a remarkable speech to a TGWU conference in Scotland urging his members to support the social contract and warning them not to take industrial action which might put their employers out of business. This strikingly vindicates the line I took with the bankers at Toronto – though I have had a letter from Angus Smart saying they all think I was sent out by HMG to propagandise about Britain.

In the evening I went to the Lord Mayor's banquet for the

bankers and merchants of the City of London, at which Gordon Richardson spoke with courage and authority. After dinner when the Lady Mayoress's guests joined us I spoke to Araminta Aldington. She said Ted Heath had no intention of resigning the leadership – 'he is like granite'.

Sunday 20 October 1974

I have been reading Nicholas Davenport's *Memoirs of a City Radical.** He is very critical of the failure to stop the spending spree which occurred after devaluation in November 1967 and says that the extra taxation which Roy Jenkins introduced in his budget of 1968 'should have been imposed at once to stop the fever rising'. He goes on to say, 'I criticise the civil servants, not Roy Jenkins [who only became Chancellor in December 1967], for allowing the public to indulge in a buying spree.' This reminded me that Roy had told me a few years ago that he had wanted to introduce a Budget in January 1968 for just this reason but that William Armstrong, then permanent secretary of the Treasury, had dissuaded him. He had always regretted taking Armstrong's advice, which he thought in retrospect was thoroughly bad. He said that Armstrong always seemed to play the role of 'vice-chairman of disaster'.

Monday 21 October 1974

I drove down to Earls Court, for a motor show lunch, with Douglas Wass. I tried out on him my belief that this country needs a national strategy, supported by all three parties in Neddy, and that we should get down to the job straight after the Budget on 12 November. Wass was sympathetic to this but said he thought the gulf between the CBI

* London: Weidenfeld and Nicolson, 1974.

and the others was too great to make it possible to reach agreement on a strategy. I asked him how in that case we could hope to avoid a really serious crisis in the next twelve months, to which he replied, 'Oh, there will certainly be some sort of shambles before we can agree on a strategy.' He said that John Hunt was doing a very effective job as Cabinet Secretary and had Wilson's complete trust as he had had Heath's.

Ray Brookes was host at lunch. I sat next to Willie Whitelaw, who greeted me very warmly though I don't really know him very well. He said the Conservatives' behaviour over the leadership would do harm to the party, which ought to be concentrating on the serious national crisis we were going through. He added that the present shambles was personally damaging to all the possible new leaders (including presumably himself) because the newspapers and the rival factions drew attention only to their faults and not to their strong points. He thought the party as a whole was very overwrought.

Whitelaw obviously doesn't think anything of Joseph. I said he seemed a very nice person if you could get past the barrier of his nervous tension but Willie said you never could do this. He was clear that Joseph would not become party leader. He was simply being manipulated by a group of MPs who formerly looked to Enoch Powell for leadership.

Willie said he knew when he became party chairman in June that the Conservatives would not win the next election, just as he had known they would lose the previous one in February. He said the central issue for the country was still the one that arose in the miners' dispute last winter – what do you do if a powerful group decides to use its power to the full to get its way? He said he was never in any doubt that we should have settled the miners' claim at the best level obtainable before Christmas last year in the wake of the oil crisis. In other words his position was exactly the same as mine. He said he regretted not having pushed this point of view harder. He was new to the job at the time and Conrad Heron and William Armstrong were advising ministers to stand firm at all costs. Willie said he should never have agreed to become Secretary of State for Employment – he should have stayed on in Northern Ireland to finish his job there – but 'it was essential to move Maurice Macmillan'.

Thursday 24 October 1974

We had a Group of 4 meeting at 11 a.m. It went on for nearly two hours. Although we probably talked more seriously than we ever have before I felt deeply depressed by it.

I began by saying that I thought we were now in a fairly considerable mess as a country. The Tory party was in disarray, the Liberals had disappeared, the Labour Party was conducting its policy debates through the correspondence columns of the *Times*, the CBI and the TUC were talking to one another by means of separate press conferences and Whitehall was waiting fatalistically for a collapse. In these circumstances we would badly need bodies which were cohesive rather than divisive. I hoped Neddy would be made proper use of, but whether it was or not I felt strongly that we must keep the Group of 4 in good shape and have regular meetings through the winter. There seemed to be general agreement with this.

I then unfolded my ideas for using Neddy to formulate a national strategy of some kind to take us through the next three to four years. Douglas Wass thought my proposal would mean that Neddy would get lost in generalities. He said that Healey was disappointed with Neddy because of the lack of continuity in its discussions and the fact that nothing happened after them. Len Murray took a similar view – he wanted Neddy meetings to result in the trade union people summoning their national officers and telling them to get cracking on some piece of action which had just been agreed round the NEDC table. There was a discursive discussion about whether Neddy had done any good over the last ten years and whether things would have been any different if it hadn't existed.

There was no hostility to Neddy in what was said – only a profound disenchantment and a desire to get Neddy discussing concrete issues 'such as energy conservation'. I said that the reason Neddy had failed was that the parties had never been willing (except in the very early days) to have a realistic discussion about the basic factors that underlay our poor national performance – they always ducked the difficult issues, with the result that their discussions were superficial. I said I thought the idea that we should discuss things like energy conservation was a similar means of evading the real issues concerning our failure to use our capital and labour resources as efficiently as other people.

We went round and round the same course with no success. But at least it was agreed that I should put a paper to the next meeting which they could all shoot down but which might get a debate going on the fundamental problems that Neddy ought to be looking at.

After lunch I went to Bristol for my speech to the Junior Chamber of Commerce. I had taken a lot of trouble over this and sent copies to a number of Neddy members and to the Chancellor and No. 10. But after the morning's meeting of the Group of 4 I was a bit nervous about its reception. When I got to Bristol I learned that ITN wanted to interview me about it. I went to the studio and did an interview with Peter Sissons, who was in London – the first time I have done one with the questioner somewhere else. I then went on to the Bristol Club and delivered my speech, which so far as I could tell went down well.

My main theme was that we were in a situation which was dominated by uncertainty – about world prospects, our own economy and above all inflation. This uncertainty had very damaging effects on investment and on people's willingness to accept change, and to reduce this Neddy should formulate an agreed national strategy to take us through the next three to four years.

Friday 25 October 1974

I found that ITN had used my interview as the first item on *News at Ten*, which is something of a coup for NEDO. Press coverage of my speech was good, although the *Evening News* referred to Neddy as a 'semi-moribund organisation'.

After lunch I ran into Douglas Wass. As far as I could make out he expects a financial collapse of some sort in the next few months, followed by a political realignment involving a split in the Labour Party. He said he had a long meeting that morning with Healey about the Budget. Healey had been very realistic in his own attitude but very conscious of the party pressures on him. Douglas was dismayed by his arrogance – he simply wouldn't admit he had been wrong on anything.

George Sinclair looked in briefly as we were leaving for Throwley. It seemed clear from what he said that he is in favour of any early change of leadership in the Conservative Party – not because he disagrees particularly with Heath but because of his evident difficulty in communicating with the electorate. I must say one hears this on all sides now from 'ordinary' non-political people as well as MPs.

Tuesday 29 October 1974

The Queen's Speech turned out exactly as one would have expected – no more and no less than the party manifesto foreshadowed. For some reason the evening papers are full of references to 'state grabs' and 'wholesale nationalisation'. As far as I can see this is quite misleading.

Thursday 31 October 19974

I went to see Eric Roll in the morning. I told him of my recent talks with Healey and in particular of his reluctance to let Neddy get involved in questions of economic strategy. Eric's immediate reaction was that this was the brief given him by the Treasury – they want Neddy out of their hair but it suits both them and Healey to have it active in Tony Benn's field.

Eric feels strongly the need for Neddy to concern itself with macro-economic questions concerning distribution of resources, balance of payments and so on. He said he would speak on these lines at Council – but I wonder if he will? Generally he is, like me, full of foreboding. I said that I would expect that the Budget might be followed by a short period of euphoria (because Healey is bound to do something to ease industry's cash flow problems). My guess was that ten days or so later confidence would be even lower than it was now. Eric agreed with this.

Friday 1 November 1974

At lunch I went to Chatham House to hear a talk by Christopher Soames.* He spoke for about twenty minutes, from notes, about the EEC's external relations and then began to read from a prepared text about Britain's current problems. His remarks on these were pungent and well phrased and ranged far beyond the question of our membership of the community. I got the strong impression from this part of his speech that Soames had his eye on the Conservative Party leadership – indeed I would say he has deliberately thrown his hat in the ring.

---

* Sir Christopher Soames was the senior British European Commissioner and a vice-president of the Commission.

Monday 4 November 1974

In the evening I went to see Tony Benn at the House of Commons. Peter Carey was there. As usual Benn was very bland and when we left I said to Carey that I had no idea what was really going on in his mind. Carey said that there was no question that he was after the leadership of the party. He didn't get on with Len Murray or the TUC bigwigs generally and was therefore seeking to build up a power base through his influence with shop stewards and other 'lay' trade unionists. Peter added that there was no doubt that Benn intended to use the NEB to gain control of important sections of private industry.

Tuesday 5 November 1974

I met Arthur Peterson at lunch. I told him the Treasury seemed unwilling to show any of their cards to Neddy. He said this was because they didn't have any – no one in Whitehall had any idea how to handle the present crisis.

In the afternoon I went to see Shirley Williams for a talk about tomorrow's council meeting. I said I thought we were in for a very rough time this winter with the possibility of some quite serious crisis occurring – triggered off maybe by some external event – and that it was important, for this reason if no other, to keep cohesive forces like Neddy in good shape. I said that I would be doing all I could tomorrow to persuade the council of the need for an agreed programme for keeping up investment, employment and productivity. I added that I hoped Shirley would approve of this – I knew she was a good friend of Neddy's and she was also caught departmentally between the need to keep prices down on the one hand and the need, on the other, to let industry have the cash and profits required for investment. Shirley entirely agreed with this and she repeated that in due course she would like to see consumer representation on Neddy.

Len Murray spoke to me on the telephone. He said that the TUC Economic Committee's meeting last Friday had been a very difficult one. He was trying to get them to agree to his proposals for stiffening up the social contract. A number of the members pressed for the discussion to be postponed – ostensibly because Murray's proposals had been leaked to the press but actually, he said, because they were somewhat ashamed of the way their own members were behaving in relation to the social contract just now. I took this to be a reference to the strikes in Scotland, most of which involved TGWU members.

Friday 8 November 1974

I took Edwin Plowden* to lunch at the Royal Thames. We talked about the CBI. Plowden said that he had never had anything to do with it before because he reckoned Tube Investments, of which he is chairman, did not need any intermediary in their dealings with government. But in the last year he had been very critical of it and so when asked if he would sit on the President's Advisory Group he felt he could hardly refuse. He said the other members of the group regarded him as 'practically a Marxist' but he was able to say what he liked because he was an old man and they knew he was not after their jobs. Plowden thinks there will be an acute balance of payments crisis in March followed by some kind of authoritarian government of the left or right. He thinks the latter is more likely and that Enoch may well lead it.

---

* Lord Plowden was a highly respected elder statesman who had been chairman of the Economic Planning Board from 1947 to 1953, of the Atomic Energy Authority from 1954 to 1959 and of innumerable committees of enquiry thereafter. His career straddled the worlds of government and industry in a way that was more typical of a French *énarque* than a British businessman.

Monday 11 November 1974

Buying the newspaper in the morning I ran into Geoffrey Howe. I asked him when the Tories were going to sort out their leadership problems. He said there was no tearing hurry – 'who cared who led the Labour Party in 1959–62?'

In the evening Doreen and I went to Covent Garden for a magnificent performance of *Boris Godunov*. We ran into Dudley Smith* among others. He said Ted Heath would quite definitely go but probably not for some time. He added that all the talk of a coming crisis tended to strengthen those who wanted to maintain the status quo. I would guess his view is very typical of the middle-of-the-road Tory backbencher.

Tuesday 12 November 1974

I went to the House of Commons after lunch to hear Denis Healey's budget – the most important since the war according to the *Financial Times*. As I got out of the car Edna Healey arrived. I asked her to wish Denis luck from me in retrospect, as it were, and said I didn't see how he could get it right whatever he did. She agreed and said, 'All he can do is keep his head down and go through with it.'

Healey spoke for ninety minutes, quietly and well. He began with a good survey of the world scene and of our own problems and even made a reference to Neddy. When he came to his measures he was less convincing. He has done a lot to ease company liquidity and very little offsetting action to please the left and he got approving noises from the Conservative benches for some of his proposals. But somehow his appeals for national unity didn't come over well and he ended on a

---

* Conservative MP for Warwick & Leamington. He had been parliamentary secretary at the Department of Employment from 1970 to 1974.

quite unrealistic note about his Budget meaning that Britain would regain 'her rightful place in the world'. Towards the end he lost the attention of the House and quite a few Labour MPs drifted out.

Gordon Richardson, who was sitting next to me in the Distinguished Strangers' Gallery, is very pleased with what is being done to provide more cash for industry, which I daresay he has done a lot to bring about. But he didn't disagree when I said that, though it would prevent bankruptcies, I didn't see that the Budget would do anything to encourage investment.

I stayed to hear Heath's reply. He was very aggressive and got quite a good reception from his own backbenchers.

Wednesday 13 November 1974

In the evening I went to a dinner at Grosvenor House given by the Machine Tools Trade Association. There were 1,200 or so people including a lot of industrial bigwigs. I had a good talk with Nicko Henderson,* who had flown in from Bonn for the occasion. He said Jim Callaghan was not a genuine convert to the pro-EEC school; the only thing he was interested in when any issue arose was how the Labour Party would react to it. Henderson said the trouble with the government was that Callaghan, Jenkins, Benn and Healey all wanted to succeed Wilson. In his view Roy hasn't a chance and he thinks Roy would have much more influence if he accepted this. As it is he thinks Shirley Williams has more influence in Cabinet than Roy.

Monday 18 November 1974

I lunched with David Scholey at Warburgs. He said he thought the present time must be rather like 1920 when a lot of people thought

---

* Sir Nicholas Henderson was ambassador to the Federal Republic of Germany.

that life was going to revert to what it had been in 1913 and were shocked to find it didn't. In the same way he thought that a great many people had not yet woken up to the significance of the shift of power to the unions. He also said we couldn't necessarily take it for granted that we should be bailed out by the USA and Germany if our economy reached the point of collapse.

Tuesday 19 November 1974

I began the day at a conference entitled 'Management of Innovation' at the Royal Garden Hotel. The Duke of Edinburgh opened it with a brisk little speech which contained one or two very subdued barbs about politicians.

I got back to the office to see another duke – Northumberland, who is chairman of our Agricultural EDC. He forecast that by next spring we shall have a national government under Jim Callaghan.

Thursday 21 November 1974

I gave lunch in the office to Toby Aldington and Ronnie Grierson and to Douglas Wass, whom they both wanted to meet. We naturally talked of the crisis. Wass said that Harold Wilson was taking it very seriously – more so than any of his colleagues. Toby said that if he wanted to improve industry's confidence he must get rid of Tony Benn. There was general agreement that the Budget would not call forth the investment we need for 1975 with confidence as low as it is.

I told Toby of Northumberland's prediction that we should soon have a national government under Callaghan. Toby said that Heath would be quite willing to serve under Callaghan – or for that matter Wilson – in a truly national government.

Friday 22 November 1974

I went to see Conrad Heron in the morning. He said he thought the NUM militants would force through a high settlement about the end of January, that this would be followed by a comparable increase for the electricity supply workers and that there would then be a balance of payments collapse. This would lead to statutory wage indexation and import restrictions. He thought a number of ministers now saw the dangers ahead, even including Peter Shore – but that Michael Foot was definitely not one of them.

Monday 25 November 1974

I took Alan Sapper* to lunch at Romeo and Juliet. He thinks that if the standard of living of working people is cut (and he agreed with me that it would have to be) there will be severe industrial strife this winter. He expects an authoritarian government of the right to emerge – followed perhaps by one on the left. He is of course totally opposed to our remaining in the EEC – and against a referendum, which he thinks can be manipulated by PR experts. He described the EEC issue as the main one which had to be resolved before progress could be made in other directions. Sapper is an agreeable lunch companion and wants us to set up a little Neddy for the cinema industry.

In the afternoon I had a meeting of EDC chairmen – attended by George Doughty, the first-ever chairman from the trade union movement. We had a good discussion, followed by drinks for which Denis Healey joined us. He made a little speech in which he talked of his desire to have a social contract with employers to maintain

---

* General secretary of the Association of Cinematograph, Television and Allied Technicians. A man of the left.

investment. I thought this was potentially important and found out that he intends to say the same thing in a speech to the Press Gallery tomorrow.

Denis obviously enjoyed himself and I think the occasion did much to cement relations between him and Neddy – it was evidently the first occasion of its kind in twelve years. I saw him out and chatted to him about our present crisis. He said there was clearly a possibility that we should have a crash by Easter, but that there was still a chance that wages could be held to reasonable levels. He had included in his Budget speech – against Treasury advice – the threat that if wages got out of hand unemployment would have to be allowed to rise sharply in order to have something to negotiate with and exert pressure on the unions. He said Jack Jones was very much concerned about the present situation and 'agonising' over it. I said that all informed people were talking of a crash within six months – we were like a country waiting for the shoe to drop and the government would have to find some way of stopping the drift before long.

Wednesday 27 November 1974

I held the first meeting of the Co-ordinating Committee* since I took over the chairmanship. Lawrence Airey from the Treasury and his opposite number in the Department of Industry turned up as well as Donald MacDougall and David Lea. It was a somewhat depressing meeting. One could see the Whitehall and TUC bureaucracies trying hard to wrest control of Neddy from its own members – in the

---

* The committee met two or three times a year. Its members were senior (though not the most senior) officials from the Treasury, the DTI and other government departments and from the CBI and the TUC. Its ostensible purpose was to exchange information about current work, reduce overlap and advise on priorities for future work by NEDO.

sense that they really want to ensure that the council deals with the matters they think important and not with those the council members think important. I suppose I was seeing the bureaucrats try to do to Neddy what the civil service does with most ministers. Fortunately MacDougall was very sensible and helpful and Lea turned out in his cross-grained way to be quite constructive, so it is probably worth persevering with the committee.

I went to lunch at 8 Smith Square with Rowland Wright, the chairman designate of ICI. Rather to my surprise he had five other ICI people with him. We spent the whole of lunch talking about Neddy and planning agreements and didn't break up until after three o'clock. The ICI people want to beef up Neddy – very much on the basis of 'keep a-hold of Nurse for fear of finding something worse'. They are extremely wary of Benn and of the left-wing people in the trade unions they deal with.

Anthony Rawlinson looked in at 6.30. He told me that the economic outlook in the USA had deteriorated quite markedly since I was there. A deep recession now seemed certain, lasting at least well into the second half of 1975.

It seems from the news that Ralph Bateman has made a speech criticising the social contract and urging the government to reconsider it. If this is a response to Healey's speech I don't think much of it. As I wrote this a bomb went off – it sounded like a big one.

I had a letter from Denis Healey's private secretary today saying that Denis had asked him to tell me how much he had enjoyed meeting the EDC chairman and that he would like to sit in on one of my meetings with them, simply as a listener. This is good news.

Thursday 28 November 1974

I evidently did Ralph Bateman an injustice. His speech yesterday seems to have been constructive and the *Times* refers to it as 'intended to be seen as a response to Healey's speech about the need for a social contract with management'. Callaghan also made a good speech to the Labour Party Conference yesterday emphasising the need for national unity.

In the course of the morning I got the text of Bateman's speech and found that near the beginning he said he was 'delighted to read the Chancellor's suggestion that the government should have a social contract with management to maintain investment and exports'. I also got the text of a major speech which Harold Wilson has made to the Labour Party conference, in which he said, 'My main message to Conference today is this: that the future of the country, of the standard of living of our people, perhaps of democracy itself, depend upon the effort we put into investment, public and private.' This was part of a long and skilful speech full of references to the importance of the NEB as a means of socialist advance etc., but in reality designed, I am sure, to reassure British industry that the government would avoid doing things which would impede investment by the private sector.

Just before I got this speech I had a call from Robin Butler at No. 10 to say the PM would not be coming to NEDC next week – partly because of other commitments and partly because he would prefer to chair a meeting early in the New Year. I suppose he fears that the economic situation may have deteriorated by then and that his unifying presence may be needed.

I then went to see Ralph Bateman. I said I had been glad to note what he said in his Nottingham speech and I thought he would do well to follow it up at NEDC next week. I said that I would always remember December 1973 as a month in which opportunities were thrown away. December 1974 seemed to offer great opportunities and I hoped we should be able to take full advantage of them. Until this week everyone I met had been talking with almost complete fatalism about the prospect of a crisis in February or March without suggesting that anything could be done to avert it. Now, with Healey's speech and those made by Callaghan and especially the PM at the Labour Party conference, I thought there was the possibility of movement. Could not the CBI take advantage of this at NEDC next week both to put pressure on the government to follow policies which would help investment and to strengthen the hands of people like Healey and Shirley Williams against the left? Senior ministers and trade union leaders like Murray and Jones were all worried now and an initiative by the CBI might be welcomed.

Bateman's response was very disappointing. He said that he found it almost impossible to discuss these issues at NEDC because Benn was present. The CBI might well want to see Healey separately and he might even take up Wilson's invitation to him to ask for a talk whenever he felt it really necessary. But he gave no impression of urgency. He doesn't strike me as a leader or a man with any breadth of vision.

I went on to the Treasury for a talk with Chris France, Healey's private secretary. I told him in general terms of my talks with Bateman and my phone conversations with Harold Watkinson (who made an excellent speech in the House of Lords) and Edwin Plowden. I said I would like Healey to know what I was up to and would be glad to get a reaction from him. France said that Healey was keen to get an accommodation with the CBI – 'as a means of strengthening the social contract with the TUC' (I am not sure what he meant by that) – and would be sympathetic to what I was trying to do.

Friday 29 November 1974

I went to see John Partridge in the morning and stayed nearly an hour with him. I told him of my recent conversations and urged on him the opportunity which seemed to exist for introducing some movement into the situation. John listened attentively and asked some pertinent questions. He is very apprehensive about the way things may develop next year and spoke of the real risk of some kind of social collapse following a high miners' settlement and a run on the pound.

Tuesday 3 December 1974

Dick Marsh rang about yesterday's CBI meeting. He said that for the first time in his life he had experienced visually the phenomenon of loss of confidence. The CBI were, he said, in a mood of near despair about their relations with government and had a terrible inferiority complex about it. They knew that Healey had complete contempt for them and were convinced that neither Foot nor Benn would pay any attention to what they said. They were therefore completely demoralised and Healey would do well to pat them on the head instead of bullying them.

I spent the afternoon reading the NIESR report on the economy and preparing for tomorrow's meeting. The report, by the director, David Worswick, is a first-rate piece of work. It is, however, very gloomy – especially about the social contract, which he no longer believes can reduce inflation. He has a nice phrase about the CBI and TUC communicating with each other from a distance 'as if through a public address system'. I worked out some proposals to put to the council tomorrow though I shall have to play it very much by ear. The proposals are that we should take special measures to encourage investment in the energy-related areas; that the government should make a public commitment to stability in the nationalised industries' investment programmes; and that we should examine urgently how to handle redundancies humanely and efficiently this winter.

I had fifteen minutes talk with Healey over the telephone and outlined what I would like to say. I added that I thought it very important that we should end the meeting with something constructive to report – it would not do simply to say that we had had a good discussion on the Budget.

After dinner Sidney Greene phoned. I told him of my talks with the CBI and Healey and explained why I thought it important to get a constructive outcome to the meeting. I also said that the CBI were in poor shape and might need a helping hand from the TUC. He said he would do his best to help.

I went to bed feeling there wasn't any more I could have done to see that we get a reasonable outcome tomorrow.

Wednesday 4 December 1974

We had a curious council meeting. Everyone was trying to be constructive without quite knowing how and provided it was the other chap who made the first move. The TUC were clearly willing to help and Len Murray and Sidney Greene both went out of their way to give me an opportunity to outline my proposals and – in Sidney's case – to give the CBI a helping hand. The CBI were conciliatory but ineffective and Ralph Bateman was downright inept. At one point Healey made a crude threat that if the private sector didn't invest, the state would have to do it for them. Instead of coming back at him hard as he should have done and telling him to get Benn off their backs etc., Bateman actually said that he agreed with the Chancellor and added, 'We shall need help from everyone.' I wish to goodness we had an articulate right-winger on the CBI team, not because I would agree with him but because he would make the argument meaningful.

I didn't speak until the end. Healey had just said that he thought we ought to spend the whole of the next meeting discussing investment and then asked me to speak. I came out with my two proposals for encouraging investment and went on to say some things about manpower policy. These went down well. Healey 'strongly welcomed them' and all agreed I should work out my ideas more fully for the next meeting.

As a result of all this, I was able to give a positive briefing to the press afterwards and to say that I had sensed a quite new willingness on the part of the three parties on Neddy to find common ground on tackling our economic problems, despite their many differences.

Thursday 5 December 1974

We had a very good press this morning – balanced reports with a good deal of prominence given to NEDO's efforts to be constructive.

Friday 13 December 1974

Nora Beloff of the *Observer* called. She wanted to know why I had spoken after the last Neddy meeting about a new willingness to co-operate and said she could see no signs of it herself. I explained the background but she clearly couldn't believe that trade union leaders (whom I think she regards as the devil incarnate) could be constructive.

Wednesday 18 December 1974

I went to the CBI's annual dinner for permanent secretaries. Ralph Bateman came up to me after dinner and had a long chat. He told me that the CBI's private dinner with Healey had gone well and that they hoped to have another soon so that they could put across to him their worries about profitability, investment and so on. In answer to a question from me, he said he could never use Neddy for this purpose 'as it is much too political'.

I had a pleasant evening sitting between George Burton and Norman Kipping at dinner.* It was at this dinner a year ago that I had so fierce an argument with Conrad Heron about the miners' strike that I had to ring up to apologise the following morning.

Thursday 19 December 1974

In the evening I went to the NIESR annual general meeting and party – my first time as a governor. Over drinks afterwards Alan Neale† said he thought that we might be in a siege economy by midsummer – if the currency collapsed we couldn't take it for granted that the Canadians would still be willing to sell wheat to us.

Wednesday 1 January 1975

Roy and Jennifer Jenkins came to lunch. Roy told me he thought that the Labour Party would split under the strains which the economic crisis and Europe would put on it. He wants a coalition government and expects to see one in the first half of this year. He said he was keen that if this happened it should split the Conservatives as well as the Labour Party – in other words he wants a genuine realignment of political forces in this country. Roy said he wouldn't mind whether Wilson or Callaghan led the new government but made it clear that he would expect to succeed whichever of them took it on – and implied that he would expect to do this quite soon.

He said that Wilson had recently asked him whether he would feel it necessary to resign if members of the present Cabinet were left free to speak and vote for or against our staying in Europe during the run

---

* George Burton was chairman of Fisons. Sir Norman Kipping had been the last director general of the FBI before it was transmogrified into the CBI in 1965.
† Sir Alan Neale was permanent secretary of the Ministry of Agriculture.

up to the referendum. Roy's answer had been that it would depend entirely on whether Wilson and Callaghan were publicly recommending support for our remaining in Europe. If so, he would happily remain in the Cabinet – if not he would feel obliged to resign in order to lead the campaign for staying in.

Thursday 2 January 1975

Chris Lucas and I went to BSC for a talk with Monty Finniston and Dick Marsh about next week's Council. Monty was pleased about his knighthood – Marsh said what he wanted was the Star of India, which entitled one to a green turban and a diamond brooch.

Friday 3 January 1975

I saw Denis Healey in the morning. He said he liked our paper for NEDC. The Treasury were advising him to forget about investment and simply batten down the hatches and deflate in preparation for the crisis they predicted. I said that there was clearly a 50-50 chance that a crisis would come in the next six months – as a result either of some external event or of developments at home – but that didn't make it any less important to do anything we could to sustain investment. Healey wasn't prepared to admit that we could have a crisis triggered off by domestic pressures but said that there might well be a Middle East war which would provoke a crisis of a kind he couldn't see his way through at all.

Saturday 11–Sunday 26 January 1975

We were away skiing.

Wednesday 29 January 1975

I opened a conference on energy conservation at the Institution of Mechanical Engineers. In the course of it I suggested that the government should make funds available on a substantial scale to support companies which embarked during the recession on investment projects that would lead to significant savings in energy and increases in productivity. This is an attempt to suggest a way in which Healey might get more money into the business sector without running into difficulties with his left wing.

Thursday 30 January 1975

I went to see Robin Butler at No. 10. He told me that Wilson and Healey had been surprised at the reaction of Bateman and Adamson to their talk at No. 10 earlier in the month. Butler thought that the CBI realised they had taken the wrong line at the Neddy meeting on 8 January and that they were determined to erase the impression when they saw the PM. They had urged on Wilson and Healey the need to toughen the social contract guidelines and to set up some kind of tripartite monitoring body on wages but the ministers had firmly ducked these issues. Wilson had, however, told them that he would make a major speech about the Industry Bill which would reassure the CBI and that he would show the draft to Bateman in advance. Butler told me that Harold Wilson had been pleased with the last Neddy meeting and had said after it that he would like to chair meetings once a quarter. I gathered he also had it in mind to ask us to take on some new responsibilities in connection with the nationalised industries.

Monday 3 February 1975

I had an hour's talk with Douglas Wass at the Treasury. He agrees with me that the prospects of a crisis or collapse in March have receded and that we are more likely to drift along through the summer. He is very concerned about the external financial situation, which could go wrong on us at any moment. We evidently need £400 million of new money from abroad every month – so far we have been getting it but we can't count on doing so if we don't look as though we have a grip on our affairs.

In the evening Peter Jenkins came in for a chat and stayed an hour and a half. He has moved a long way to the right – he is now a tidy-looking member of the Establishment. He thinks that there is no prospect of maintaining genuine tripartite talks just now and would like to replace Neddy by some sort of Parliament of Industry as proposed by Peter Parker and others. I warned him against scrapping Neddy, which is the last remaining manifestation of the tripartite idea, unless one were very sure that its replacement would last.

Peter Jenkins thinks that Heath is unlikely to win the Conservative leadership in the first ballot and that this means Willie Whitelaw will get it at a later ballot. He says Whitelaw wants very badly to be leader and would be a good one.

Tuesday 4 February 1975

Jack Jones spoke to me on the phone about last night's dinner with the CBI. He said the atmosphere had been very good indeed. His view was that regular interchanges must continue and that they must concentrate on those matters on which it is possible to agree and leave aside the rest. He sounded just like a director general of Neddy.

At 4 p.m. we got the news of the first ballot for the Conservative leadership. To my astonishment – and great regret – Margaret Thatcher got more votes than Ted Heath.

At 5.30 I went to No. 10 to see the PM at his request. He told me he would like NEDO to take on the job of advising on nationalised industries' investment programmes, which the select committee had recommended should be given to an independent body of inquiry. He said nice things about NEDO's independence and previous work in this field in order to persuade me to take the assignment on. While we were talking the news came in that Ted Heath had given up the leadership. Wilson said that like me he was surprised that Margaret Thatcher had got more votes than Ted. He said that the Conservative Party would not be willing to have her as leader and that Whitelaw would win in the second ballot. Downstairs I met Joe Haines,* who thought that with 130 votes in the first ballot Thatcher would be very hard to stop. I am inclined to agree.

Wednesday 5 February 1975

The job Wilson wants us to do turns out to be a very wide one indeed. The select committee's report recommended an inquiry into 'the role of the nationalised industries in our economy'. Healey referred briefly to this at the beginning of the Neddy meeting, which went off well. After the forceful line I took last month I thought it best to play my own hand in a low key this month. The discussion was practical, down to earth and generally friendly. In contrast to last month, ministers took an active part, although as usual Foot said nothing. We reached as firm decisions as we could on the various items and the hope is that I can persuade the newspapers that our discussions are really going to lead to action.

At lunch afterwards Healey told me he had expected Heath to get

---

* The Prime Minister's press secretary.

more votes than Thatcher; and like the PM he expects Whitelaw to be the next leader. I asked him if (a) he and (b) his advisers wanted me to take on the assignment that the PM had spoken to me about. He said he did but that Treasury officials would not necessarily take the same view.

Friday 7 February 1975

I had a letter from Robert Armstrong[*] this morning sending me, at the PM's request, an advance copy of the speech he is to make this weekend about the Industry Bill etc.

Monday 10 February 1975

In the evening I saw George Sinclair. He said Margaret Thatcher would win on the second ballot and implied that he would vote for her, which is surprising as he is on the left of the party.

Tuesday 11 February 1975

After various meetings I went to Birmingham for a private dinner with the Chamber of Commerce. As I arrived we got the news that Margaret Thatcher had won the second ballot outright, beating Willie by sixty-seven votes. I don't think anyone expected quite such a decisive result as this.

Wednesday 12 February 1975

Healey is reported to have said last night that if wage settlements are not moderated the nation will go bankrupt.

---

[*] The Prime Minister's principal private secretary.

Tuesday 18 February 1975

I lunched with the directors of Spencer Stuart, the headhunters. Richard Meyjes of Shell was there and reminisced a little about his time in Whitehall as the leader of Heath's team of industrial advisers. He was responsible for setting up the CPRS and thought, as I do, that it was a very good move; but he thought it needed a maverick like Victor Rothschild in charge and suspects that the civil service mandarins put Ken Berrill* there after him in order to make sure the CPRS did not get out of line with the established machine. I fear he is right.

Otto Clarke was there – more piano than in his days as permanent secretary of the Ministry of Technology, when I used to think him very arrogant. There was a lot of talk of the IRC, which Otto and I had a good deal to do with, and everyone round the table thought Heath had made a great mistake in getting rid of it.

Thursday 20 February 1975

I went to the consulting engineers' dinner as the guest of Bill Atkins, the founder of W. S. Atkins and Partners. Eddie Shackleton and Judith Hart were the speakers.† Shackleton was good. Hart was quite amusing but the thought that she has influence in the field of industrial policy is terrifying. Evidently she chaired the Labour Party committee which conceived the Industry Bill – which explains a lot about it.

---

* Sir Kenneth Berrill had previously been chief economic adviser at the Treasury.
† Lord Shackleton had held several ministerial appointments in the Wilson governments of the 1960s. Dame Judith Hart was minister of overseas development.

Monday 24 February 1975

I lunched with Donald Taylor* and various of his partners and guests in a private room at the Carlton Club. Donald asked the guests, who apart from myself were mostly from the City, what we thought the prospects for the country were. We all gave very gloomy replies and there was much talk of collapse and perhaps authoritarian rule. The setting – with various nineteenth-century Prime Ministers looking down on us from the walls – made the whole thing seem rather macabre.

Tuesday 25 February 1975

I lunched with John Hunt at the Charing Cross Hotel. He has been to Washington and Moscow with Wilson in the last month and is off to Jamaica and Dublin with him soon. He says Wilson has recaptured his interest in world statesmanship and travel.

John also said that Whitehall still had no answer to our crisis – most permanent secretaries laboured under the illusion that ministers would soon do 'all the right things' including a statutory wages policy, which John is quite sure they will not.

Wednesday 26 February 1975

I went to the first day of the *FT* conference on the state and industry. Charles Villiers† is chairman today and I shall be tomorrow.

Tony Benn spoke about his Industry Bill. For the first thirty minutes (of speech and discussion) he spoke very well and made an impression even on that very critical audience. In the last fifteen

---

* Senior partner of the surveyors and property advisers Weatherall Green.

† Sir Charles Villiers was chairman of Guinness Mahon and soon to be chairman of the British Steel Corporation.

minutes he lost them. One thing he said towards the end was that he did not think that British industry would ever again be able to generate the funds it needed for investment – the electorate would throw out any government which followed policies involving the necessary degree of inequality.

Thursday 27 February 1975

I spent all day chairing the *FT* conference. Hugh Scanlon was the first speaker. He did very well, especially in the discussion afterwards, when he was realistic and candid about trade union matters. He was followed by Michael Heseltine,* who made a party political broadcast kind of speech about reds under the bed etc., which didn't go down well with the audience. In winding up I said I thought the differing style and content of the two speeches would give the audience an insight into 'the difficulties facing those of us who through professional duty and personal conviction are trying to bring about the consensus on industrial policy without which this country will perish'.

Monday 3 March 1975

I lunched with Arthur Knight, the finance director of Courtaulds. Rather to my surprise he feels strongly that the City has 'let down private enterprise'. He believes that the insurance companies and pension funds which hold 40 per cent of the equity of most large companies must use their power to improve management performance, keep up high investment rates etc.

We dined at the Plowdens'. Jim Prior said that he had done all he could to persuade Ted Heath to step down after the October election

---

* Opposition spokesman on industry.

but he would have none of it. It seemed clear that there is no love lost between Prior and Margaret Thatcher. Edwin Plowden told Doreen that he saw no prospect of arresting our national decline for at least a generation.

Tuesday 4 March 1975

We went to the Palace with our niece, Elizabeth Dolan, for my investiture. I was first to go of all – followed by 'C' (Maurice Oldfield), Charlie Chaplin* and Alan Walker, the chairman of Bass Charrington. However sceptical one may feel about the honours system one couldn't fail to be impressed. The Queen was on her feet for an hour and a half and must have handed out honours to 300 people but her smile was as natural looking for the last (a lance-corporal) as it had been for me.

Wednesday 5 March 1975

Quite a good Neddy meeting. Healey, although very tired, put a lot of effort into the chairmanship. Unfortunately, I found myself at odds with the CBI almost throughout.

In the evening I went down to the Heathrow Hotel to speak at a transport dinner. I referred to Katherine Whitehorn's[†] image of the nation's leaders spending their time 'rearranging the deckchairs on the *Titanic*'. I said I had dreamed that we held an Neddy meeting on the *Titanic*. 'The TUC were cheerful – they looked over the side saying, "That's not an iceberg, it's just the Northern Lights." The CBI were gloomy – down in the saloon singing, "Not so much a

---

* He arrived in a wheelchair with tears of emotion streaming down his face.

† A widely read columnist for the *Observer*. Her brother was a deputy director general of the CBI.

contract, more a way of death" – while the ship's officers were holding a referendum on whether to put the helm to port or starboard.' It went down pretty well.

Thursday 6 March 1975

I lunched with Bill Rodgers at the House of Commons. He told me he was now on very good terms with Wilson and had some influence with him – 'I have learned to live with the bastard.' He predicted that the pro-Europeans would win the referendum on a 70 per cent poll. I said that I was sure that if the poll was as high as that it would go the other way. But my own guess is that the working classes, who are anti-European (or at best neutral) to a man, will stay at home and that the cause will be won by the pros on a distinctly low poll.

Monday 10 March 1975

Douglas Wass, Campbell Adamson and Len Murray came to my office for a meeting of the Group of 4. I said I thought Neddy ought to get down to a discussion of macro-economic issues. Wass said he couldn't see any point in this but to my great pleasure not only Campbell but Murray argued quite strongly in support of me. It really is foolish of the Treasury to resist all suggestions of reasonably open discussion of our economic prospects and I am sorry to see Wass and Healey taking the same line as all their predecessors.

After Murray had gone Wass said he thought we were in for a very difficult summer indeed.

In the evening I went to a pleasant dinner given by the Long Range Planning Society in the Skinners Hall. Peter Parker made a good speech, in which he introduced the concept of the 'industrial citizen', who was (as I understood it) to be neither manager nor worker but someone who worked in a factory in any capacity and took his due share of decision-taking.

Tuesday 11 March 1975

I spent most of the day at the Long Range Planners' conference. Harold Watkinson spoke first, on industry–government relations, and made a strong plea for government, CBI and TUC to 'put more life into Neddy' and to use it as their central instrument for reaching agreed policies on the contentious economic issues of the day.

In the afternoon Len Murray spoke and he also urged that greater use should be made of Neddy, which he thought had great potential.

I had to give the closing address and delivered a carefully prepared speech in which I called for 'a national planning effort to be initiated by Neddy'. This would be in two parts. Firstly, Neddy would try to agree on the nature of our crisis, the constraints we operate under and the policy options open to us. Secondly, we should launch a new productivity drive to get people to put into effect the simple things which everyone knew could lead to a significant increase in productivity – but which 'through inertia, self-interest and defeatism we habitually brushed under the carpet'. I said that if need be Neddy could be enlarged somewhat and that 'to make the planning effort truly national' conclusions reached at NEDC might be debated in Parliament.

Wednesday 12 March 1975

My speech was very well reported today. It led the business news in the *Times* and the *Guardian*. I have sent copies of it to the PM, all Neddy members and various other people. What I am trying to do is get a groundswell in favour of a national planning effort going over the next few weeks so that we can take advantage of opportunities for consensus-building which I believe will occur in the second half of this year – when we shall have the Budget, the Industry Bill and the referendum behind us and there will be a lull (until October) in wage bargaining.

This afternoon the Swiss ambassador came to see me to find out what I thought of our national prospects. He is an agreeable man and an Anglophile but he does not see how we can get through our difficulties successfully. I spoke in mildly optimistic vein, along the lines of yesterday's speech of which I gave him a copy.

We dined with the Bond-Williams at the Stafford. The other guests were Howard French and his wife. He used to edit the *Daily Sketch* and since it was merged with the *Mail* he has been a director of Associated Newspapers. He said he believed in the conspiracy theory of history and reds under the bed. He doesn't approve of trade unions.

Thursday 13 March 1975

I spent the morning at a meeting of the Mechanical Engineering EDC. It was very depressing. The members of the EDC all want to make tripartism work and to get us out of our national mess but the management members in particular can do nothing but criticise others – mostly the government and the trade unions. I suppose it is a sign of an unsuccessful and perhaps disintegrating society that everyone looks for alibis. I got rather annoyed and at one point very nearly told them we would do well to wind up the EDC. But I held myself in check and in the end they decided to devote the whole of their next meeting to problems of skilled manpower.

In the evening I went to the London Business School to hear Sam Brittan deliver the Stockton Lecture. He spoke very well – in favour of the market place and against corporatism (in which by implication he included Neddy). There was an impressive audience, including many prominent businessmen, and a very pleasant dinner afterwards.

Saturday 15 March 1975

The two main headlines in the *Times* this morning are 'Militant consultants threaten to close NHS hospitals' and 'Troops to move into Glasgow tomorrow'. This really does look like a collapsing society.

Monday 17 March 1975

This morning I went to Parkside Colliery, near Liverpool, where I made my first underground visit in this country (years ago I went down a coalmine in West Bengal). I enjoyed the visit. We went down about 2,500 feet and then walked and rode about a mile to the coalface. The conditions were better than I expected. Being a miner in this sort of pit doesn't seem too bad a job but no one would think it worthwhile, I imagine, unless they were pretty well paid for it. I gather that since the last rise the men do think they are reasonably well paid and that morale is good.

In Manchester I had dinner with eight or nine members of the CBI Regional Council. We discussed the prospects for the country very freely. They were fairly gloomy about the outlook but without exception moderate and constructive – and not so preoccupied with politics as their counterparts in London.

Thursday 20 March 1975

I went to the Canada Club dinner and found myself almost in the place of honour between old Lord Amory and Eustace Roskill.*

---

* As Derrick Heathcoat Amory, Lord Amory had been Chancellor of the Exchequer from 1958 to 1960. Sir Eustace Roskill was a Lord Justice of Appeal and later became a Law Lord.

Lord Amory, who is quite delightful and made a very funny speech (not bad at seventy-five),* clearly doesn't think anything much of Margaret Thatcher, nor (I think) of Ted Heath. He urged me to do everything I possibly could to strengthen Neddy and get the government and industry to give it more authority.

Roskill and I discussed the National Industrial Relations Court and the Court of Appeal's reversal of some of Donaldson's judgments. He said that Donaldson, who had volunteered for the job of president of NIRC, was much too political for a judge.

Friday 21 March 1975

I went to No. 10 to see Bernard Donoughue.† As I went in I ran into Denis Healey, who said, 'I wish you would stop making my Budget speech for me,' from which I infer that he will make some of the points I made in my Long Range Planners' speech.

I had an interesting hour with Donoughue. So far as he is concerned the object of our nationalised industries study is to circumvent Whitehall. I don't mind being used for this purpose as I think that departments' relationship with nationalised industries has been in general very bad – too much interference in detail and too little guidance about strategy – and I believe that civil servants are more to blame for this than ministers. Donoughue is brisk and intelligent though not, perhaps, profound. He told me that Wilson is a good friend and supporter of Neddy, which I believe is true.

---

* Thirty years later I can only echo Georges Clemenceau's remark, as he watched the girls walking down the rue de la Paix: 'Oh to be seventy-five again!'
† Senior policy adviser to the Prime Minister.

Monday 24 March 1975

I have had another letter about my Long Range Planners' speech. This one is from the managing director of a large engineering company who said he was immensely encouraged by it and would like to reproduce it in his house newspaper. Evidently Ralph Bateman doesn't speak for all his members.

Mrs Fisher rang today to tell me that Pat was dying. He will be a great loss. I had become very fond of him and the respect in which he was held in the trade union movement was invaluable to us. It is very distressing that he should be cut off like this at fifty – if he had lived I daresay he would have succeeded me at NEDO.

Tuesday 25 March 1975

In the evening I went to an advertising dinner in Carpenters' Hall at which Margaret Thatcher was the guest of honour. So far as I know it was her first major speech to a business audience since becoming leader. It was an accomplished performance but the content was pretty thin. Paul Bryan* was at the dinner and talked about the election for the Conservative leadership, in which he managed Willie Whitelaw's campaign. He said that forty people, of whom he was one, voted for Margaret Thatcher in the first ballot simply to make sure Heath lost – and by doing so they enabled her to do so well that she became unstoppable. There were a number of Tory MPs and peers at the dinner and none of them seemed to have any idea beforehand what line their leader would take.

I met George Brown there. He told me solemnly that he had made it clear that he would only come back into politics as a member of a national government; that there would probably have to be such a

---

* Sir Paul Bryan was Conservative MP for Howden.

government after the referendum; and that he would be part of it. But it was a sad conversation because we both knew that he would never be a minister again and he knew that I knew it. He is a completely busted flush.*

Wednesday 2 April 1975

I had lunch with Bob Ramsay of Ford at the Café Royal. He told me that Ford UK's labour costs compared quite well with their counterparts in Germany etc., except for one thing – namely, the constant interruptions due to industrial disputes of one kind and another. These pushed their productivity right down and Ford's overriding aim was to reduce or eliminate them. They had come to the conclusion that to achieve this they needed to involve the shop stewards much more in the running of the plant and to give them far more information than hitherto – indeed virtually any information they wanted about the company's affairs.

Friday 4 April 1975

Pat Harrison gave me lunch at the RIBA.† The main purpose was to tell me that he and his council would like to do more to support the work of Neddy and to help the building industry to take a wider view of its responsibilities through the Building EDC.

I decided to issue a statement to the press over the weekend saying that Neddy would have an opportunity to give the lead for which so many people were waiting when it discussed finance for investment

---

* I had worked closely with George Brown in the Department of Economic Affairs from its inception in October 1964 until he became Foreign Secretary in 1966. Like many others who worked for him, I had an admiration and liking for him despite his obvious weaknesses and had watched him self-destruct with sadness and regret.
† Harrison was secretary of the institute.

next Wednesday. I said that this should not be the subject of party political controversy or of disagreement between management and trade unions and that it would be a good thing if the City took a less detached attitude to manufacturing industry and sought new ways of co-operating with management and trade unions in pursuit of nationally agreed objectives. This is a deliberate attempt to put pressure on my fellow members of Neddy. It may backfire on me but it needs doing – if we can't get agreement on finance for investment we shall not get it on anything.

Thursday 10 April 1975

The Neddy meeting was fully and positively reported in this morning's press.

I lunched with Leighton-Boyce and his chairman Alastair Pilkington* at Brooks's. They are a very nice, humane pair but Pilkington said he would go to prison rather than conform with the provisions in Tony Benn's Industry Bill about disclosing information to the government and unions. The contrast with Bob Ramsay's attitude earlier in the week was striking. Leighton-Boyce is a member of my advisory committee on finance for investment and was very pleased at the result of yesterday's meeting.

In the afternoon I got a very unhelpful letter from Douglas Wass refusing to agree to my hiring David Stout as economic director. I was angry and upset by it – it is a simple case of the Treasury wanting to show their power and to use it (as they so often do) for a negative purpose.†

---

* Sir Alastair Pilkington was chairman of the glass company which bore his name; Leighton-Boyce was its finance director.

† In retrospect I have sometimes wondered if I was unduly critical of the Treasury in my diary. It was reassuring to read Edward Heath's considered opinion seventeen years later: 'In all my experience of Neddy, the Treasury was a pain in the neck.' (Hansard, HC Deb, vol. 209, col. 779, 16 June 1992.)

We met Douglas Wass and his wife in the evening when we went to Covent Garden for a beautiful performance of *Eugene Onegin*. We were guests of Claus Moser and thus received royal treatment.*

Tuesday 15 April 1975

Doreen and I had lunch at the Royal Thames and then I went to the House of Commons to hear the Budget. It was long, didactic and in my view misguided – though Denis Healey showed great political courage in what he said about wage inflation and unemployment. My fear is that the big increases in indirect taxation will stimulate inflation. Even if they don't reopen existing settlements, most groups who have any industrial power (which at present means mainly those in the public sector) will use it when they next negotiate to recover the fall in their standard of living which the Budget will bring about. It is also clear from the Budget that public expenditure and the borrowing requirement are right out of control.

Wednesday 16 April 1975

Ronnie Grierson came into the office at 9 a.m. for a talk about the proposed new committee on finance for investment, of which he can really claim to be the originator. Then Harold Watkinson came for a talk which lasted over an hour about the work of Neddy. He had some CBI staff people with him and said that he intended to try to get the CBI to make a strengthened Neddy the centrepiece of their policy. The news that he is to be the CBI's next president is foreshadowed in the press today – and is very welcome indeed.

---

* Sir Claus Moser, formerly Professor of Statistics at the London School of Economics, was director of the Central Statistical Office. He was chairman of the Royal Opera House board at the time.

Thursday 17 April 1975

I set off at crack of dawn for Aberdeen to pay a quick visit to the Scottish TUC. It was a left-wing affair, more or less completely controlled by the Communists. They passed a resolution yesterday deploring the Budget and another today opposing pay restraint in any form. Michael Foot made a speech shortly after the latter resolution was passed in which he passionately defended the social contract and vigorously denied that the Budget had in any way weakened it. He was heard quite friendlily but didn't seem to make any impression on the delegates. Immediately after it Mick McGahey, who was very much in evidence, told the press that the social contract had 'gone for a Burton'. One had the feeling that the People's Republic of Scotland had already arrived. At lunch George Smith of UCATT said he was considering taking his union out of the Scottish TUC because it was so Communist dominated.

After a dinner given by the STUC I went to a reception given by the *Morning Star*, where I was told all the principal delegates would be. I saw Mick Costello* and went up to him for a chat. He introduced me to McGahey who was beside him and at that moment the band struck up the 'Internationale'. So I found myself singing what I could remember of the words in company with two of the best known Communist Party members in Britain. Ah, well.

Monday 21 April 1975

Roly Gribben's interview is in the *Telegraph* today. It is the main item on the City page and is headed 'Five point plan for consensus to avoid disaster'. It ends by quoting me as saying that 'the trouble with this country is not that we don't agree about everything but that

---

* Industrial correspondent of the *Morning Star*.

we can't agree about anything'. It reads quite well and will, I hope, reassure some of my friends and/or critics in industry.

After lunch I went to the Bank of England to see Gordon Richardson and his deputy, Jasper Hollom, about the committee on finance for investment. I kicked off by saying that he with his large and prestigious organisation and I with my small one were among the very few people in public positions who were entirely independent of vested interests and that I hoped we could, as it were, forge an alliance between us.* Gordon strongly welcomed this and we then had a talk about the new committee, towards which he seemed to be taking a constructive approach.

For the first time in my presence Gordon was strongly – one might say venomously – critical of the government. He said Harold Wilson had no will to put things right and that he had told outright lies to industry about the content of the Industry Bill. He also said that public expenditure was totally out of control and that this would do untold damage to the economy. The trouble was, he said, that central bankers had said this so often that no one paid any attention to them any more. I said I planned to say something in a speech this week about the need to regain control over public expenditure, to which Gordon said, 'They won't like you for that.' I said that if they wanted to, they could always get another DG for NEDO.

Thursday 24 April 1975

In the afternoon Jasper Hollom phoned to say that the governor had talked to various people and that he thought we should now get down to working out specific proposals for the new committee on

---

* Richardson knew Neddy well. As chairman of the merchant bankers Schroeder Wagg he had been a member of NEDC from 1971 to 1973, and he was again a member from 1980 to 1983 as governor of the Bank of England.

finance for investment, which would include the trade unions and might have a joint secretariat from NEDO and the Bank. This is a breakthrough – the City fathers have resisted all previous attempts to set up standing machinery of this sort.

Monday 28 April 1975

I went to a prestigious lunch at the *Times*. The guest of honour was Elliot Richardson, the new American ambassador. Margaret Thatcher was also there. I sat between the two editors, William Rees-Mogg and Harold Evans. I had a lively conversation with Evans, whom I hadn't seen for a long time. I explained my theory that after the referendum, with the Industry Bill out of the way and a lull in wage bargaining, we should have a great, though short, opportunity to develop a national plan or strategy. I said we needed a new approach and that this should be positively slanted so as to give people some hope. We should not settle for an incomes policy but go for a really imaginative programme designed to eliminate overmanning by the time the next upswing occurs. Evans expressed great interest and said that the *Sunday Times* would back an approach on these lines wholeheartedly. I told him that the CBI and TUC would shortly make a joint statement urging support for national planning through a strengthened Neddy. (I read their paper just before lunch – it is not at all bad and will do both Neddy and the country good.)

After lunch I spoke to Margaret Thatcher about Neddy and remarked that so far as I knew she hadn't had anything to do with it as a minister. 'I went to one meeting', she said, 'and it was a total waste of time.' I then told her that Harold Watkinson was about to become president of the CBI and was anxious that they should give much more support to Neddy. 'A cold and ruthless man,' she said. 'I am sorry to hear he is going to take over at the CBI – he will not go over well on TV.' After a few more unfortunate remarks on my part, for all of which I was picked up sharply, she said it would be a good thing if I explained the work of Neddy to her and a group of her colleagues. She was not personally unpleasant but sharp and prickly – so far at least I can't see her as a party leader of stature.

Monday 5 May 1975

In the late afternoon we had a conference to launch a big report by our Building EDC on the Public Client and the Construction Industry. Gerald Kaufman* came for the government. He seemed very tense and I subsequently discovered that he was furious because he had been kept waiting by our security people, mistaken for a junior civil servant by Sir Kenneth Wood (the chairman of the committee which produced the report) and made to wait for three minutes because I was on the phone when he arrived.

Wednesday 7 May 1975

We had an extraordinary council meeting. Half way through the discussion of finance for investment, Tony Benn said he wanted to make some general points. He thereupon delivered a speech (which is unusual at NEDC) about investment and its financing on the lines he had used in public recently. The main burden was that it was unrealistic to think that industry would be able to raise the money for the huge amount of investment we needed and it would accordingly have to come from the state. He looked very tense throughout the meeting and I thought – probably wrongly – that he looked like a man who did not expect to remain a minister for long.

After one or two people had come into the discussion Shirley

---

* Minister of State at the Department of Industry.

Williams spoke – also for quite a time. She said the real trouble with Britain was that we had no continuing policy for industry which commanded bipartisan support. There was far too much chopping and changing, for which politicians were largely to blame. To help to get a consensus it might be a good thing for the new government members of Neddy to meet the opposition from time to time. Her speech was applauded – the first time I have seen this happen at NEDC.

Benn then intervened to say this amounted to recommending a coalition, which Shirley strenuously denied. Healey made no attempt to stop the argument. After the meeting Shirley told me she was sure that the story of her argument with Benn would leak and asked me to do anything I could to refute reports that she had advocated a coalition.

At 3.15 I gave my usual press conference but did not of course say anything about the Benn–Williams argument. At 5 p.m. Malcolm Brown of the *Times* rang me to say that he had heard on very good authority (Healey?) that there had been 'a blazing row' between the two of them at NEDC. I said I couldn't comment nor would I volunteer any information, but if he found out more and wanted to check it with me I should probably be willing to guide him. Shortly afterwards the *FT* rang up and I told them much the same.

At 8 p.m. Malcolm rang with a remarkably accurate account of the meeting. I told him he had done his homework well and spoke to No. 10, Shirley and the offices of Healey and Benn to let them know what was afoot.

Thursday 8 May 1975

The press is full of the argument at NEDC. We got a very good first leader in the *FT* and favourable comment in the *Telegraph* for our new committee on finance for investment. I am very pleased about this. A new committee may not seem much but it is the first time the City institutions and the TUC have ever agreed to sit down together in a standing body and there is quite a chance that good may come of it.

Tuesday 13 May 1975

I spent the evening at the biennial conference of the MNAOA.* Peter Shore spoke first – a straightforward speech as minister of shipping. Then the chairman presented me with a tie and a car badge as an old member of the union 'who had made good ashore'. I gave a short speech in which I described the DG of NEDO as like a navigation beacon marking the middle ground of some winding and dangerous channel, able to flash a light and give the signal 'you are straying into danger' but powerless to stop the vessel driving onto the rocks if the ship's company are bent on it. Altogether it was a very friendly occasion and I was pleased at the association's gesture in inviting me.

Wednesday 14 May 1975

I was interviewed on the BBC *Today* programme after the eight o'clock news by John Timpson. He had picked up something I said in Liverpool about our being in danger of throwing away our biggest national asset, our tolerance of widely differing views. I liked Timpson very much – it is the first time I have been on the *Today* programme.

---

* The Merchant Navy and Airline Officers' Association. I had served in the Merchant Navy from 1939 to 1945, for the last three years as navigating officer.

Thursday 15 May 1975

A nice letter of support for what I said on radio from John Read, the chairman of EMI, and an unusually enthusiastic one from Len Murray about our recent meeting with TGWU shop stewards. I find there is a steady trickle of letters in the morning mail now supporting what we are trying to do.

In the afternoon I went to the Bank to see Gordon Richardson. I asked him what his mood was now. 'One of intense irritation that we manage our affairs so badly that we are the despair of our friends abroad.'

Monday 19 May 1975

I had lunch at the Stock Exchange with the chairman (George Loveday), the chief executive (my old colleague Bob Fell) and three or four others. They were quite intelligent and reasonably forward-looking but like so many stockbrokers they cultivate an artificial and anachronistic kind of manner. However, they too pledged support for our efforts to bring the City, the trade unions and others together to consider problems of investment.

Tuesday 20 May 1975

I had cocktails at the German embassy and then went on to the CBI dinner. Harold Wilson was the main speaker. He followed Ralph Bateman, who was waspish and small minded. Wilson spoke for an interminably long time and as a result completely lost his audience, whom he was presumably trying to woo. The general drift of the speech was strongly anti-Benn.

Wednesday 21 May 1975

I flew to Edinburgh in the morning. I called on Eric Mackay, the editor of the *Scotsman*, who told me that when he had met Harold Wilson at a private lunch some months previously the PM had suggested that there should be a Neddy for Scotland. But Mackay advised me against following this idea up – he said I would do much better to work through the Scottish Council for Industry.

I went on to lunch with Willie Robertson, the director of the Scottish Council. Robertson, who is a nice, quiet, serious man, said that he would give full personal support to anything I tried to do through Neddy to stop the country falling apart through economic mismanagement. He is obviously very much afraid of a left-wing takeover of some kind.

Friday 23 May 1975

We flew out to BP's first production platform (120 miles out in the North Sea) and flew over various pipe-laying barges etc. The scale of the North Sea operations is very impressive and cheers me up every time I see it.

Tuesday 27 May 1975

I lunched with Harold Evans at the *Sunday Times*. Two Oxford economists* were there plus Peter Wilsher, Malcolm Crawford and others from the business staff. Harold made us talk about investment, wages and productivity throughout lunch. It was a

---

* Walter Eltis and Robert Bacon, who wrote a series of influential articles for the *Sunday Times* on the problems of British manufacturing industry. Eltis subsequently became the last director general of NEDO.

somewhat ragged discussion but some good points came out and one could see how he was trying to evolve a line which the paper could usefully take after the referendum. I plugged the need to concentrate on productivity and not get obsessed again with incomes policy.

Wednesday 28 May 1975

We spent the morning at Westminster Abbey at the 250th anniversary of the Order of the Bath. A beautiful and impressive piece of pageantry in the course of which the Queen installed the Prince of Wales as Grand Master. So he is now my boss in the Order of the Bath and in the Royal Thames.*

The new Archbishop of Canterbury, Donald Coggan, gave a splendid address – relevant, courageous and to the point – in which he spoke on such controversial topics as the referendum and abortion. If he goes on like this he will be a great prelate.

Thursday 29 May 1975

I lunched at the Orion Bank with David Montagu, the chairman. He is a dedicated 'centrist' and spoke very sensibly about the need to construct a political programme which all moderate people could support without necessarily giving up their party allegiances. He thinks we are certainly heading for a financial crash next winter. I said I had been hearing for more than a year that the crash was only three months away. I thought we should probably get through this winter without one but that if we didn't put our house in order we should run into a tremendous crisis in 1977–8, when world trade should be booming again. This is because I fear we shall run into all

---

* The Prince of Wales was then Commodore and is now Admiral of the Royal Thames Yacht Club.

the old bottlenecks again – shortage of skilled labour, plant capacity
and so on.

Monday 2 June 1975

I had a talk with Chris France at the Treasury about the post-
referendum prospect and the council meeting on 17 June. He said
that the government had virtually ceased to exist – for the last two
weeks there had been no collective decisions or discussions about
anything. With Healey in Paris for three days after the referendum
he couldn't see how the government could set a collective strategy
until quite late on in June.

Tuesday 3 June 1975

I flew up to Renfrew with John King, Tom Carlyle and other
Babcock directors to see their main engineering plant. At my request
the works manager had arranged a meeting with the shop stewards –
about twenty-four people in all. The Babcock management had been
very sceptical about the value of this but in fact it went off very well
and they were pleased that I had asked for it. I am sure it is right that
when I visit a plant as DG of NEDO I should make a point of
meeting the trade union representatives as well as the managers.

Friday 6 June 1975

The referendum result is wonderful and against all my own
predictions and expectations. I had forecast a low poll and a narrow
margin – in the event there was a high poll and a substantial margin.
The clearcut nature of the result is especially good.*

---

* 67 per cent voted 'yes' and 32 per cent 'no'.

Monday 9 June 1975

David Howell called this morning and stayed for an hour or so. He spoke very sensibly and moderately and really seems indistinguishable in his general outlook from the social democrats in the Labour Party. He said that the left of the Tory Party really believed in a statutory wages policy and the right believed in monetarist policies – but that virtually all the shadow Cabinet thought the right thing to go for was as strong a voluntary incomes policy as we could get. On this, he said, there was nothing between the Conservative leaders and Healey. I asked him what the chances were of getting a bipartisan approach to a wider range of economic and industrial policies – to which he said that there were none until the Labour government showed by deeds that it wanted one. For example they should drop the nationalisation of shipbuilding and aircraft.

In the afternoon I held the first ever meeting of independent members of EDCs.* Quite a lively and constructive occasion and obviously appreciated.

Tuesday 10 June 1975

I had lunch with Geoffrey Howe. He spoke much as David Howell had done. Like David he is worried stiff (as I am too) about the uncontrolled growth of public expenditure and wants cash ceilings for all public services.

After lunch I went to the House of Commons to talk to the Conservative Party's Trade and Industry Committee. Heseltine was in the chair but had to leave early for a meeting of the Industry Bill Committee. There was a pleasant and I thought quite good

---

* Most EDCs had one independent person (often an academic) as a member, in addition to their independent chairman.

discussion after my opening remarks. John Biffen* made an anti-big-business speech – aimed at the CBI and perhaps therefore indirectly at Neddy. But fortunately I had begun my talk by saying that I very much wanted to create a link between Neddy and Parliament – precisely in order to avoid accusations of a corporate state approach.

Wednesday 11 June 1975

I had a talk in the morning with Lord Limerick, the President of the ABCC, who would like his organisation to be represented on Neddy. I would personally be in favour of this – we need some change to break out of the rut in which CBI and TUC thinking keep us.

In the afternoon I held an EDC chairmen's meeting – a good deal better than usual. I had asked Campbell Adamson and Len Murray to join us for the end of the meeting. They both came and spoke helpfully and it was a good thing for them to meet the chairmen, who are quite a strong bunch of people.

Thursday 12 June 1975

I went to the House of Commons to see Denis Healey, who has refused to back me in my appeal to reverse a decision by Douglas Wass that I can't pay David Stout the salary he requires if he is to come to NEDO as economic director. The Treasury are in my view being deliberately unhelpful. They have never really supported NEDO and I expect they want to clip my wings as well. Anyway I have decided, after talking it over with Doreen, that it would be better to pack the job in than try to carry on without proper staff at the senior level.

I explained my point of view to Healey at some length and with a

---

* MP for Oswestry.

good deal of force. So far as I could tell this made no impression on him at all. He kept telling me that there was a system for dealing with these matters and I must abide by it, but I pointed out to him that the system was what the permanent secretaries wanted it to be at any given time. At the end of the interview, in which Healey was definite though not personally unpleasant, I said I would feel bound to take the matter up with the PM.

As soon as I got back to the office I arranged to see Robin Butler at No. 10. I told him the story and said (a) I couldn't and wouldn't do the job without proper staff; (b) I expected the Treasury to respect NEDO's independence and treat it sensibly and not by the book; and (c) I was fed up with being messed around. Butler was sympathetic and said he thought the PM would want to help provided he could do so without overruling Healey.

Monday 16 June 1975

I called in at No. 10 to see Ken Stowe,* at his request. He told me that the PM was sympathetic to my difficulties over senior staff and had suggested that Douglas Allen might take the matter in hand with a view to settling it forthwith. I said I would be entirely content with this.

Tuesday 17 June 1975

NEDC in the morning. We had had all sorts of indications in advance that Wilson wanted to play it in a low key. In the event he took a more lively interest in the proceedings and was a more active chairman than I have seen him for a long time. He gave the impression of being less

---

* He had succeeded Robert Armstrong as the Prime Minister's principal private secretary.

physically and mentally lethargic than recently, though his threshold of boredom is very low. He was, as usual, friendly to Neddy and to myself and helped the discussion along.

Apart from the nationalised industry reports (which were well received) the main item was the first CBI–TUC paper on the role of Neddy. They pressed their case on this quite hard and pushed Healey into being more forthcoming about making Treasury information available to Neddy than he had intended at the start. The government are to give their reaction to the CBI–TUC paper next month. As he left after drinks I said to Wilson that I hoped he would see that the government gave a constructive response. He replied, 'I thought he [i.e. Healey] came a long way during the meeting, didn't you?'

As a result of intensive preparatory work on my part we got agreement to the new finance for investment committee at this meeting. The TUC did not press their desire to have its terms of reference extended to cover the use of manpower in the City – which would have killed the proposed committee stone dead.

Wednesday 18 June 1975

The papers are full of reports that Healey said at yesterday's NEDC that the pick up in world trade was likely to come later than he had earlier thought. This point arose from a misunderstanding by the PA reporter (who is notoriously apt to get things wrong) of something I said at yesterday's press briefing after the Neddy meeting. I didn't think anyone would get excited about it since it is fairly clear that the recession will go on longer than most people (though not myself) had expected but I learned in the course of the morning that Healey was very angry. I stuck to my fixed policy – not to issue any corrections myself but to raise no objections to anyone who thinks I misquoted him from doing so and I gather Healey intends to issue a statement disavowing the press reports.

In the afternoon I made a speech to a BIM conference. When I got back in the evening I discovered that the Treasury had issued a strong statement to the effect that I had misquoted the Chancellor yesterday. John Palmer of the *Guardian* phoned me about it and pressed me hard to make a comment. I refused to do so and said he needn't try ringing later because I was going for a walk.

Thursday 19 June 1975

The *Guardian* today reports the disagreement between Healey and myself and says that 'when asked to comment Sir Ronald said he was going for a nice walk'. This is bad journalism – to quote an informal remark by someone who has been as helpful to the *Guardian* as I have. It won't help my relations with Healey.*

Sunday 22 June 1975

Doreen's birthday. John and Madeleine Hunt were down for the weekend. We set off for a week's sailing in South Brittany with the Bond-Williams. We were both physically and mentally near the end of our tether and very ready for a break.

Tuesday 1 July 1975

Back to work, refreshed by excellent cruising in *Bowstring*. Although we were only away a week we came back to find the general

---

* That this was a correct forecast is confirmed by the entry for 24 June 1975 in Bernard Donoughue's *Downing Street Diary* (London: Jonathan Cape, 2005): 'We went to the Cabinet Committee on Ministerial Economic Strategy at 11. Discussed the future of the NEDC – including Healey's statement that if its director Ronnie McIntosh continues to act the prima donna he would send him "for a very long walk".'

atmosphere dramatically changed. The pound has fallen very low and there is a mood of near hysteria and incipient collapse around.

Healey has put round a paper about the role of Neddy which is very negative and really rather bad. It also ends with a disagreeable sentence about the need for post-Council press briefings to stick to what was said at meetings. Apparently the original version of the paper contained another sentence: 'The standing of NEDO is not enhanced when Ministers have to issue statements denying opinions wrongly attributed to them.' Chris Lucas got Healey to take this out – presumably because he thought it might provoke me into resignation. Fortunately, having had a week's holiday I am quite relaxed about it.

In the afternoon Healey made a crisis statement giving notice that wage settlements must not exceed 10 per cent in the next wage round and that, if need be, the government would take statutory powers to enforce this. The statement came more or less out of the blue after a Cabinet meeting this morning. Len Murray and Campbell Adamson both said they were given warning of it very late last night.

Wednesday 2 July 1975

Before the Neddy meeting Len Murray told me he had talked to Healey last night and he thought that as a result Healey would now want to open the meeting with a statement about the government's new approach to inflation. This is what in fact happened. Denis began the meeting by saying, 'Ronnie has suggested that I should say something to you about my statement yesterday,' and then went on to talk for some time about the economic situation and the government's intentions.

After that we spent the whole morning discussing the Treasury paper on the role of Neddy. It got a vigorous hammering from all the non-government members. The TUC hit it particularly hard and towards the end Murray put the pressure on by becoming mildly unpleasant – a familiar trade union tactic but not one I have seen him use against Labour ministers before.

By the time I came in to speak most of my points had been made for me – but I kept the pressure up for a greater government commitment to Neddy and the need for a return to some form of consensus planning if we were ever to get out of our national economic crisis. Healey put up a strong resistance but the council would not accept his summing up and it was left that we would return to the subject next month.

At lunch Healey was quite genial and my relations with him seem more or less back to normal.

I talked privately to both Alf Allen and David Basnett about the proposed new incomes policy. Alf said he might end up alongside the left-wingers opposing the policy, the effect of which might be to hold retail prices down to such an extent that shop workers' wages would be quite disproportionately depressed. Alf was very critical of Jack Jones – the trade union movement would not stomach 'the cult of the individual' for much longer. Basnett was deeply disillusioned about the whole business and seemed inclined to opt out.

Thursday 3 July 1975

In the afternoon I went to see Margaret Thatcher at the House of Commons. Michael Heseltine was also there. She greeted me by saying, 'You are the man who stopped me from giving the teachers their London allowance' – a reference to my activities as chairman of the Official Committee on Pay three or four years previously.* We

---

* I was at that time helping Robert Carr, the Secretary of State for Employment, to run an informal policy of wage restraint (known as n minus one) which is regarded by many as the most effective method of reducing wage inflation which we had in the 1960s or 1970s.

talked a little of the current situation and I said I was still resolutely opposed to a statutory pay policy, as I had been under the Heath government.

I then opened up by saying what my philosophy on Neddy was. I said I thought this country must find a way of developing a consensus on the hard core of industrial and economic policies which would survive a change of government. I said that my starting point was the assumption that we faced a prolonged period of economic crisis and political instability and that this called for a degree of consensus planning and a strengthening of those forces in the country which made for cohesion. Without exaggerating what Neddy could do, I thought it had a substantial contribution to make and I was anxious to maintain close relations with the main political parties.

This all seemed to go down reasonably well but what struck me very forcibly was the lack of any kind of strategic approach in Mrs Thatcher's comments. No doubt she had her mind on a lot of other things and her job as leader of the opposition this week can't be an easy one. Nevertheless, it was painfully clear that she hadn't really got her thoughts on anything further ahead than tomorrow or next week – in this respect she was very much a Tory Harold Wilson. Heseltine told me afterwards that with the exception of Keith Joseph more or less the whole of the Tory party now supported the approach I had outlined to Mrs Thatcher and that they would back Neddy to the hilt.

Friday 4 July 1975

Douglas Allen has sent me the draft of his report to the PM about my staffing problems. It is excellent and will give me everything I want.

Sam Brittan has a very good article in today's *FT* in which he comes out strongly against statutory wage control. I agree with him. It might hold through this winter but the danger that some militant unions will again destroy a policy endorsed by Parliament is very real and in my view too great a risk to run. My position is a mixture of right and left. Like the left I find legal controls on wage bargaining distasteful – they are an unwarrantable interference with personal rights and freedoms. Like the right I believe that the government's priority should be to deal with the two contributory causes of inflation which are – or ought to be – under its control, namely public expenditure and the money supply. Its failure to tackle the alarming growth of public expenditure and the public sector borrowing requirement will catch up with it in the end; and my guess is that before this year is out we may have the worst of all worlds – statutory wage controls, steeply rising unemployment and savage and ill-considered cuts in public expenditure. Very few people in authority would agree with me – it is nice to think that Sam Brittan (who is unusually perceptive and intelligent) does.

I have just seen a leader in the *Guardian* of 27 June, when we were away. It says, 'Neddy has survived the comings and goings of administrations and has built up a valuable stock of authority and expertise. Indeed its reputation probably stands as high now as it has ever done.'

Wednesday 9 July 1975

I went to the Scientific Instrument Makers' lunch at the Savoy. Unexpectedly, Peter Jay* was the principal guest. He made a witty, devastating and wholly destructive speech about the government's handling of the economy. Its theme was that incomes policy is an almost totally ineffective weapon against inflation so long as public

---

* Economics editor of the *Times*.

expenditure and the money supply are not strictly controlled. He forecast that political pressures would make the government reflate later this year or early next year; that inflation would remain at least at its present levels; and that in 1977/8 we should be engulfed in a severe crisis which our democratic institutions would not survive. Broadly speaking I think he is right though he may have overpainted it a bit.

Friday 11 July 1975

The PM announced the government's new anti-inflation package. I don't think it has any chance of working; no approach which makes incomes policy the central instrument will ever work. There is no sign that the government means to tackle public expenditure – indeed the new package will lead to some increases in expenditure. There is not to be any immediate statutory back up for the pay policy but the government says it will introduce legislation if the policy seems not to be working. This gives us the worst of all worlds – it really means that ministers will be committed to introduce a Bill to impose legal curbs on wages as soon as some large militant union calls a strike to support an over-the-odds wage claim. That looks like a recipe for disaster.

I don't think that the package will hold beyond the autumn – and I believe its failure will lead to some political change.

Monday 14 July 1975

Doreen and I gave a splendid party in the evening for Sid Greene and his wife. Sid was a founder member of Neddy and has served without a break until now. He will give up in September, when he ceases to be chairman of the TUC Economic Committee. He is a very nice man and has been a very good influence in public life and

I was keen to do him honour when he left us.

We had asked past and present members of Neddy plus current EDC chairmen and their wives, along with others who had been closely associated with Neddy. It was all very relaxed and friendly and our guests seemed genuinely to enjoy themselves.

Selwyn Lloyd* made a delightful little speech in which he referred to the setting up of Neddy and how he had enjoyed chairing it 'until for reasons which even now I do not wholly understand I was removed from the scene'. Harold Wilson followed and said among other things that Neddy had never been stronger than it was now – and then Sid made a nice little speech in the course of which he referred very pleasantly to 'our friend Ted there'. Altogether a good occasion.

Monday 21 July 1975

I took John Lyons, the general secretary of the EPEA, to lunch at Romeo and Juliet. He is one of the most intelligent trade union leaders I have met and a man of independent mind. We talked usefully about our nationalised industry enquiry.

Friday 25 July 1975

We got up at 5.30 a.m. on an unbelievably perfect day to take part in the bicentenary celebrations of the Royal Thames Yacht Club. A couple of hundred yachts of all shapes and sizes set sail from the Hamble to Cowes, where the club's admiral, Lord Mountbatten, took the salute. We were on board David Nicolson's yacht *Deerhound*,†

---

* Speaker of the House of Commons.

† David Lancaster Nicolson was a descendant of Robert Lancaster, who had rescued and taken to England in his yacht *Deerhound* the captain of the Confederate ship *Alabama* after she had been sunk off Cherbourg by a Yankee warship in 1864.

followed by *Morning Cloud* with Ted Heath at the helm. It was a marvellous nautical occasion.

Wednesday 30 July 1975

The other day I rang Ken Stowe at No. 10 to find out what on earth had happened to Douglas Allen's report on my senior staff needs. He said that No. 10 had dealt with it in twenty-four hours and he was astonished that I hadn't heard from the Treasury about it yet. Today I got a letter from Healey's private secretary saying in somewhat ungracious terms that the Chancellor accepted Allen's recommendations. Peter Carey says that the Treasury will never forgive either Allen or me for this.

I also circulated the paper I have prepared for next week's Council with my ideas on planning and the role of Neddy. I worked very hard on it and in the end felt it came out reasonably well. I have sent copies to various people in and outside Whitehall in order to try to drum up support for it.

Michael Heseltine came to the office for a talk about the EDCs. He had Tom King and John Stanley* with him. Heseltine seems incredibly well disposed to Neddy and much more sensible in his general approach than he was a few months ago. King is like a KGB man appointed by Thatcher to see that Heseltine doesn't commit the party to Heath-like policies.

I had a visit from a Saudi Arabian sheikh – a sophisticated and very sceptical sort of a person. It is somewhat disturbing to know that our economic future depends on people like him – I don't think they have any intention of taking their money away from London but if it suited their book to do so they wouldn't hesitate for a second.

In the evening I had dinner at the House of Commons with

---

* Conservative MPs for Bridgwater and Tonbridge & Malling respectively.

Liberal MPs and peers. The host was Jeremy Thorpe, whom I found just as attractive a person close to as he is on television. When we broke up sometime after ten Thorpe took me up to his room for a nightcap. We talked about the first general election of 1974 and the talks he had had with Heath immediately after it. He said that the first time he went to No. 10 after the election Heath read out some notes instead of simply talking to him in a natural manner. Thorpe seemed to think that this was something to do with Heath's personality but I imagine that Heath was in fact pretty tightly bound by a Cabinet decision on how far he could go with the Liberals. Anyway, Thorpe evidently raised the question of electoral reform quite early on in the conversation but Heath seemed unprepared for it and said he would have to consult his colleagues. This depressed Thorpe, who considered that, if the Tories were serious about a coalition, they should have known the question of electoral reform would arise and should have decided on their attitude in advance.

I told Thorpe that Doreen and I had both voted Liberal at both elections in 1974 but that we had been greatly disappointed that they had not increased their vote in October. We talked about the possible emergence of a centre party but I don't think that Thorpe believes in it any more than I do.

I left after half an hour or so still impressed by Thorpe's likeable personality – but he doesn't give the impression of a man who seriously expects to hold ministerial office as leader of the Liberal Party.

Thursday 31 July 1975

I had a nice letter from Heseltine saying that our talk confirmed his strong impression that no government had ever allowed Neddy to realise the great potential it has.

Sunday 3 August 1975

We motored down to Southampton and caught the ferry to Cowes for a cocktail party given by the Duke of Edinburgh for the Royal Thames on *Britannia*. It was a perfect evening. We assembled at the squadron steps – the men in reefer jackets and white trousers and the women in long dresses with a crowd of sight-seeing tourists to see us off. It was pure fantasy and full of the spirit of 1913.

Monday 4 August 1975

I spent the day preparing for Wednesday's council meeting. I am very apprehensive that the government will take a negative line and simply let the discussion run into the sand, which would be a very bad thing for Neddy – and I believe for the country. Chris Lucas has been lobbying departments hard to prevent this.

Tuesday 5 August 1975

Going to work I ran into Len Neal.* I asked him how he was, to which he replied, 'Like everyone else, waiting for the collapse.'

Wednesday 6 August 1975

In the event the Neddy meeting, about which I had been getting increasingly gloomy, went off very well. Healey made a long and very constructive opening statement on the planning item, in which he went out of his way to compliment NEDO on its work in the last

---

* Sir Leonard Neal had been chairman of the Commission on Industrial Relations (established by the Heath government's Industrial Relations Act) from 1971 to 1974.

eighteen months (we had circulated a number of papers for this meeting which were generally recognised to be of high quality). In the course of the meeting he was pushed quite a long way by the CBI and others to 'open up the Treasury books' and encourage wider discussion of macro-economic policy and he yielded to this pressure quite significantly. I said that it wasn't Treasury forecasts which people really wanted to have but a more open discussion of their assumptions and of the constraints under which the government's economic policy had to be framed. I think Healey now accepts this.

Eric Varley took a more active part than usual in the meeting. I had the impression that we were witnessing the end of the Healey–Foot alliance and the beginning of the Healey–Varley alliance. Healey talked a great deal during the meeting and at the end Foot made a quip about 'taciturn Yorkshire men'. It was all pleasantly done but I thought there was an undercurrent of antagonism between the two men.

Anyway, the government are now committed to putting a paper on a new industrial strategy to the council for discussion in October. This is what I have been pressing for in speeches and papers for about a year now.

Roy and Jennifer, Piers Dixon and the Seligmans came to supper. The Jenkins seemed a bit low – I don't think Roy enjoys government much just now but I suppose he is more or less trapped in it. I told Roy about my recent difficulties over staff etc. with Healey but said that our relations had greatly improved and that Denis had gone out of his way to say pleasant things about NEDO. Roy warned me to pay no attention to this. He said that Healey's personal relations were entirely governed by political expediency.

Monday 1 September 1975

Back to work after a splendid break – which included a very good week's sailing from Lymington to Salcombe and back with our old sailing friends John and Mary Masterman.

I had lunch with Edwin Plowden at the Tube Investments offices at Bridgewater House. It is a marvellous building though I should think it is quite unsuitable for the headquarters of a large company. Plowden said the board would get rid of it as soon as he retired.

We talked mostly about the CBI. Plowden is carrying out an inquiry into its role and organisation and is also looking for a successor to Campbell Adamson.* He told me that until two or three years ago he never had anything to do with the CBI because he reckoned that his personal contacts with politicians and civil servants would be of more use to his company than the CBI would ever be. But he acknowledged that this had been a mistake and said he was now giving a lot of time to its affairs. He likes and admires Ted Heath, though he finds him almost impossible to talk to, and regards Margaret Thatcher as of no account.

I told him that the CBI seemed to me to have two glaring defects (both of which are often to be found in major British institutions). One is that it doesn't seem to have any clear idea of what its objectives are; the other is that – compared for example to the TUC – it is very unprofessional. I think this is a real handicap nationally – we need a strong body to speak for private sector manufacturing interests, which can hold its own with the bureaucracies of Whitehall and Congress House, and the CBI as at present organised just doesn't match up to this requirement.

Tuesday 2 September 1975

I went to Blackpool in the afternoon for the Trades Union Congress. I arrived in brilliant sunshine and for the first time in my experience

---

* After seven years at the CBI Adamson had decided to move on. He became chairman of Abbey National in 1978.

both Snowdonia and the Cumberland hills were clearly visible from the beach.

Wednesday 3 September 1975

The economic debate took place today and Congress decided by a two-to-one majority to give up free collective bargaining for the next twelve months and to support the government's policy of a £6-a-week increase instead. Jack Jones and Len Murray spoke very powerfully in support of the policy, using economic arguments which would come easily from the most conventional official in the Treasury or Bank of England. Jones's main non-economic argument was that unless the trade union movement exercised voluntary self-restraint on wages, the Labour government would be swept aside by hyper-inflation. His support for the Labour government was expressed in most extreme terms – in anyone else it would have seemed sycophantic but Jones's influence over government policy is strong enough to make it certain that they will dance to his tune rather than vice versa. However, he did speak in a very responsible way. Murray made a good, strong speech in which he spoke very realistically about our economic difficulties. He was of course able to do this because of Jones's support for the policy – without that he would, I think, have had to make a rather different speech.

Murray said that the government had promised 'a major initiative in the field of commercial and industrial planning in the autumn'. This was presumably a reference to the paper on industrial strategy which Healey has promised to put to the October meeting of Neddy. John Elliott tackled me about this as I left the auditorium. I told him of the discussions at our last three Neddy meetings and said, on the record, that in my view what the TUC and the government were doing to bring inflation under control would be so much wasted effort unless we used the next twelve months to get to grips with the underlying problems of industrial structure and productivity which we have talked about and neglected for these past ten years.

Doreen arrived in the evening – for her first Congress.

Thursday 4 September 1975

The lead story in the *FT* is a piece by John Elliott about a new move towards national planning in which my statement about the need to tackle the underlying problems of industry is given prominence. After lunch I spoke to my office in London and learned that the Treasury were concerned about Elliott's piece, which gave too much prominence to Neddy's role. What a crabbing, unhelpful lot they are.

In the evening we gave our party for the General Council and the trade union people who sit on little Neddies. It seemed to go very well – Doreen's presence as hostess was a great help and the trade union people clearly enjoyed bringing their wives. There was a good turn out – about 120 in all and almost all the bigwigs of the movement attended.

Friday 5 September 1975

We left Blackpool after breakfast. The last two people we saw were Frank Chapple and Dai Davies, both of whom told Doreen how little they thought of their fellow trade union leaders. Davies said that the movement was a mere shadow of what it had been ten years ago and was in the hands of the left. Chapple referred to the ineffectiveness of most moderate trade union leaders – 'they give me a pain in the arse with their poncing around' was his phrase.

Wednesday 10 September 1975

I lunched at Great Universal Stores headquarters with Leonard Wolfson, the managing director, and his finance director. Lucien Wigdor of the CBI was also there. Wolfson is very entrepreneurial and anti-bureaucratic in his approach but reacted very favourably to what I said about my aims for Neddy. He is very anti-Wilson, whom he despises. I said I thought we owed Wilson a debt of gratitude for taking us through the referendum so successfully – but Wolfson replied (with some justice) that the referendum was quite unnecessary and that all Wilson had done was 'thrown the girl into the water and then rescued her'. Wolfson is pro-Thatcher, Callaghan and Jenkins. His attitude to industrial relations is civilised.

Thursday 18 September 1975

In the afternoon Donald Maitland called to see me before taking up his post as ambassador to the EEC. He is a real apparatchik and I think he will do the job very well indeed. There was some doubt whether Wilson would approve his appointment because he had been very much identified with Ted Heath when he was press officer at No. 10, but apparently this difficulty was overcome. In the old days of 1964–70 Wilson would certainly have blocked the appointment of anyone who had been personally close to a Tory Prime Minister.

Donald said he thought it very important that I should go on saying the things I said in my recent speeches. He said Jim Callaghan would strongly support them. He (Callaghan) had kept off domestic affairs in Cabinet while the negotiations leading up to the referendum were on but Maitland thought that he would take a much more active part now and throw his weight firmly on the social democratic side.

Friday 19 September 1975

Jeremy Thorpe is reported in today's papers as having told the Liberal Assembly that opposition parties should be represented on Neddy.

Tuesday 23 September 1975

I made a lunchtime speech at the Hilton to the joint Brimec–NEDO conference on investment. I had decided it was time I made a somewhat right-wing speech so I talked about the appalling effect which inflation and price control have had on manufacturing industry. I gave some figures showing the declining share of manufacturing in our national output and pointed out that the manufacturing sector as a whole had had cash flow deficits in four of the last five years. I described this as a recipe for contraction and obsolescence whose implications for the age and quality of our capital stock in five years time were frightening. The conference came to a sudden end halfway through the afternoon because of a bomb scare.

Thursday 25 September 1975

In the afternoon Oliver Wright called. He is just about to go to Bonn as our ambassador. Like Donald Maitland he is a warm supporter of Neddy.

Friday 26 September 1975

My 56th birthday. Ron Smith came to see me to tell me about an imaginative scheme the BSC (of which he is a director) are going in for to provide new work for those of their employees who become redundant as they run down the old steel plants and cut overmanning. It is a very intelligent idea and I hope it works – without schemes of this sort we shall never get our manning scales down to competitive levels.

Tuesday 30 September 1975

Nicky Kaldor* took me to lunch at the Reform. I was interested to find out why, as he and I have never been close and I don't know him well. It turned out that Denis Healey has been giving him some of our recent papers about the state of British industry etc. and that these have greatly impressed him. In particular he shares to the full the ideas I expressed at the Brimec conference about manufacturing industry. I suppose he saw it all long before I did and recommended selective employment tax as a result.† Anyway, the upshot is that I have forged a new alliance with him and we can count on him to give our ideas a fair wind within the Treasury.

Monday 6 October 1975

Contrary to expectation, we had a good Neddy meeting. This was the meeting at which we should have taken the government's paper on a new industrial strategy but they couldn't get it ready in time so we had to make do with some 'fill-in' items about the nationalised industries and manpower. However, the discussion was clear and positive – one really begins to feel that the council will soon get down to the real problems facing this country.

---

* Nicholas Kaldor was Professor of Economics at Cambridge and had been given leave of absence to become special adviser to the Chancellor. He and his compatriot Thomas Balogh both had Rolls-Royce minds but as economic advisers to successive Labour governments they were not an unqualified success.

† Introduced in 1967, selective employment tax was designed to encourage the movement of labour from service industries to manufacturing.

At lunch Harold Watkinson told me there was still quite a significant faction of CBI members (though small in number) who wanted to break off co-operation with the government and would be prepared to withdraw from Neddy as a symbolic gesture. He and Eric Roll spoke about the hostility of the official Treasury towards Neddy – now and previously. Eric thought that it occurred below permanent secretary level only and was part of a continuing power struggle.

At my press briefing I announced that the next meeting of Neddy will be held at Chequers under the PM's chairmanship and will last all day.

Thursday 9 October 1975

Doreen and I arrived yesterday in Toronto, where I had been invited to speak at a conference on the business outlook. I had to speak at lunchtime to an audience of six or seven hundred. My speech was about Britain's current economic and industrial situation – how we had got into it and how we might get out of it. I had taken a lot of trouble over it and was glad to find it seemed to go over well. It is very difficult in a speech of this sort to strike the right balance. One must show some optimism but if you overdo it an audience like this will simply switch off.

Things have changed a lot in Canada since I was here a year ago. Now the talk is all of inflation and strikes: Ontario has a minority Conservative government for the first time for over a generation and the official opposition is socialist. I can't remember experiencing such a marked change of mood in twelve months. Perhaps for this reason there was more interest in what I had to say about problems in Britain than one might have expected.

Monday 13 October 1975

We flew to Ottawa and arrived in time to hear the Prime Minister, Pierre Trudeau, give a very uninspiring TV broadcast announcing the introduction of new wage and price controls – he was flat and unconvincing and if I had shut my eyes I would have thought it was any British Chancellor of the last ten years talking.

Thursday 16 October 1975

I went to the Mansion House for the Lord Mayor's dinner for the bankers and merchants of the City of London. Denis Healey spoke complacently about the size of the borrowing requirement and about the level of public expenditure, which everyone knows is out of control. Gordon Richardson spoke well and with increased authority in terms which did not accord easily with Denis's speech.

Monday 27 October 1975

Flew to Frankfurt in the morning – my first visit there and only my second time in Germany since the war. The town was disappointing – rather like Sheffield and with none of the panache of the North American cities we saw earlier this month. I was, however, very hospitably received by the consul general, who had laid on a lunch for me. The German guests were a very agreeable and civilised lot, consisting of a banker, the chairman of the editorial board of the *Frankfurter Allgemeine Zeitung*, a director of Hoechst and a man from the automobile industry. They were self-assured without being in any way assertive and showed a friendly and intelligent interest in Britain's problems without being condescending. They said that the high level of unemployment in Germany had not so far created any social problems – unemployment insurance was generous and the unemployed did not suffer much loss of earnings in the first six months at least.

Thursday 30 October 1975

I went to lunch at the Bank of England, where I sat next to Maurice Laing. He said he always avoided Cecil King when the latter was a Bank director because he suspected he was keeping a diary.* I kept quiet.

Sunday 2 November 1975

Doreen and I went after lunch to King's Cross to board a special train laid on by BP to take people to the ceremonies marking the opening of the Forties Field. There were about 300 people on the train.

Monday 3 November 1975

On arrival in Aberdeen we were taken in coaches to Dyce, where BP had erected an enormous marquee – said to be the biggest ever made – outside their offices.

The arrangements for the rest of the day worked like clockwork. The Queen arrived by car in the middle of the tent, where there were about 1,000 invited guests. The ceremony itself was fairly short, with speeches from the Queen, the PM and Eric Drake,† and the proceedings were televised.

The whole thing was magnificently done and BP really pushed the boat out. It must have cost a fortune but I think on the whole that

---

* Sir Maurice Laing was chairman of John Laing and Co and a director of the Bank. Cecil King was a former chairman of the *Daily Mirror*, whose diary for 1965–70 was published in 1972.
† Sir Eric Drake was chairman of BP.

it was justified. The North Sea operation is a very impressive one and BP have done extremely well to get oil ashore by pipeline less than five years since the first discovery – and by making a splash and having the whole thing televised with the Queen present they may have got some feeling of the scale of the achievement across to the public.

Tuesday 4 November 1975

In the afternoon I went over to the House of Commons to see Michael Heseltine, who had Tom King and John Stanley with him. I told him about the papers which would be in front of the Neddy meeting at Chequers. I said that Wilson would be giving a televised press conference but that I thought there was a good chance that there would be a constructive outcome which might lead the way towards a more sensible, less partisan approach to our industrial problems. I said I hoped that Conservative frontbenchers would not feel obliged to come out in instant opposition to the meeting's conclusions. Heseltine and co. listened warily to what I had to say. Michael himself was, I think, entirely sympathetic but he said there would be plenty of people in the Conservative Party who did not believe that a consensus could be achieved while the present Labour government was in power. He did say, however, that two-thirds of the shadow Cabinet would be prepared to support policies which were genuinely aimed at getting to grips with the nation's problems. King seemed less sure – he evidently represents a harder school of thought within the party and I doubt if he believes in consensus or the middle way at all. We left it that they would wait to see what emerged from Chequers. I was glad I made the approach – at least it can do no harm and it might just possibly do some good.

Wednesday 5 November 1975

I worried most of the night about what I should say at Chequers and redrafted my notes in the car on the way down. The meeting started at ten and we had an absolutely full house. All the members of Neddy were there (twenty-five counting the PM) and there was a strong contingent in the back row. John Cousins attended for the first time as a member of the NEDO staff.*

Wilson was in cracking form – much more alive and active in the chair than I have seen him for some time. He brought with him the text of the statement he was going to make after the meeting and amended it as the discussion proceeded.

Healey spoke rather well – and more briefly than usual – about the mistakes of government policy in the past and the need to give more continuous priority to manufacturing industry. On the whole it was one of his best statements to NEDC and included several friendly references to NEDO's work and role.

Then it was Varley's turn. He was less convincing – probably because they have only the haziest idea of how their new strategy is going to work. I can't make him out yet – he is still fully acceptable to the left but the ideas he expresses on industrial matters are entirely conventional and indistinguishable from those of his civil servants. They say he has a highly developed political sense – but I would guess also that he is easily influenced.

I spoke next – in fairly low profile but emphasising the dangerous condition of manufacturing industry and the need for continuity of policy extending beyond the lifetime of a single parliament. Nearly everyone took part in the discussions after that. The two who spoke best were Monty Finniston and Campbell Adamson. Harold

* John Cousins, a former national officer of the TGWU and son of a previous general secretary, had joined NEDO as manpower director after Pat Fisher's death.

Watkinson told the PM that if he wanted industry's support he should declare Neddy as his 'chosen instrument'. However, the trade union people were not good. Jack Jones was in an awkward mood. He and Scanlon had a hate against all committee activity – they wanted 'action now'. But when the CBI said that price control should be modified to help investment they said that would need 'very careful study' before any conclusion could be reached on it!

On balance the mood was very constructive. There was an encouraging sense of urgency and everyone was agreed on the need to give manufacturing industry higher priority even at the expense of social objectives. A number of people, including Jones, were critical of Wilson for having the meeting at Chequers – it would arouse expectations which couldn't be fulfilled, they said. The fact is that people *are* expecting a lot from this meeting because they realise the mess the country is in and desperately want to see action taken to put things right.

After lunch we had a brief discussion of a paper by Michael Foot which was embarrassingly bad. His contribution to Neddy and the economic debate generally seems to me to be precisely nil. After that Wilson summed up by saying that despite serious reservations on some points the council had generally endorsed the government's proposals for a new industrial strategy – which is, I think, true.

We then rushed back to London, where I joined Wilson, Healey and Varley for the press conference. Wilson's opening statement was good and very helpful from my point of view – 'Neddy is to mastermind the whole programme,' he said.

Thursday 6 November 1975

The press is absolutely full of Chequers. Quite rightly there is much scepticism but the *FT* has a warily favourable leader and most of the others regard the outcome as mildly encouraging. But Peter Jay in the *Times* is very critical – so is the *Morning Star*.

I went to the House of Lords for a drink with Tommy Balogh. He said a decision would soon have to be taken about whether we should ask the IMF for a loan.

Friday 7 November 1975

I drove to Luton airport and flew to Teesside. George Chetwynd – whom I had known very well in 1963 when he was director of the North East Development Council and I was helping Hailsham* – met me at the airport. We spent the morning in a launch on the river seeing the industrial developments connected with the port. These are very impressive – Teesside really does look the growth point which I always thought it had the potential to become.

The trip had been laid on for Jack Jones, who was up with his wife and Moss Evans to open a new TGWU office in Middlesbrough. He told me he thought the Chequers meeting had been useful and that it had got a better reception in the press than he had feared it might.

I flew back to London in the evening and spent an hour in a traffic jam inside the multi-storey car park. While waiting, I read the *Spectator*, which has a very hostile article by 'Skinflint' called 'Let Neddy die', critical both of the institution and of me personally. One way and another it has been quite a week.

Tuesday 11 November 1975

I spent an hour with Antony Part and Tony Rawlinson† at the

---

* Lord Hailsham was appointed Minister for the North-East in 1963 and I was the senior full-time member of this staff.

† Rawlinson had been posted to the DoI when his term as economic minister in Washington had come to an end.

Department of Industry to discuss the government's new industrial strategy and our relationship with the department. It was a satisfactory meeting and should help our two organisations to work harmoniously together. I wish I could get the same relationship with the Treasury.

Thursday 13 November 1975

John Sackur of Spencer Stuart came to see me to discuss possible successors to Campbell Adamson. He said that Harold Watkinson had specifically instructed him to ask if I would let my name go forward. I said no.

I had a working lunch in the office with Geoffrey Owen of the *FT* and three of my own staff to discuss the work of the EDCs. Geoffrey plans to do a feature article about them. He asked at the end whether tripartite industry committees such as EDCs would not do better if they had civil service chairmen, as in France. I said definitely not. In Britain civil servants are entirely subject to ministers and have to follow all the shifts and turns of policy which arise when individual ministers change, governments run into unexpected difficulties or a new party comes into power. The great merit of the Neddy system of independent chairmen is that they can provide continuity with relatively little regard to changes of ministerial policy. Also, industry trusts Neddy in a way it doesn't trust government departments.

Friday 14 November 1975

The *Investor's Chronicle* has an unsigned profile of me which is hostile and vindictive. It begins, "'The trouble with Ronnie McIntosh", snapped a leading political figure contemptuously, "is that he thinks he's Jesus Christ – only Ronnie McIntosh and NEDC can save Britain.'" Coming after Skinflint's piece in the *Spectator* it looks as though someone is pursuing a vendetta.*

Tuesday 18 November 1975

In the morning I drove down to a hotel at Heathrow to speak at a conference. I made a short and mildly optimistic speech referring to Chequers – and the G7 summit meeting at Rambouillet, which ended yesterday – as perhaps signifying 'the beginning of the beginning'. In talking about our economic predicament and our efforts to get out of it, I also used that excellent phrase of Bill Slim's about 'the British always fighting their battles at the bottom of a hill at a point where two or more maps join', which went down well.

Doreen and I went to dinner with David and Davina Howell. John Nott† and his wife, Ronnie and Heather Grierson and another MP and his wife were there, and Geoffrey Howe joined us after dinner. There was a great deal of talk about Neddy, Chequers and so on.

Nott gave the impression of great scepticism about Neddy and the consensus. He and the other MP seemed to belong to the rightish end of the Tory party, which thinks that the middle ground is wishy-washy and that we can only be saved if we return to Conservative principles, i.e. market forces. But they were open to argument and showed no hostility towards our efforts at Neddy – indeed they were all extremely friendly. They were all agreed that Margaret Thatcher was the only possible leader for the party at the moment and they all seemed to think she was making a good job of it. Once again I thought Geoffrey Howe was much the best frontbench Conservative that I know. It was a nice evening and interesting for us to spend one with a group of young and able Conservative MPs just now.

---

* I did not ask the journalist whether my chairman was his source.
† Conservative MP for St Ives.

Thursday 20 November 1975

I have had a letter from the chairman of the ABCC about the Chequers meeting in which he says they very much hope that Neddy will be the central instrument for devising the new industrial strategy. I have sent it on to No. 10 and to Healey.

Sunday 23 November 1975

We drove to Penshurst for lunch with Carol and Tony Howard. Tony, who works for a French chemicals firm here, said he didn't think that French management or workers were any better than ours – the main difference was that whereas huge funds had gone into the property boom in Britain, the French government had seen to it that savings were channelled to manufacturing investment first.

Monday 24 November 1975

I held a meeting of EDC chairmen at 4.30 p.m. They were all there bar one, who is abroad, and Eric Roll joined us as chairman designate of the Committee on Finance for Investment. The *FT* had a big feature about the EDCs this morning, which aroused interest in the meeting, and before it began the *Times* took a photograph of us all. At 5 p.m. Denis Healey and Eric Varley joined the meeting. Neither had anything new to say and it is clear that the government is in a great muddle over what the new strategy is supposed to be and do. But the two ministers listened well and the chairmen spoke sensibly and constructively. I thought the meeting was well worthwhile and I was gratified that two such busy ministers were willing to spend over two hours with us.

Wednesday 26 November 1975

I had lunch with Robert Carr* at Brooks's. We had an enjoyable talk about current problems and past mistakes. He said that 'if you trod on Margaret Thatcher's toe the cry of pain would come out on a right-wing note' but that, like all Conservative leaders, she knew that the party wouldn't win unless its appeal was sufficiently broad to capture at least a part of the middle ground vote.

Robert is still a convinced believer in an incomes policy and did not agree with me that price control was a nonsense which ought to be scrapped. And yet when I said that with hindsight I regretted having advised him to support the abolition of the PIB† in 1970 he said he thought it was the right thing to do because, partly due to Aubrey Jones's personality, the PIB had outlived its usefulness. In discussing the events leading up to the 1974 election Carr said he thought that Tony Barber had been grossly overloaded – indeed Barber himself had said that it was madness to run a system in which the Chancellor was the only Treasury minister in Cabinet. I quite agree with this and can't see why Harold Wilson's arrangement of having both Roy (as Chancellor) and Jack Diamond (as Chief Secretary to the Treasury) in the Cabinet in 1968–70 was never repeated.

Wednesday 3 December 1975

At the Neddy meeting this morning the government came under heavy fire from the TUC and CBI about their progress report on

---

* Robert Carr had been made a life peer not long before. I had greatly enjoyed working with him when he was Secretary of State for Employment in 1970–72.
† The National Board for Prices and Incomes (usually known as the PIB) was set up by the Labour government in 1965 and abolished by the Conservatives in 1970. Aubrey Jones, a former Conservative minister, was its chairman throughout.

post-Chequers work on industrial strategy. The paper was very thin and was concerned almost entirely with questions of machinery. The CBI said they were beginning to feel they had been conned at Chequers – the TUC said it was time the government showed a greater sense of urgency. I spoke in similar terms but the CBI and TUC criticisms made it possible for me to produce my criticisms of the government paper almost as a mediator. I urged that at the January meeting we should get down to the issues of substance and not get bogged down in questions of procedure, as so often happens in this country. In the course of the discussion Harold Watkinson made a very fluent statement about the CBI's opposition to planning agreements. This was not very welcome to the TUC or the government but I think Watkinson was quite right. There ought to be plain speaking at NEDC on the issues people feel strongly about.

Thursday 4 December 1975

We announced our new Committee on Finance for Investment today. It is a very strong one and the first ever to bring leading City and trade union people round the same table in a permanent body. I am very pleased indeed to have got it off the ground properly and have great hopes for it.

Monday 8 December 1975

I drove to Birmingham in the morning for a private lunch with a dozen or so leading members of the chamber of commerce. Afterwards we had a good discussion, lasting about an hour, about industrial problems. The main fear is that we shall 'miss the boom'. Having gone into the world recession later than our competitors we shall come out of it later and when trade starts booming again in 1977 they will have the capacity for it whereas we won't. There was general agreement about the need to do everything possible to bring forward into 1976 investment which would otherwise not take place until 1977 or 1978. I find these lunches in Birmingham very useful – the people there know me now and one gets a different slant on things from the standard London view.

I then drove on to Coventry for dinner with a group from the Engineering Employers' Association. They are a hard-headed lot, much concerned with union matters and pretty sceptical about Chequers and all that – but they were constructive too and, like so many people one meets nowadays, desperately anxious to get the country back on its feet. Their main message was about the need not to pump money into ailing businesses as was done with Leyland.

Friday 12 December 1975

The morning papers are full of reports – clearly inspired – that Eric Varley will resign if the Cabinet do not accept his proposals on Chrysler.* He wants to take a tough line and save public funds for more worthwhile projects; and he is said to be furious at the way Harold Lever took over the negotiations with Chrysler – presumably at Wilson's request – a week or so ago.

In the evening it was announced that the government had decided to give Chrysler £186m apparently without strings and that Varley is not to resign. The general feeling is that this will mean the deathknell of the Chequers strategy.

---

* Chrysler's UK operation, which employed around 17,000 people, was losing money and the US parent company proposed to close it unless the British government agreed to finance a rescue operation. Political opinion on the pros and cons of subsidising a 'lame duck' to maintain employment and exports was deeply divided.

Monday 15 December 1975

After lunch I gave a talk to sixty or so people from different branches of the transport industry. I told them that until last week I had begun to think that Chequers might prove to be a real turning point but that the government's decision to save Chrysler put a big question mark over this.

I drove back to London to see Eric Roll about the work of the Committee on Finance for Investment. We discussed the Chrysler business, with which Eric, as a non-executive director of the company, has been closely associated. He said that there was never any question of government letting Chrysler go into liquidation (which I believe would have been the right course) – the argument was simply about how the rescue operation should be financed.*

Tuesday 16 December 1975

In the evening Doreen and I went to the BIM dinner at the Hilton. Margaret Thatcher was the principal guest and her speech was televised live for the *Nine O'clock News*. She spoke mostly about Chrysler – attacking the government's rescue operation and saying it was quite inconsistent with the outcome of the Neddy meeting at Chequers. In doing this she nailed her colours in effect to the Chequers mast, which is helpful from my point of view. She spoke well and confidently but Edwin Plowden, who was sitting next to her at dinner, said she was very nervous and hardly ate a thing. That is in her favour – no one I know makes a good speech unless they are nervous beforehand.

---

* In 1979 the French manufacturer Peugeot took over what remained of Chrysler's European operations.

Wednesday 17 December 1975

I went with several colleagues to the House of Commons for a meeting with the Select Committee on Nationalised Industries. Russell Kerr was in the chair and there were eight or nine committee members from all three parties. We had an informal and, I thought, useful exchange of views about the problems of nationalised industries which lasted for about an hour and a half. These select committees come nearer to a bipartisan approach to industrial problems than anything else we have in this country. I wish we could develop them further.

Thursday 18 December 1975

Peter Ramsbotham called for a general talk before lunch. He is over from Washington for a few days in connection with the Queen's visit to the USA next year. He dined last night with Harold Lever and Gordon Richardson, both of whom were extremely sceptical, he said, about Chequers. Ramsbotham showed me a piece which appeared in the *Wall Street Journal* after my last Neddy briefing which he said had done us a lot of good in the States.

Tuesday 6 January 1976

After lunch we had the first meeting of the Committee on Finance for Investment. Eric Roll handled it well and we got off to a good start. Len Murray spoke very sensibly and made it impossible for the City representatives such as Ian Fraser and Frederic Seebohm* to take up the defensive attitudes which I am sure they had come prepared to do.

• Ian Fraser was deputy chairman of Lazards. Lord Seebohm was chairman of the Finance Corporation for Industry and a former deputy chairman of Barclays Bank.

Thursday 8 January 1976

I took an early train to Leeds for a meeting of the Regional Economic Planning Council. They had asked me to speak to them privately about the national economic situation. I gave them as realistic an account as I could – the gist of which was that our situation was very grave indeed but not yet hopeless. I said that a great deal would depend on what we did in the next two years. If we allowed present trends to continue we should cease by the early 1980s to belong to the ranks of advanced industrial countries. But if we really got to grips with our problems and halted the decline in manufacturing industry the 1980s could be a period of renewed growth, rising real incomes and increasing share of world trade for us.

Friday 9 January 1976

We had a Group of 4 meeting in the morning. I had a very difficult time with Douglas Wass, who is resolutely opposed to discussing economic strategy in NEDC – or, so far as I can see, anywhere else – and took a strangely complacent view of our prospects. Fortunately, Len Murray and Campbell Adamson agreed with me so that, though I found it necessary to press my point of view very hard, I got their general support. At the end of the meeting I referred to the lack of support I got from the Treasury and the extra difficulties this created for me and Wass and I parted on far from friendly terms.

Saturday 17 January 1976

I found the council meeting on 14 January very depressing. The TUC pressed the government hard on its economic strategy and so in a half-hearted way did the CBI. But Healey was not keen to have a serious discussion – he said he would talk to the TUC about the prospect for unemployment at a bilateral meeting afterwards. Generally speaking, the whole council ran away from all the big issues and refused to face up to the question posed in the paper I had circulated – which was how do you get productivity and investment up in a no-growth economy with high and rising unemployment and low profitability?

In discussing the government's proposals for an elaborate series of sectoral enquiries, Jack Jones launched into a great attack on EDCs and other committees. I got very annoyed by this – the EDCs have plenty of failings but they are in some ways more effective than the council. I reminded Jack that the men who gave up their time to sit on the EDCs were decidedly lukewarm in their admiration for the main council. In the end the TUC and CBI accepted the government's proposals but I don't think they feel any real commitment to them.

The newspapers are full of comment on our council meeting. They all seem to think the Chequers strategy is dead and most of them seem to regret it.

Tuesday 20 January 1976

We flew to Dublin in the morning for a conference organised by the CBI's Irish counterpart. When we arrived we drove straight to the ambassador's house, which is ten miles or so south of the city in lovely hilly country. The grounds were of course crawling with Special Branch men. Arthur Galsworthy turned out to be a delightful, unassuming man who was very welcoming and went out of his way to make our stay pleasant. He told me he couldn't see any way out of the Troubles – although he would never say so in public he thought that one day the British people would get fed up with seeing their soldiers shot at in Ulster and just decide to clear out.

Wednesday 21 January 1976

I spent the whole day at the conference. I had put a lot of effort into preparing my speech and was pleased to find it went down well.

At the conference lunch and the reception afterwards I talked to a great many Irish industrialists and civil servants and found them without exception intelligent and likeable – with no sign of hostility to Britain at all. I had an interesting chat with the permanent head of the Irish Foreign Office, who said he thought that if Heath had remained in power he might just possibly have solved the Ulster problem on the basis of the Sunningdale agreement. Reminiscing about that period he said that Heath had arrived at the Copenhagen summit exhausted by the Sunningdale talks and this, combined with the fact that (as we now know) Pompidou was dying, had made the summit a fiasco. (It also made a bad start for the talks on the miners' strike which followed immediately.)

Thursday 22 January 1976

As we left Arthur Galsworthy told me that my speech at the conference had done a lot of good for Britain, which I was pleased about.

Monday 26 January 1976

In the evening I flew to Paris and went straight to the British embassy, where Nicko Henderson* had a cold supper waiting for me. We had a talk about the political situation at home of the usual kind. Like me, Nicko has a very high opinion of Ted Heath but doesn't see him ever becoming Prime Minister again. He thought Roy would

---

* He had left Bonn and was now ambassador to France.

make a very good Foreign Secretary and that if he got the job it would transform his personality. 'Roy doesn't enjoy looking after policemen's helmets at the Home Office,' he said.

Nicko said the French didn't think much of us just now – one had to run very hard to keep our standing in their eyes from slipping even further. In general he takes a pretty gloomy view of the prospects in Britain – and he is very anti-Treasury.

Tuesday 27 January 1976

I spent the morning with a delightful and articulate trio at Electricité de France, followed by a dull and unimaginative trio at SNCF,* discussing problems of relationships between government and nationalised industries. It is clear that these are solved in France by the nationalised industries doing what the government tells them to do.

This was followed by a very pleasant lunch with Ripère, the president of the Commissariat Général du Plan, and a couple of his colleagues in their offices in an old house on the Left Bank. Ripère is highly intelligent and has spent a large part of his life in the Commissariat. He reports direct to the President, who is said to be less enthusiastic about the benefits of planning than his predecessors. This evidently clips Ripère's wings as, like all French officials – whether in or outside formal ministries – he does precisely what the Elysée wants. It is a much more unified, essentially autocratic, system than ours or even the Americans'.

After lunch I saw various high officials in the Treasury and the banks. The general impression I got was that they were all rather unself-confident about France's prospects. Like me, they don't expect the revival in world trade to be especially vigorous and are

---

* French railways.

very conscious that all the main industrial countries will be trying to solve their problems by exporting more. They seem less sure of France's ability to come off well from this process than one might expect.

Wednesday 28 January 1976

I went to a lunch at the Royal Lancaster for the participants in the first day of a two-day *FT* conference, which John Partridge and I are chairing in succession. Shirley Williams was to have been the main speaker but has evidently got flu. So her good social democratic speech was made for her by a nice young parliamentary secretary called Robert Maclennan,* whom I hadn't met before. I sat next to Martin Redmayne and we talked about Selwyn Lloyd, who founded Neddy and is retiring as Speaker next week. Redmayne was Chief Whip at the time of the night of the long knives, when Lloyd was sacked. He said that Harold Macmillan agonised over the sackings for six weeks during which he went over the pros and cons with Redmayne virtually every day, until Redmayne felt like telling him for God's sake to make up his mind and be done with it.

Thursday 29 January 1976

I spent all day chairing the *FT* conference. I thought there were far too many speakers but they all in their different ways did well and the audience showed great stamina. My most interesting speaker was John Pardoe,† a man of considerable ability and charm who is often spoken of as a possible leader of the Liberal Party. He said he didn't really think the British people would put their affairs in order until

---

* Labour MP for Caithness & Sutherland and later leader of the SDP.
† Liberal MP for Cornwall North.

they had 'been through the abyss' – by which it appeared he meant some kind of monetary and social collapse à la Weimar. I wound up in a mildly pessimistic way, which appeared to reflect the general mood.

Friday 30 January 1976

John Methven's appointment to succeed Campbell Adamson is announced today. I don't know him at all well but from what I have seen and heard of him it seems a first-rate appointment.*

Friday 27 February 1976

In the evening I drove Geoffrey Howe to Heathrow, where we joined a party bound for Hamburg for a conference organised by the Anglo-German Industrial Foundation. On the way to the airport Geoffrey and I talked about the events of the winter of 1973–4, which are the subject of long articles in three successive issues of the *Sunday Times*. Geoffrey was at the famous Neddy meeting on 9 January 1974. He was the only senior minister apart from Barber who was present and it is clear from what he told me that he quite failed to appreciate the seriousness of the TUC offer. He doubted, however, whether if he had he could have done anything much about it as suspicion of the TUC within the Tory Party was by then so strong.

Saturday 28 and Sunday 29 February 1976

The conference turned out to be an interesting and from my point of view encouraging affair. The purpose of it was to discuss Neddy and

---

* Methven, formerly of ICI, was an effective and well-respected director general of the CBI until his untimely death in 1980.

Germany's Concerted Action, which, though very different in form, were set up with similar considerations in mind.

As so often happens with conferences like this the mood swung quite decisively half way through. In the beginning almost every speaker expressed great scepticism about the value of Neddy and CA and emphasised how few concrete achievements one could point to. The Germans complained that CA was too big (apparently about fifty people attend its meetings) and that the main participants simply spoke for the record and often released their statements to the press before they made them in CA. Some British speakers similarly stressed the talking shop atmosphere of Neddy and took the line that although it did no harm it didn't do much good either.

The procedure was that one of the Germans spoke about the founding of CA; then came Aubrey Jones, who gave an interesting but very negative account of Britain in the 1960s (when he was chairman of the PIB); then I spoke about what Neddy was doing now and one of the German 'wise men' did the same for CA. After lunch we had contributions from Malcolm Rutherford, the former Bonn correspondent of the *FT*, about CA as seen through British eyes and from the London correspondent of *Die Welt* about Neddy. Then we all went off on a conducted tour of Hamburg, which was looking beautiful in the cold spring sunshine.

When we started again the discussions began to take on a more positive note. Peter Carey and Dick Marsh spoke up for Neddy on the British side and several of the Germans thought the scepticism about CA was overdone. The following morning we had two out-standing contributions, both very constructive. The first was from Alastair Pilkington, who spoke very strongly in favour of Neddy – I was particularly encouraged by this because he was the leading British industrialist present and has no direct connection with our work. The second was from Herr von Bismarck, a direct descendant of the great man, an industrialist and an active CDU member.

I was asked to sum up the whole discussion. My main theme was that after 1945, when Germany and other countries had to concentrate on reconstructing their manufacturing base, we had been preoccupied with two quite different things. One was to carry through successfully the great social reforms which had been conceived by the coalition government and were implemented by the post-war Labour government. The other was to liquidate the Empire, a process which was started by Attlee in India and continued by Conservative governments, notably Macmillan's, in Africa and elsewhere. I said that on the whole we had done these things well because our political leaders and administrators understood the problems and had been trained to deal with them. But all this time manufacturing industry was neglected and when the seriousness of its decline came to be recognised, our governments mishandled the issues because most politicians and civil servants in Britain simply didn't understand how industry or the trade unions worked. From this I led on naturally to Neddy and the need for a bipartisan approach based on industrial realities. And finally, in answer to points raised by several German speeches, I said that the corporate approach of Neddy posed no threat to our democracy – the real danger to democracy was the possibility of continued economic failure.

All in all it was a worthwhile visit; I learned a lot about Germany and was very much interested (and encouraged) to hear the comments of my English colleagues on Neddy and our current activities. The weekend confirmed my impression that Geoffrey Howe is much the most intelligent of the present Conservative front bench.

Monday 1 March 1976

In the afternoon I had a meeting of my Skilled Manpower committee. It was much the best we have had so far. In the middle of it the trade unions and employer members suddenly got on to a new and unusually constructive wavelength and started discussing problems about the use of craftsmen in a more open way than (according to one employer member) they have ever done before. This is the real value of our Neddy committees – sometimes they can bring about a breakthrough in the handling of an old, familiar problem such as this.

Tuesday 2 March 1976

I had lunch with Jim Prior at the Royal Thames. He knew about our Hamburg conference and said that Geoffrey Howe had come back from it expressing very different views from those he had held before it. On Neddy affairs he said the biggest criticism I would have to meet within the Conservative Party was that we were 'corporatist'. He also told me, sadly, that he saw little nowadays of Ted Heath, who had not forgiven him for taking a job under Mrs Thatcher.

Wednesday 3 March 1976

Harold Wilson took the chair at this morning's Neddy meeting. We had quite a good discussion about the medium-term outlook in which the CBI and TUC put pressure on Healey to discuss his objectives for the medium term. We also had a reasonably good discussion about the effect of price control on investment. I underlined the way in which industrialists contemplating capital-intensive investment were deterred from going ahead with schemes because they feared that if they could operate them at reasonably full capacity (when unit costs tend to fall dramatically) they would not be allowed to keep the resulting profits. This was a good deal more radical than anything the CBI said.

Wilson was friendly and relaxed and chatted to me over drinks about Oxford days before the war.

Over lunch we talked à propos the *Sunday Times* articles about the Neddy meeting in January 1974. Shirley Williams asked why Barber had rejected the TUC offer so abruptly as he seemed to do. I said I was quite clear that he did it with his eyes open because he wanted an election on 7 February, when he thought – probably rightly – that the Tories would win. Alan Bailey, who was his private secretary at the time, doubted this. He said that Barber simply wasn't prepared for the TUC offer and reacted without thinking. But the general opinion was that it was in any case too late by then – the gap between government and TUC thinking was too wide to bridge.

Thursday 4 March 1976

This afternoon I had a somewhat offensive letter from Len Murray about the press reports of yesterday's Neddy meeting. I was able to reply that the reports he took exception to were all based on Healey's paper about the medium-term outlook (which had been given to the press) and not on anything I said at my press briefing. I have now been criticised, in relation to post-council briefings, by all my shareholders – Barber, Healey, the CBI and now the TUC. This must, I think, show that I really am independent of them all.

Tuesday 9 March 1976

I had lunch with John Hunt at the Thames. He told me (à propos the *Sunday Times* articles) about William Armstrong's breakdown in January 1974. Apparently there were two critical occasions. One was a meeting with ministers when Armstrong virtually prevented them from speaking and forced them to listen to his own dire warnings about the consequences of 'giving in' to the miners. The other was a meeting of permanent secretaries where he had all the doors locked before the discussion started. This was evidently the one at which his mental instability became too obvious to ignore.

Friday 12 March 1976

I flew to Washington and after checking in at Bill Ryrie's* house in Kalorama Circle went straight to the embassy for the meeting which was the object of my visit to the States. There followed a very pleasant and so far as I could judge successful evening.

We assembled at the residence at 5 p.m. under Peter Ramsbotham's chairmanship. The US side consisted of George Ball, who had been Undersecretary of State in Kennedy's time; Bob Schaetzel, formerly US ambassador to the EEC; Bingen, chairman of the board of Honeywell; Reg Jones and Parker of General Electric; and Mark Shepherd of Texas Instruments. The British consisted of Peter Ramsbotham, Reg Prentice† and myself, plus Bill Ryrie and Tom Bridges from the embassy. Apart from the resident diplomats everyone seemed to have flown several thousand miles in the last twenty-four hours to attend the meeting.

Ramsbotham organised the discussion well. We started with 'North–South' problems. Reg Prentice led off on this, stressing the growing problems of the 'fourth world' (i.e. the very poor countries) and the inadequacy of Western aid. George Ball followed him with a gloomy account of US opposition to and disenchantment with substantial aid programmes. There followed a good discussion which confirmed Ball's views. I was very depressed by this, not having appreciated how far the US attitude to aid had changed since I was last in touch with it.

---

* He had succeeded Anthony Rawlinson as economic minister at the embassy and UK director of the IMF and World Bank.
† Minister for Overseas Development.

About 7.30 we switched to the problems of recovery from world recession. The discussion on this was led by Reg Jones, who was born in England and came to the US when he was about eight. He spoke for about half an hour and gave a very effective presentation of the prospects and problems of the US economy till 1980. This was a good deal less optimistic than I had expected – he thought that there would be great difficulties in financing the investment required and envisaged unemployment continuing at fairly high levels for some years to come.

We then adjourned for dinner. When we came back I gave a British view of the prospects for recovery in the world and the UK. This was followed by a general discussion of what Jones and I had said and we then went on to discuss the growing problem of protectionist attitudes in the USA and elsewhere, about which Tom Bridges evidently felt very strongly. The meeting adjourned about 11 p.m. The British contingent stayed on for a nightcap with Peter Ramsbotham, who reported that the Americans had been very pleased with the discussion and gratified that Prentice and I should have crossed the Atlantic to take part in it.

Saturday 13 March 1976

The Ryries gave a pleasant dinner party for Reg Prentice and me. The principal American guest was Bob McNamara, the president of the World Bank. I had not met him before and had assumed from the reputation he acquired as US Secretary for Defense that he would be a hard, machine-like sort of person. In fact he turned out to be enormously attractive and impressive.

I told McNamara how depressed I had been by what I had heard last night about the US attitude to aid. He agreed that it was depressing now but said that there would be a substantial change after the presidential election. He said that the administration was now deeply divided over many policy issues and Gerald Ford's authority was weak because he was not an elected president. All this would change if, as McNamara seemed to expect, Ford was elected in November.

Wednesday 17 March 1976

Harold Wilson has announced his intention to retire as Prime Minister as soon as the PLP has elected a new leader. He issued a long statement which included an agreeable reference to Neddy. I am pleased that he should have chosen to chair the last council meeting to take place during his long period of office.

Friday 19 March 1976

I wrote to Wilson wishing him well for the future and thanking him for his encouraging support for Neddy.

PART FOUR

ON THE EDGE OF THE ABYSS

21 March 1976 to 4 January 1977

If (as I surmised) Harold Wilson had grown bored with economic problems, his resignation was well timed. By the time his successor was elected a few weeks later, the outlook for the economy had taken a dramatic turn for the worse.

There was no single event which triggered this. It was rather a question of a growing recognition that the underlying problems of high inflation, low productivity and excessive public borrowing, which had been ignored during the previous year's drift, were getting steadily worse and that there was no solution for them in sight.

There was a widespread perception – especially overseas – that Britain was in a state of terminal decline which it had neither the will nor the ability to reverse. The effect on the currency was predictable: at the beginning of April 1976 the pound fell sharply and the decline continued without let up until the IMF arrived six months later. There was much talk of imminent national collapse and there were plenty of people who believed that we would not put our house in order until this had occurred.

Meanwhile, the 'industrial strategy' launched at the Chequers meeting of Neddy in November 1975 was beginning to make progress. The decision to rescue Chrysler had severely dented its credibility but the work being done in the little Neddies to improve productivity in individual industries was gathering momentum and, as the diary shows, the new Prime Minister, James Callaghan, and the Chancellor, Denis Healey, gave it their strong personal encouragement and support.

It was obvious that if this work was to lead to real improvements in industrial performance, a sustained effort extending beyond the lifetime of a single parliament would be required. For this reason it seemed to me important that it should have the support not only of the interests represented on Neddy (including the government of the day) but of a broad spectrum of parliamentary opinion as well.

To this end I took every opportunity to explain to MPs of the three main parties how Neddy operated and what we were trying to achieve.

I also delivered a series of lectures and speeches in which I set out what I believed to be the main causes of our national decline and emphasised the need for continuity in industrial policy, commanding a degree of bipartisan support, if the decline was to be arrested. These speeches, which attracted a good deal of publicity, were generally well received, although from time to time they got me into trouble with some of my fellow council members. The diary relates how these events unfolded in what was to prove a turbulent beginning to Callaghan's premiership.

Sunday 21 March 1976

I phoned Roy to wish him luck in the election for the Labour Party leadership. He expects Callaghan to win (as most people do) but clearly has some hope that he himself may pull it off and admitted that he felt exhilarated by the whole thing. I told him how I had been with Wilson last year when the result of the first round of the Tory leadership contest became known and how Wilson had been sure that Whitelaw would win – which shows how even the experts can get their predictions wrong.

I then spoke to Bill Rodgers, who is managing Roy's campaign. He says that Callaghan is ahead of Roy just now but that his support is likely to erode quite quickly unless he does very well in the first ballot. Bill's estimate for the first ballot is Foot 90+, Callaghan 80, Jenkins 70, Healey 40. He doesn't think Foot can possibly win – he puts his maximum support at 125. Bill said that all his efforts would go into trying to get Roy ahead of Callaghan in the first ballot, though I don't think he really expects to achieve this.*

I must say that on policy as well as personal grounds, I very much hope that Roy makes it. He stands more nearly than any other politician for the things I believe in and he has the quality to make a better Prime Minister (as opposed to party leader) than the others.

Tuesday 23 March 1976

This evening I went to the Athenaeum for a dinner given for Robert and Elinor Birley by a group of people whom he had taught at Charterhouse and Eton.† In proposing Robert's health, Paul Gore

---

* The actual figures for the first ballot were Foot 90, Callaghan 84, Jenkins 56, Benn 37, Healey 30, Crosland 17.

† Charterhouse, where I was at school in the 1930s, was Birley's first head-mastership. It was an outstanding success.

Booth,* who was at Eton in the 1920s, said that in those days there were seventy King's scholars who spent all day at their books and whom nobody knew, and 1,050 other boys who were dedicated to the proposition that if you avoided work altogether at school you stored up energy which ensured you success in banking, diplomacy or whatever in later life. He said that Robert's great contribution to Eton was to persuade it to abandon this outlook in the 1950s.

Sunday 28 March 1976

I phoned Roy this evening. He didn't sound too low and said he was pretty sure that he was right to stand and right to withdraw when he did. (I quite agree.) He said he thought that Callaghan and Foot would come pretty close on the next ballot with Healey getting perhaps 45 votes.† I asked him if Foot really wanted to be Prime Minister, to which he said, 'Yes – very much indeed.' I said that if Foot did win I should probably resign from NEDO.

Tuesday 30 March 1976

I lunched with Edwin Plowden. He said he could see no prospect of any real improvement in our economic performance unless and until we had a really acute crisis – the cold shower syndrome one so often meets in businessmen. However, Plowden devotes a great deal of time and effort to trying to make things run better and more constructively and so, I suppose, to stave off the collapse he expects. He is an honest and likeable person.

---

* Former permanent secretary of the Foreign Office. He had been high commissioner in India during my posting to Delhi.
† Jenkins, Benn and Crosland having withdrawn after the first ballot, the result of the second ballot was Callaghan 141, Foot 133, Healey 38. The final figures (on the third ballot) were Callaghan 176, Foot 137.

I told him I thought I would want to give up my present job in the summer of 1977. It involves an expenditure of nervous energy which one can only put up with for a certain time and anyway I shall probably be persona non grata with my shareholders by next year – none of them really like the director general to be an independent-minded person.

Thursday 1 April 1976

The pound had an appalling day. It is down to $1.88 and we seem to have spent very large sums in a vain effort to stem the run.*

Friday 2 April 1976

Paul Martin, the Canadian high commissioner, came to see me. He maintains a heavily qualified optimism about our prospects. In particular (unlike most foreign observers) he thinks that our trade union leaders are behaving very responsibly and that this is a substantial advantage which we have over, for example, Canada.†

Monday 5 April 1976

I went to the Royal Society of Arts, where Michael Edwardes, the chairman of Chloride, gave an excellent lecture about our national predicament. He put a great deal of emphasis on the need for more incentives – especially but not solely for management. He also stressed – as all sensible people do – the need for a bipartisan

---

* By October it had fallen below $1.60.

† Martin, who had been Secretary for External Affairs in the 1960s, admired the Neddy concept and wanted to see it adopted in his own country (P. Martin, *The London Diaries 1975–1979* (Ottawa: University of Ottawa Press, 1988)).

approach to industry and argued that the opposition should be represented on Neddy. I have never been in favour of this – I fear it would simply reproduce in our council room the conflicts which now take place on the floor of the House.

Tuesday 6 April 1976

I went to the House after lunch to hear the Budget. At 3.10 Jim Callaghan arrived for his first Prime Minister's Questions. The House was full and he got a fairly enthusiastic welcome from his own side. As far as I could see, Roy was the only member of the Cabinet who was absent. The first question was in fact about Neddy: when would he chair a meeting of Neddy? Callaghan said he would hope to chair Neddy from time to time but he had no immediate plans to do so. Jeremy Thorpe said he hoped the new PM would use Neddy to bring about a bipartisan approach to our economic problems. Callaghan handled it all with skill and good humour, watched benevolently by Harold Wilson.

Wednesday 7 April 1976

The Neddy meeting was almost all taken up with a discussion of the Budget. The TUC don't like being put on the spot. They reacted adversely to Healey's proposal to link tax cuts with the wage norm and Len Murray said that they would want other things – food subsidies, price control and so on – brought into the discussion. Hugh Scanlon and Alf Allen both told me afterwards that there was no chance of the TUC agreeing to a 3 per cent wage norm.*

---

* The proposal was to raise tax allowances and so increase take-home pay if, but only if, the TUC agreed to keep wage increases within a pre-determined 'norm'.

We went to a crowded party given by Phil and Hannah Kaiser.* Most people seem to think that Healey has been clever in making the TUC take responsibility for how much tax relief we get; I don't share this view.

Thursday 8 April 1976

The *Sun* has a front-page editorial headed 'Who the hell is Len Murray?'. It is very anti-TUC and calculated to make the average taxpayer turn against the trade unions. This is just the reaction I feared.

In the evening Doreen and I went to a wonderful performance by the Royal Shakespeare Company of *The Merry Wives of Windsor* in modern dress. It was a delight to see such good acting and production.

Friday 9 April 1976

I took Geoffrey Drain to lunch at the Thames. He readily accepted my offer of the chairmanship of our new committee on the paper industry. I am pleased about this. Geoffrey is a very sensible man and it is useful to us to have a second member of the TUC Economic Committee in the family. He is distinctly left of centre but he is also a strong pro-European and this means that his opinions are less predictable and stereotyped than those of many other trade union leaders. He confirmed that there was no chance of the TUC agreeing to a 3 per cent wage norm but he assumed they would work out some agreement with the government involving a higher figure.

---

* Philip Kaiser had been Minister at the American Embassy in the 1960s and now lived in London. A Rhodes scholar, he had been an undergraduate at Balliol before the war – like Ted Heath, Denis Healey, Roy Jenkins, Maurice Macmillan, Madron Seligman and myself – and had many friends among British politicians.

Monday 12 April 1976

Reflecting on the Budget and our economic situation generally, I have a sense of doom today. For the first time I feel that the financial collapse, which so many people have said was imminent at various times in the last two years, may really be on its way. The fall in the value of sterling which has taken place in the last few weeks is very dramatic and shows that foreigners simply don't believe we are capable of managing our affairs effectively. The inevitably complicated manoeuvres over Healey's wage/tax proposal will reduce their confidence even further and there is a clear risk of another massive run on the pound any time in the next couple of months. It seems to me quite likely that before the end of July we shall experience a financial crisis so severe that it brings about some kind of political realignment.

Tuesday 13 April 1976

I had lunch at ICI with Stanley Lyon, the deputy chairman. Neither he nor Peter Thornton* (whom I saw at a meeting in the afternoon) share my fears about a financial collapse this summer.

Wednesday 14 April 1976

Doreen and I went to lunch with the Jenkins at Ladbroke Square. Roy was very relaxed. He said he had decided that if he couldn't be Prime Minister he would like to be Foreign Secretary and was therefore a bit put out when Callaghan didn't offer it to him. He was, however, happy to become president of the European Commission if (as he expected) he received a firm offer of it. He said he realised

---

* Sir Peter Thornton, a former school-fellow of mine, was permanent secretary of the Department of Trade.

it might be the end of his career in British politics but he couldn't see any future for himself in the Labour Party, as at present constituted, anyway.

Wednesday 21 April 1976

I took a morning flight to Edinburgh and then drove up with John Cousins to Perth for the Scottish TUC.

The atmosphere was very different from last year at Aberdeen. Jack Jones had been in Perth since Sunday organising support for the government's pay policy. On the day before we arrived there had been a long debate on all aspects of economic policy and the Communist-inspired resolution criticising the government was defeated 3-1 on a card vote.

Today there were two more votes on economic issues – one on the Budget and the other recommending a return to free collective bargaining. The first was a composite, which, though critical of the government, did not oppose its policies outright. This was carried, with little opposition, on a show of hands. The second was defeated 3-2 on a card vote.

It was altogether rather an odd business, with general secretaries travelling up from London to use their card votes to prevent the Scots from coming out in favour of collective bargaining. But it all went off quite good-humouredly and a lot of my trade union friends enjoyed seeing the left well and truly clobbered.

Thursday 22 April 1976

The Scottish TUC seems to have been badly reported on the BBC and to some extent in the press. The result is that, although the Congress was in part a success from the government's point of view, the pound has again fallen sharply.

I went to a buffet at the German embassy in the evening. This was for German trade union people who are over for the European TUC meeting, which is being held for the first time in London. I had a short talk with Jack Jones, who said it had been hard work persuading his delegation at the Scottish TUC to vote the way they did.

I had a long talk over dinner with Karl-Günther von Hase, the ambassador, who considers that the fall in sterling (which closed today at only just over $1.80) is very grave. Len Murray then came over for a talk. He was in an odd mood – I would guess that he is highly strung about the attempt to reach agreement with the government on wages policy. He told me it was a waste of time for me to go to the STUC, but didn't explain why. I told him that I thought the fall in the pound was a very serious matter and that, even if the TUC made a good agreement on pay restraint, this wouldn't restore confidence for more than a fairly short period; the only thing which would restore confidence in the longer run was a cut in the public sector borrowing requirement, to which, rightly or wrongly, foreigners attached great importance. Len said darkly that in that event more drastic measures of a different kind (by implication import restrictions and exchange controls) would have to be taken 'as my chaps won't agree to cuts in public expenditure'.

Tuesday 27 April 1976

In the late afternoon I took Bernard Asher* to have a drink with Peter Carey, whom he hadn't met. Peter entirely shares my views about the pound and the probability of a really serious crisis later in the year.

---

* A very able businessman who had joined NEDO as industrial director on secondment from the American telecommunications company ITT.

Wednesday 28 April 1976

I went to lunch with Sir Thomas Waterlow and the editorial committee of the *Three Banks Review*. They were a pleasant lot of Scots bankers whose views about employment and labour relations seemed to be based exclusively on their experience with ghillies and gamekeepers.

Thursday 29 April 1976

The pound has picked up a little – mainly because the government's talks with the TUC seem to be going reasonably well. Jim Callaghan told the House that he intended to chair the next Neddy meeting. Unfortunately it may have to be postponed because of the special meeting of the General Council which the TUC will probably convene next week.

Tuesday 4 May 1976

I went to lunch at Chatham House to meet Wilhelm Haferkamp, the German vice-president of the European Commission. He gave a good talk in which he expressed great concern about the way in which the gap between the weak and the strong economies in the EEC is widening. He thought that unless we made a combined effort to prevent this, the Community would find it difficult to survive. He also thought that any such effort should be made on a tripartite basis involving 'the social partners'.

At 6 I went to hear Victor Rothschild give the first Israel Sieff Memorial Lecture. He spoke extremely well about planners and planning. He was very witty – mostly at the expense of politicians and civil servants, especially the latter. He had two phrases that stuck in my mind. The first was that governments should have a self-imposed period of three months after an election in which they took no action – 'a sort of political Ramadan'. The other, à propos appointments to public bodies, was that 'Clemenceau – or was it Tully? – said that patronage is too serious a matter to be left to the outsider'.

In the evening Doreen and I went to a splendid party given by Nancy-Joan and Madron Seligman at Cadogan Place. There were eighty or so people present including a number of Conservative politicians, among them Ted Heath. Towards the end of the evening Tony Barber came up to chat to me. We quite quickly became involved in a fairly considerable row. Something he said made me tell him I had never forgiven him for the public rebuke he gave me in December 1973 over the statement I made after a Neddy meeting about the effect which the oil price rise would have on our standard of living. He accused me of being political and pro-Harold Wilson and when I said that most businessmen had agreed with me and not with him he said it was always easy to curry favour with industrialists if you didn't have responsibility. We then got into a real slanging match which lasted for several minutes. It was all a bit unfortunate but I am glad to have got it off my chest. The Barbers left immediately afterwards but Doreen and I stayed to dance. It was altogether a very good party.

Thursday 6 May 1976

I lunched at Carmelite House with Vere Harmsworth and Howard French, the managing director of Associated Newspapers. This morning's papers were full of the agreement between the government and the TUC under which wage increases will be held to 4.5 per cent next year. I said I thought the deal was quite a good one and would probably stick but that unless it was complemented by cuts in public expenditure it wouldn't restore confidence in sterling. My hosts shared this view.

After lunch I heard the Duke of Edinburgh give a lecture at the Royal Society of Arts about the place of the individual in society. He spoke very well, with originality and forthrightness.

The pound has not strengthened as a result of the wage pact – indeed it seems to have weakened a bit.

Monday 10 May 1976

A heavy day. I spent the morning with the nationalised industry chairmen explaining to them the proposals we had in mind to improve their relations with government. It was one of the most difficult meetings of my working life. With Bill Ryland* in the chair, the chairmen's first reactions were predictably negative and we had to try to prevent them from hardening into outright opposition before they had had time to reflect on our proposals. Their opinions seemed to swing a bit in our favour during the meeting and I heard afterwards that they regretted having started off by being so immediately negative. Apparently we were greatly helped by the fact that they entertained Margaret Thatcher to lunch after we had gone and her attitude to nationalised industries' problems was so unattractive to them that ours shone by comparison.

After lunch I attended a meeting of Eric Roll's Committee on Finance for Investment – an uphill business as the sharp difference of view between the bankers and the TUC is now coming into the open. Ian Fraser in particular made no attempt to conceal his contempt for the trade unions' approach, which didn't improve Len Murray's mood.

In the evening I went with Doreen to a dinner arranged by the German Chamber of Commerce to meet the Erste Burgomeister of Hamburg. It was a pleasant occasion, marked for me by the fact that

---

* Sir William Ryland was chairman of the Post Office Corporation.

Tony Barber, having had a friendly word with Doreen, came up and apologised for his part in the row we had at the Seligmans' the other evening. I did the same and we and our wives parted on friendly terms.

Tuesday 11 May 1976

I went to dinner at the Reform Club, where I had to speak to an industrialists' dining club called the 1969 Club. As they were practical people, many of whom I knew quite well, I told them what I really thought – that our prospects were dismal and we should probably have a thumping great crisis later this year. After I had spoken Campbell Adamson chipped in and said he thought I had got it all wrong. He then gave a very optimistic picture of our situation à la Healey. I find it impossible to believe he is right.

Wednesday 12 May 1976

We had a short Neddy meeting in the afternoon – curtailed because Len Murray and Alf Allen, the only TUC men present, had to leave early. As a result we only talked about the progress so far made with work on the industrial strategy and how it should be handled when the working party reports are ready. We decided on an all-day meeting in July which I expect Callaghan will chair.

Tuesday 18 May 1976

I took Ron Spiers, the American Minister, to lunch. He said that the US businessmen who were invited over by the British government last year (the Mansergh mission) left with a poor impression of the way the country was going. Spiers had seen them shortly after their final interview with Wilson and had seen Wilson shortly after that. Harold evidently thought the whole thing had gone very well but the

US businessmen had made it clear to Spiers that they had not been impressed by what they saw and heard here.

In the afternoon I went to the House to talk to the Industry Group of the PLP. It was a small meeting with Giles Radice* in the chair and only half a dozen others present. Perhaps because of this we had a very good discussion without the need for me to make a speech. The frustration of those interested and intelligent backbenchers was very striking – indeed they ended up by asking me what they could do to help to persuade the government to go in for more sensible economic planning!

After that I went to the CBI's annual dinner – a large affair at the Dorchester. Jim Callaghan was the principal guest and pleased his audience by making a conciliatory and undoctrinaire speech in which he went out of his way to stress that the government understood industry's worries (over such things as price control) and would try to meet them.

Before dinner I had a chat with Callaghan over a drink. He said he was looking forward to chairing the Neddy meeting in July and hoped we could show some real progress in easing bottlenecks. There was some talk of the pound (which had had a bad day) and Callaghan said he was glad he had a Chancellor to worry about it. I said I thought sterling would be vulnerable as long as the public sector deficit remained at its present levels. Callaghan didn't disagree but said, 'The trouble is, where do you make the cuts?' He also said that although Wilson had frequently told him of his intention to retire he hadn't really believed him. Now as he walked down the stairs in Downing Street he felt the eyes of his predecessors following him sardonically.

---

* The former head of the research department of the GMWU who had become Labour MP for Chester-le-Street in 1973. He subsequently wrote a perceptive book about Tony Crosland, Roy Jenkins and Denis Healey, *Friends and Rivals* (London: Little, Brown, 2002).

Friday 21 May 1976

The pound fell sharply today – more than on any other day since the recent pressure on it began – and the Bank of England raised the minimum lending rate to counter it. It looks as though my fears are going to prove justified.

Thursday 27 May 1976

I went to a small lunch at the Connaught given by Jack Scamp, chairman of Urwick Orr. The other guests were mostly industrialists, and we had been warned that we should be expected to take part over coffee in a discussion of relations between the public and private sectors. James Meade* led off with a nice little macro-economic lecture in which he urged the need for an effective incomes policy. I came in a little later on, saying that my previous experience with incomes policies had left me totally sceptical about them: if they were effective the price which had to be paid to secure trade union agreement (in the present case high public expenditure and damaging price controls) was altogether excessive.

Friday 28 May 1976

Last night's House of Commons debate on the nationalisation of shipbuilding produced two extraordinary results: the first division was a tie, the second gave the government a majority of one. The Tories think – I should guess justifiably – that the government won the second division on a cheat and the House evidently erupted into scenes of unprecedented violence. Roger Moate told me this

---

* A distinguished Oxford economist who won the Nobel Prize for Economics in the following year.

morning that the whole affair was very unpleasant and even rougher than the newspapers suggest. He said that it was not just a handful of Tribunites who sang 'The Red Flag' (and thus provoked Michael Heseltine into seizing the mace) but a solid phalanx of eighty or ninety.

Saturday 5 June 1976

Connie Campbell took us to see *Falstaff* at Glyndebourne. I met Peter Carrington in the interval. He asked me whether I thought we were really heading for disaster and I said the short answer was 'yes'. He said he was one of those who thought we should not be able to improve things until we had been through some kind of collapse. When I told him I thought we could still avoid the collapse if our political leaders would agree to try to work out a programme of recovery, his answer seemed to be that the leaders were powerless until the national mood changed. The trouble with people who expect and almost welcome the prospect of collapse is that they always assume its cathartic effect will be beneficial. It seems to me there is at least an equal chance that it would leave things worse than they are now.

Monday 7 June 1976

Denis Healey announced in the House today that he has negotiated a new $5 billion line of credit from the USA, Germany, Japan and Switzerland. This will take the pressure off sterling for a while but won't make any lasting difference.

Monday 14 June 1976

Our twenty-fifth wedding anniversary. We gave a party on a boat on the river Thames.

Thursday 17 June 1976

We drove down to Ascot. Neither of us had been before but we thought we had better go this year in case Jack Jones gets it abolished. In his puritanical and class-conscious way, Jack has been making speeches about the way the rich spend their time at Ascot while the sons of toil work away in the factories. In fact it turned out to be a much less privileged affair than one might have expected. Racing is after all a working man's sport and the crowds milling around the bookies were a complete mixture of social types, with no distinction between those in morning dress and those in shirt sleeves. So far from giving an impression of a socially divided country I thought it showed the free and easy way in which the various groups mix.

Monday 21 June 1976

We drove down to Torquay after lunch for the CSEU conference. For the second time this year we arrived at the Imperial in glorious sunshine with a beautiful view across the bay to Brixham from our bedroom.

We went to the Torbay Hotel for dinner. Les Buck, this year's president of the CSEU, made a genial speech of welcome and two employers' representatives replied. Unlike most of the other guests we stayed on for the dance and cabaret after dinner and had a pleasant evening with Hugh Scanlon, Les Dixon, George Doughty and their wives. It was a very relaxed and friendly occasion and at midnight Doreen got her first birthday kiss, from an executive councillor of the AUEW.

Wednesday 23 June 1976

I went to the House of Lords to talk to an all-party group about Neddy. We had a pleasant hour's meeting in which I first gave a talk and then answered questions. I went back to the House of Commons for dinner with a group of Tory backbench MPs. They belonged to a dining club founded by Nicholas Scott, which is now chaired by Charles Morrison and consists of MPs from the liberal wing of the Conservative Party.* I found the evening a really enjoyable one which restored my faith in the Tory Party. The fourteen MPs present were courteous, well informed and open minded; there was none of the arrogance and bigotry that one often finds among Tory MPs. Charles Morrison told me that there would be fifty or so backbenchers in the Tory party of similar views.

Friday 2 July 1976

We had a truncated Group of 4 meeting – just Douglas Wass, John Methven and myself as Len Murray has not yet recovered from his heart attack. I was pleased that Wass took the trouble to come – the Group of 4 is a useful piece of machinery to have in reserve and I don't want it to get rusty for lack of use.

I wrote again to the PM saying I hoped that if next week's meeting went well, he or another minister would make a statement in the House about it so as to reduce the criticism that Parliament is always bypassed on these occasions.

Tuesday 6 July 1976

I spent the day preparing for tomorrow's Council. At 5 p.m. I went

---

* The club was known as Nick's Diner and, I believe, still exists. Scott's constituency was Kensington & Chelsea; Morrison's was Devizes.

across to No. 10 to see the Prime Minister. He was in the garden and we spent half an hour talking about the meeting and how it might go. Callaghan clearly wants a good result from it. He hopes it will be possible for him to give a joint press conference with the CBI and the TUC after it but we agreed that this would have to depend on how the meeting went. I again pressed him to arrange for the outcome to be reported to Parliament.

Wednesday 7 July 1976

We began the Neddy meeting at 9.30 a.m. with an absolutely full house. As I expected, the TUC were in a difficult mood – especially Jack Jones, who has no great love for Neddy and used the meeting to put pressure on the CBI and government to do something to reduce unemployment. The general discussion went on for over two hours and it wasn't until about noon that we got on to the substance of the sector working party reports. Callaghan was a little bothered about the slow progress but I told him that Neddy meetings always went best if one let the parties get whatever was concerning them off their chests at the beginning.

Over lunch Callaghan persuaded Harold Watkinson and Alf Allen to join him at the press conference. Discussion in the council after lunch went a good deal better, though we had to avoid some financial subjects on which Jones was known to have very strong views, as he had to leave the meeting early. Alex Jarratt made one of the few really honest statements of the day when he told the trade unions it was unrealistic to think one could raise efficiency without at least a temporary increase in unemployment. Anyway, one way or another we got through the afternoon and maintained quite a reasonable level of discussion.

At 4.30 we went down to the cinema in our building for the press conference. Callaghan took it, flanked by Watkinson and Allen and with Healey, Varley and myself on the platform. The PM handled it very well and got excellent support from the others. He made no attempt to paper over the differences between the parties but said that they had all affirmed their support for the new industrial strategy, with its emphasis on priority for manufacturing industry, and all wanted the work of the sector working parties to continue. They had 'stopped grumbling at one another' and were now determined to make the mixed economy work. The impression that came over was one of a national strategy, worked out in Neddy and involving management and unions just as much as government. All in all I think it was a good day's work and I was much impressed by Callaghan's chairmanship, especially the way he handled Jones and the rest of the TUC team.

Thursday 8 July 1976

The Neddy meeting is the lead story in all the papers, including the populars. The meeting has shown that Chequers was not simply a one-off meeting but that we have begun to follow through effectively. Watkinson's constructive attitude tipped the balance by giving the whole thing a national, non-party flavour.

Eric Varley made a statement in the house yesterday about the Neddy meeting – the first time this has ever been done, I think. He got a rough reception from his own left-wing backbenchers, who think the government have sold out to the CBI. Michael Heseltine gave the statement a grudging, rather ambivalent welcome. In the Lords, however, the Tory spokesman (Niall Drumalbyn) expressed warm support for Neddy and this week's agreement.

Before going home I phoned Harry Evans, the editor of the Sunday Times. I said his chaps on the Business News were always very sceptical about Neddy meetings but that this one really had gone well and had been greatly helped by the series of articles about the decline of manufacturing industry which the paper had carried earlier in the year. Evans said he was thinking of writing a leader and would bear in mind what I had said.

Sunday 11 July 1976

The first leader in today's *Sunday Times* says, 'The British economic miracle is a conceit which ministers now allow to cross their minds . . . A modicum of scepticism should be preserved just yet, but if the miracle ever acquires substance there can be little doubt that the Neddy is where it will begin. Last week's Neddy meeting was a considerable success . . .'

Tuesday 13 July 1976

I went to see Eric Varley about our nationalised industry enquiry. I thanked him for making the statement about Neddy in the House. On my way in I ran into Willie Whitelaw, who was very friendly, and Michael Heseltine, who told me that Margaret Thatcher had given her prior approval to every word of what he said in response to Varley's statement last week.

Wednesday 14 July 1976

I was principal guest at the annual lunch of the industrial engine-makers' trade association. I made a speech about Neddy and the new industrial strategy and took the opportunity – as I knew I had a sceptical audience – to justify the attempt to secure consensus. I described the consensus we want as not depending on brushing the awkward issues under the carpet but seeking to take account of the realities of power and self-interest. It is three years ago this week since I took up my present job and despite all the difficulties I feel pleased with the progress made in developing this kind of consensus.

Thursday 15 July 1976

I spent a couple of hours in the morning with Russell Kerr and his colleagues on the Select Committee on Nationalised Industries. They are a sensible lot with a genuine desire to produce good and reasonably bipartisan reports but they have no power and not very much influence – and they know it.

Friday 16 July 1976

It looks as though another row with Whitehall may be brewing up. They will not realise that the only reason a lot of industrialists support the strategy is that it is being developed in Neddy and not in Whitehall – if they try to make the industrial strategy too government dominated they will lose management support and ensure that the whole thing is killed stone dead if the Tories get back to power.

I had a useful lunch with Don Ryder and others at the NEB. Ryder said he had been to a lunch for Ted Heath earlier in the week. It had gone very well until the host said he hoped Ted would soon be back on the Tory front bench – whereupon Heath froze and said nothing more until he left.

Heath has made a speech in the House in which he had some interesting things to say about Neddy and Parliament. I am more than ever convinced that we need to create what Robert Carr called in a recent Lords debate an organic relationship between Neddy and Parliament.

Tuesday 20 July 1976

I went to the House of Commons to talk to the Conservative Party's

Industry Committee. Heseltine was in the chair and there were twenty-five MPs present. It was a friendly occasion and will, I hope, have helped to strengthen our links with Parliament.

Wednesday 21 July 1976

I went to a curious lunch at the Building Societies Association, where the guests were Margaret Thatcher and her PPS, Francis Sandilands (the chairman of Commercial Union), the deputy chairman of Tarmac and myself.

There was no general conversation until coffee, when the Tarmac man, who was forthright and intelligent, opened up with an innocuous question about the Conservatives' housing policy. Margaret Thatcher immediately jumped down his throat – saying it was all in the manifesto and if he had done his homework he would have known the answer to his question before he put it. She was sharp and aggressive throughout – no doubt it's due to strain and tiredness but it creates a very bad effect, especially on people like the Tarmac man, who is just the sort of chap she should be getting on her side.

After lunch she spoke to me briefly about our recent Neddy meeting and asked me if I could let her have the sector working party reports, which I promised to do.

Thursday 22 July 1976

This afternoon Denis Healey announced his long-awaited package of economic measures. He has reduced the borrowing requirement by £2 billion but only half of this is through cuts in public expenditure – the rest is by an increase in the employers' national insurance contribution of 2 per cent. This will bring in £1 billion in a full year.

At 7 p.m. I recorded an interview for BBC radio commenting on the measures. I said I was personally very sorry to see industrial costs loaded with an extra £1 billion and that there must be a question mark over whether these measures would achieve their aim of restoring confidence.

Friday 23 July 1976

We had a good meeting of the Group of 4 in the afternoon. We discussed the government's measures. Methven was less critical of the increase in employers' contributions than I was. Murray was unenthusiastic about the whole package and seems to think the cuts in public expenditure were not really necessary. Douglas Wass told us that the Treasury had prepared a good paper on the medium-term prospects for next month's Neddy meeting.

We had a useful discussion about the composition of Neddy in which Murray and Methven both reaffirmed their strong support and said quite emphatically that they were against having any comprehensive review of council membership just now.

Saturday 24 July 1976

Doreen and I drove down to Poole to join the Mastermans on *Tugradog*. We had a lovely week's sailing – to the Fal, the Helford, the Yealm and the Tamar. Conditions were more or less perfect throughout and we were both greatly impressed by the Cornish coast.

Monday 2 August 1976

I had lunch with Harold Watkinson at the Stafford. While we were away sailing he complained strongly about the increase in national insurance contributions and in a well-publicised encounter with the Prime Minister he accused the latter of going back on the undertakings given at the Neddy meeting in July. In my view Harold is right on the substance of the issue; but unfortunately he didn't handle it very well and he is getting a bad press for it. He was a bit subdued at lunch and repeated what he has often said before – and is I am sure quite true – that he only took on the CBI presidency out of a sense of public duty. I have the impression that he is running into a good deal of criticism from CBI members as well as from the press – which is unfortunate as it will weaken his position at the very time when the CBI needs a strong president.

Wednesday 4 August 1976

The main item on the NEDC agenda was the Treasury paper on the medium term. It was not a good effort but revealed more Treasury thinking about the prospects for the next few years than is normal – perhaps more than has ever been done before.

Characteristically, we spent almost the whole time discussing whether to release the document and virtually none discussing the substance. Denis Healey was strongly in favour of publishing his paper – he made out that this was because large extracts from it had been published in this morning's *Guardian* but I am sure he had decided on publication before he saw this. Jack Jones, as is usual nowadays, was in a difficult mood and wanted two sentences (to do with wages policy) rewritten. John Methven was against publishing the document at all.

After a while I lost patience and reminded the council that Chancellors were always being pressed to make more of their thinking about the future public – it would be a bit much if, when one of them was prepared to do so, Neddy were to stop him. This swung the debate and it was agreed the document should be released. But the discussion then took an odd turn as Jones proposed that, provided his two amendments were agreed, the council should pass a resolution endorsing the document. This was absurd because all the document really says is that if we go on as we are we shall be in the soup, but that if we increase our share of world markets things will be much better. However, Jones's proposal was agreed and so the council passed what we think is the first resolution in its history.

After the meeting John Cousins came to see me in a very contrite mood. He confessed that he had given the *Guardian*'s labour correspondent a copy of Healey's paper as background information!

Thursday 5 August 1976

After lunch I went with Dick Homan and others from NEDO to the House of Commons to discuss our nationalised industry study with shadow ministers. Those present were Geoffrey Howe, Michael Heseltine, Nicholas Ridley and Adam Butler. It was a disappointing occasion. Neville Abraham* gave a good presentation of our findings. Nicholas Ridley then said that there was only one course for us to recommend – 'denationalise the lot'.† After that the discussion never really got off the ground. Michael Heseltine echoed Ridley and Geoffrey Howe kept pretty quiet. It was all very depressing.

Tuesday 10 August 1976

After lunch I had a visit from James Swaffield.‡ The GLC now want to get on to the industrial strategy band-wagon. I told him I would

---

* Neville Abraham was a management consultant and a member of the team which drew up our report on nationalised industries.
† This now strikes me as a rather sensible suggestion. At the time I thought it bizarre.
‡ Sir James Sutherland was director general of the Greater London Council.

welcome this in principle – the more support the exercise gets the more likely we are to trap people into consensus, whether they want it or not.

Thursday 12 August 1976

Cob Stenham* gave me lunch at Unilever. When he was a member of our advisory group on finance for investment he was cynical and critical. Now he is a changed man – a strong supporter of Neddy and very critical of the City. Times change.

Friday 13 August 1976

Peter Ramsbotham came in for a glass of sherry and a talk before lunch. He told me that the letter I had sent him early in the summer – predicting a severe financial crisis later in the year – had not surprised him all that much. I said that things looked somewhat better now – what I had not expected was Callaghan's ability to stand up to the Tribune group and to put through public expenditure cuts without splitting the Labour Party.

Friday 3 September 1976

Back to work after a delightful break at Throwley, which we both badly needed. I had lunch at Bridgewater House with Brian Kellett[†] and the three most senior directors of Tube Investments. They are a moderate, middle-of-the-road crowd but I was interested to find them adamantly opposed to the idea of workers on their board. Since the Bullock inquiry is virtually certain to recommend this it looks as

---

* Finance director of Unilever.
† Brian Kellett had succeeded Lord Plowden as chairman of Tube Investments.

though we are in for a sharp conflict between management and unions over this issue next year.*

Tuesday 7 September 1976

I drove down to Brighton for the TUC Congress. I first started coming to them in 1970 so this will be my seventh in a row.

In the evening we gave a dinner for some of the senior trade union officials who are not on the General Council. We had a very good evening with them. Among other things we had a long argument about whether the present level of unemployment was really such a social evil as the TUC are making out. Moss Evans† was sure it was and drew heavily on his experience as an unemployed man's son in the 1930s to prove it. The others were much more doubtful and told us of instances when they had fought to prevent redundancies at factories only to find that their members were quite happy to lose their jobs in return for a decent cash payment. It was all very good natured and rather refreshing to be able to discuss one of the labour movement's sacred cows so openly with them.

Wednesday 8 September 1976

This was the day of the economic debate. It was a very dull affair. All the controversial motions had been 'composited' and Cyril Plant (who is chairing the Congress very effectively) took them all together, thus mixing up resolutions about incomes policy and unemployment. The left were very piano; no one really bothered to

---

* The report of the Committee of Enquiry on Industrial Democracy, chaired by the distinguished historian Alan Bullock, was published in 1977 and buried shortly afterwards.
† Moss Evans was national organiser of the TGWU. He was elected to succeed Jack Jones as general secretary the following year.

challenge the General Council's moderate line and all the votes went as the platform wanted.

This debate showed clearly the strength of the current alliance between the TUC and the Labour government. The economic policies which the TUC leaders advocated in the debate – on wage restraint and unemployment – are in principle repugnant to most of them but this is far outweighed by their determination to keep the Labour government in power. Their dislike of the present Conservative leadership is almost pathological and they would do anything to keep Mrs Thatcher out.

Thursday 9 September 1976

Today's proceedings at Congress were completely dominated by the seamen's decision to strike for higher wages. No one here expected them to call an all-out strike, especially as the ballot of their members gave only a tiny majority in favour of industrial action. The newspapers are full of references to the 1966 seamen's strike and Harold Wilson's description of its leaders as a 'tightly knit group of politically motivated men'. But I don't think the motive is political on this occasion. Mick Costello of the *Morning Star* told me that the motion to call a strike was moved by a left-wing member of the NUS executive and seconded by a right-winger and I have no reason to disbelieve him.

The debate at Congress came alive late this afternoon on – of all things – the subject of devolution. George Smith of UCATT moved a motion against any form of devolution with eloquence and passion and in a broad Scots accent. But the General Council and the Communists were against him and he went down 9-1 on a card vote. 'We lost by a whisker,' he said to me ruefully later.

As a result of this, the proceedings went on long past the normal 5 p.m. finish and immediately afterwards the TUC Economic

Committee began talks with the seamen's representatives.

Friday 10 September 1976

The seamen have suspended their strike for two weeks while six members of the General Council of the TUC see how they could be given more money through an increase in fringe benefits without breaching the pay policy. Evidently the idea is that they might be compensated for the fact that they find things more expensive when they go ashore in foreign countries because of the fall in the pound. Shades of 'washing-up time' in the miners' strike of 1973–4 – it's ironic and a bit sad to see how the TUC have dug themselves into the same hole that Heath dug then.

Sunday 11 September 1976

I phoned Roy, who has resigned as Home Secretary. He said he was enjoying his European activities – indeed, provided he could keep the emoluments, he thought that to be president elect of the Commission would be the ideal job.

Tuesday 14 September 1976

Hugh Overton, our economic minister in Bonn, gave me lunch at his eponymous restaurant in St. James's.* He said that though the Germans were generally well disposed to us they took a very bleak view of our economy and the way we run our affairs – much more so, he thought, than the Americans.

---

* Overton's was an excellent fish restaurant which, alas, no longer exists.

Wednesday 15 September 1976

In the evening John Horam came in for a drink with Doreen and myself. He said he had hesitated a good deal before agreeing to enter the government. He had enjoyed his position as chairman of the Manifesto Group* and thought he could have used it to exercise some real influence in favour of the middle ground, social democratic politics in which he believes. As a member of the government he could not do this and would have to work with some people with whom he has less in common politically than he has with some Conservatives.† However, he accepted that to know anything about government you had to work within it for a time at least and he likes Bill Rodgers, who will be his Secretary of State.

John thought the civil servants in his Ministry were very able. But their attitude was one of déjà vu: 'I'm afraid that's all been tried before, Minister, and never worked.'

Tuesday 21 September 1976

In the morning I went to see John Read, the chairman of EMI, to ask him to chair an Electronics EDC. He is a great believer in what we are trying to do and agreed at once.

I lunched with Andrew Railton,‡ who told me that despite the general atmosphere of doom and gloom, which he basically shared, his companies were doing remarkably well.

---

* A group of about eighty Labour MPs from the social democratic wing of the party.
† Horam, who was Labour MP for Gateshead West, had been appointed parliamentary secretary in the Department of Transport. He later joined the Conservative Party and became a junior minister in John Major's last government.
‡ A successful entrepreneur who, after some years as a big company executive, had founded the Anduff group, of which he was chairman, in 1968.

Wednesday 22 September 1976

After an hour or so at the office I took a train to Birmingham International for the machine tools exhibition lunch. The Prime Minister was the guest of honour and devoted most of his speech to the recent report of the Machine Tools EDC and the importance of the industrial strategy. He called it the Neddy strategy and made an agreeable reference to my own presence at the lunch.

Tuesday 28 September 1976

In the evening we had a pleasant dinner with Gloria Stacey, a talented painter – if that is the right word – of collages. Jean Wahl, the minister at the French embassy, said that the reputation for being hostile to the Anglo-Saxons which Raymond Barre, the new Prime Minister of France, had acquired during his time at Brussels was undeserved – he simply thought that our economic weakness would be a liability for Europe. Wahl made it clear that in his view Barre could not reasonably be faulted for this.

Wednesday 29 September 1976

The pound plummeted today. The Labour Party conference voted yesterday against the government's public expenditure cuts and the foreign exchange markets reacted immediately. Jim Callaghan made a very orthodox right-wing speech with all the right noises but our creditors are evidently no longer interested in mere words.

At one time the dollar rate fell to $1.63 to the pound. Healey was on his way to Heathrow at the time – about to fly to Manila for an International Monetary Fund conference – but he turned back to London before the plane took off. I fear that the prediction I made in the spring – that we should have a sterling crisis severe enough to provoke political change before the year was out – may be about to come true.

Thursday 30 September 1976

Healey flew up to the TUC in Blackpool and made a somewhat strident defence of his policies – I wonder if the present run on sterling has really taken him by surprise? John Cousins, who has been in Blackpool, told me today that the journalists there were all talking of a scene at Heathrow on Tuesday in which Gordon Richardson practically forced Healey to change his plans and return to London.

Callaghan has made a speech in which he spoke of the possibility of dictatorship if we don't solve the present economic crisis. It seems to me that some political change is bound to occur in the next few months – and although the IMF loan will give us a breathing space it could well happen before the end of the year.* The present Labour government certainly could not survive another sterling crisis, which seems inevitable unless public expenditure is cut pretty substantially; but the signs are that the Labour movement could not stand up to the strains which large cuts would impose on it.

Margaret Thatcher has a huge opportunity at next week's Conservative Party conference to show that she could be a national leader. I shall be surprised if she can grasp it and even more so if she can make her shadow front bench appear credible.

Tuesday 5 October 1976

I had lunch with Roy at Brooks's. He was on good form and clearly interested in his job in Brussels. But like me he thinks the sterling

---

* The government had announced on the previous day that it was applying to the IMF for a conditional loan.

Lord Watkinson (right), president of the CBI, with his successor Hedley Greenborough in 1977, when things were evidently looking a little brighter. (Mike Stephens/Central Press/Getty Images)

CBI top brass at Downing Street in 1975. Left to right: Sir John Partridge, Ralph Bateman, Campbell Adamson. (Dennis Oulds/Central Press/Getty Images)

Sir Douglas Allen: the ablest mandarin of his time. (Anglo-German Foundation

Edward Heath with OPEC's chief negotiator, Sheikh Yamani, as the oil crisis intensified in November 1973. (George W. Hales/Fox Photos/Getty Images)

Harold Wilson leaving Millbank Tower after a meeting of NEDC, which
he always enjoyed chairing, accompanied by myself.

Edward Heath, Jeremy Thorpe and Harold Wilson shortly before the second
general election of 1974. (*Evening Standard*/Getty Image*s*)

Anthony Barber in 1970, shortly before he learned he was to be Chancellor of the Exchequer. (Central Press/Getty Images)

Denis Healey addressing the Labour Party conference in 1976. The strain of
managing the British economy took its toll even on him. (*Guardian*)

James Callaghan in 1978. (Central Press/Getty Images)

Margaret Thatcher in 1975: 'a new generation, with new ideas and values'.
(UPPA/Photoshot)

With members of the Balliol mafia at our silver wedding party on the Thames in 1976. To Doreen's left are Andrew Railton, Roy Jenkins and Nigel Foulkes; to my right (in front of the table) are Neil Bruce and Madron Seligman.

Doreen and myself on board RFA *Lyness* at the Queen's Silver Jubilee naval review, Spithead, 1977.

crisis could produce political change and said a little wistfully that he wondered whether he had been right to leave British politics at this time.

After lunch I had a visit from the Japanese ambassador. He wanted to know more about Neddy and how we operate and would like to develop some continuing relationship between his embassy and NEDO.

In the evening I went to dinner with Nigel Foulkes and the executive directors of the BAA. Speaking informally after dinner I said we had now reached the point where the collapse of which many people had spoken for so long was in sight. I added that it seemed to me the crisis would require a political rather than an economic solution and that I thought some political change was certain within the next six months.

Wednesday 6 October 1976

Ted Heath made a forceful speech at the Conservative Party conference at Brighton in which he echoed exactly the things I had been saying at the BAA dinner last night and even used the same phrases: 'Britain has reached the end of the road', 'collapse is in sight' and so on.

I had a busy day in the office. It began with a long talk with Denis Rooke,* who is just coming on to the council. He has a reputation for being sharp and forthright and I warned him he might find Neddy a disappointing and puzzling body at first – especially at a time like this when there are likely to be strong political undercurrents. I then saw John Cuckney,† who says the construction industry is thoroughly demoralised and pessimistic about the future.

---

* Sir Denis Rooke was chairman of the British Gas Corporation.
† Chairman of the Building EDC.

Later I had a talk with George Smith, who confirmed Cuckney's description of morale in the building industry. When I said it was clear that big public expenditure cuts were on their way (either by government decision or imposed by events) he did not disagree at all – the sensible trade union leaders understand the realities of our economic situation very well.

I then went on to see John Hunt at his request. He was in a very gloomy mood. He said that if the next set of measures taken by the government did not restore confidence he could see no way out of the crisis – there would be no more shots in the locker.

John told me he had urged the Prime Minister a little while ago to put increasing effort into 'the Neddy industrial strategy'. I said that the need to support this industrial strategy to the full was even stronger following the latest run on sterling. But I reminded John that I had predicted this crisis many months ago. I told him I was sure that confidence would not return unless there were substantial cuts in public expenditure and that some political realignment would almost certainly be needed. Our talk ended abruptly as John had to go off to see the Prime Minister. We were interrupted by several phone calls and the general impression was one of imminent crisis.

After a quick change I went on to a dinner at the Hilton given by the BIM for the Prime Minister. This was arranged some time ago to give the PM an opportunity to say something nice to managers. There was a large turn out which included more big company chairmen than I can ever remember seeing at a single dinner before. The BIM chairman, Derek Ezra, made a fulsome reference to the new NEDO–BIM committee which I have set up in order to provide them with a formal link to our activities. The Prime Minister then gave what I thought was a good speech about the importance of management, his understanding of their difficulties and so on. The applause at the end was only lukewarm and rather to my surprise I found that most people had thought it disappointing – mainly, I think, because of some remarks he made about industrial democracy at the end. I think the BIM people did Jim less than justice – he really was trying to be constructive and to hold out an olive branch to management. At the same time one must recognise that his speech did not measure up to the gravity of our crisis – one has the feeling that he would be quite a good 'peacetime' Prime Minister but that we are really in a wartime situation now.

Thursday 7 October 1976

We got our nationalised industries report off to the printers. To my great delight all the members of my advisory group (Berrill, Pennock, Stanley, Foulkes and Young)* have authorised me to say in my introduction that they agree with our recommendations. This will give our report considerable authority – if it doesn't get lost in the turmoil of a political crisis.

In the afternoon we learned that minimum lending rate had gone up by two points to 15 per cent – a crisis level which we have never had before.

At six o'clock we had a Group of 4 meeting. Douglas Wass had flown in from Manila yesterday and was obviously dead tired. He tried to persuade us that the rise in the MLR was purely a technical move to 'squeeze the bears' and that it didn't represent any change in the government's general strategy. He didn't persuade me or, I think, John Methven, who thought it was bound to have a quite serious effect on investment. Len Murray was in a very nervous mood. He obviously doesn't know how the main TUC people will react to the

---

* It was a strong group. Sir Kenneth Berrill was head of the CPRS, Ray Pennock was deputy chairman of ICI, Bryan Stanley was general secretary of the POEU, Nigel Foulkes was chairman of the BAA and Michael Young was president of the Consumers' Association.

present crisis. He was very anxious to avoid any discussion of the crisis at Monday's Neddy meeting because he evidently doubts if he could keep his own team under control. Fortunately Wass said he thought that Healey would want to make a statement about the economic situation at Neddy; but he, like Murray, wanted to keep the discussion very low key. I said I thought it was time that Neddy faced up to the real issues – on public expenditure and the like – and had a serious, off-the-record discussion about them.

Friday 8 October 1976

There is to be an emergency debate on the economy on Monday. Healey is coming to NEDC to say something on the economic crisis and will then hand over the chair to Harold Lever.

I went to see Harold in the morning. He was very busy so I travelled in his car with him from the Cabinet Office to Harley Street. Despite his stroke he was mentally very much on the ball. He is appalled at the failure of Healey and others to foresee the crisis and thinks that yesterday's measures will be very damaging to industry. Harold's remedy for the present situation is heavy cuts in unproductive public expenditure – not involving any cuts in capital projects – offset by tax cuts to avoid undue deflation of demand.

Monday 11 October 1976

The Neddy meeting began with a low-key account from Denis Healey of the reasons for the sudden rise in interest rates last week. He said that if it achieved its purpose – to enable the authorities to sell more gilts – the squeeze might last for only a few weeks. I shall be very surprised if it is over so soon. Healey was not his usual forceful self and asked the CBI what they thought the effect of the squeeze would be. They replied cautiously that it would all depend on how long it lasted but pointed out that industrialists were bound to take a pessimistic view about the chances of relaxing it and that its effect on new investment projects could be significant. I said I hoped that if the government had to take any further measures (as I am quite sure they will) they would avoid action which would add to industry's difficulties – e.g. by raising its costs. This was an obvious reference to the increase in national insurance contributions last July and did not please Healey. He stayed for about fifty minutes in all and Harold Lever then took over for the rest of the meeting, which was quiet, serious and quite useful.

After lunch I gave my usual press briefing and then went over to the House to hear the opening speeches in the debate. Healey was again low key and took care to avoid saying anything which would upset either the IMF or the Tribune group – in other words he said very little. Geoffrey Howe followed with a poor speech which let the government completely off the hook.

I went back to the office to give an interview to Vincent Duggleby for *The Financial World Tonight.* He was just back from the IMF conference at Manila, where he said our failure to send a minister out had gone down very badly with everyone. Douglas Wass, who was leading our delegation, had inevitably kept a very low profile – I don't suppose he knew much about what was going on in London as it was still under discussion in Cabinet. In the end, according to Duggleby, the representatives of the British joint stock banks bullied Kit MacMahon (the senior Bank of England man present) into giving a secret briefing to a number of American bankers, who were so mystified by our behaviour that they were losing all confidence in sterling. Presumably Kit gave them some indication of the coming rise in interest rates.

I went to the House of Commons to hear the PM and Margaret Thatcher wind up a debate on the economic situation. Thatcher made a very effective speech, with a scathing attack on Healey, which brought her supporters cheering to their feet. But though excellent House of Commons stuff, it was entirely partisan and didn't contribute at all to the solution of our crisis. Jim Callaghan followed with a moderate but very ordinary speech which didn't begin to match up to the needs of the occasion.

Wednesday 13 October 1976

Piers Dixon took me to lunch with Keith Joseph at Brooks's. We talked about the present crisis and the reasons for it. A great deal of what Keith says is good sense which one can readily agree with but he does very much see things in black and white. He seems convinced that all forms of government support for industry must by definition be harmful. I said I agreed entirely that civil servants can't take business decisions but I tried to persuade him that some sectors of British industry were now so run down that government support was needed to keep them from disappearing altogether. He wouldn't have this because he believes that if market forces lead to an industry disappearing it wasn't worth saving anyway. Keith was, however, delighted to find that I share his opposition to prices and incomes policies.

We talked after lunch about the possibility of achieving some consensus of the political centre. Keith thinks that would simply mean agreement on the soft options and surrender to trade union blackmail. However, he said that if only Callaghan would live up to the speech he made at Blackpool – in which he attacked the left's economic views – the Conservatives could give him support in the crisis.

Keith is a nice man and a serious and lucid thinker. But he is too logical and rational. So he will make the same mistake that the Tories made in 1970 over the Industrial Relations Bill. They had it all worked out logically and rationally but they left real life out of account – with consequences that led directly to the imprisonment of the Pentonville dockers, the strengthening of the TUC and the debacle of 1973–4. Keith hasn't learned anything from this.

Thursday 14 October 1976

I went to Vic Feather's memorial service at St Martin in the Fields. Incredibly he is the only general secretary of the TUC to die in the fifty years of its existence. His three predecessors, Walter Citrine, Vincent Tewson and George Woodcock, were all there. Jim Callaghan read a passage from *The Pilgrim's Progress* in the presence of two ex-Prime Ministers; Len Murray gave a straightforward address; and the Grimethorpe Colliery Band played the TUC centenary march.

In the evening Doreen and I went to Wychwood House for dinner with the American minister. It was planned in honour of his ambassador, Anne Armstrong, but she wasn't there as she flew to the US unexpectedly yesterday. Tobin, her husband, was there and said to Doreen that he was baffled by the situation here and gave the impression that he thought this country had passed the point of no return. Dickson Mabon,* who was also there, said that Shirley Williams would beat Foot for the deputy leadership of the PLP. The middle-of-the-road MPs as well as the Manifesto group were so sickened by the behaviour of the left at Blackpool that they would flock to Shirley's banner.†

Friday 15 October 1976

Adrian Hamilton took me to lunch. He said that Sam Brittan and he

---

* Minister of State at the Department of Energy.
† In the event Foot won by 166 votes to 128.

were being criticised by some of their seniors at the *Financial Times* for taking too gloomy a view of things. He thinks editors all get too easily seduced by invitations to private briefings at No. 10. I agree – although I have a high regard for the *FT*, I think its leader writers have always been too ready to be guided by the Whitehall establishment. Hamilton has a robust view of his job – he says that businessmen are being misled about the nature and gravity of the crisis and that the *FT* ought to let them know the unvarnished facts even if these are unpalatable to the authorities.

Monday 18 October 1976

After lunch I went to a meeting chaired by Ken Berrill and attended by four permanent secretaries to discuss a paper by Peter Carey on the difficulty of attracting good graduates and school leavers to industrial management. This is, of course, an immensely important subject and Peter wanted to circulate his paper among educationalists, businessmen and so on. The others found all kinds of reasons for stopping him and in fact succeeded in doing so. I had forgotten how awful these Whitehall meetings are – no wonder the pound is down to $1.65.

Tuesday 19 October 1976

At five o'clock I gave a little party for all the people who worked on our nationalised industries study. All our advisory group came and everyone seems very pleased with the report. I sent it to the Prime Minister today and to ministers, permanent secretaries and nationalised industry chairmen. It will be interesting to see what reaction it provokes and whether Whitehall tries to suppress it.

I then went on to the German embassy, where von Hase had a party for the trustees of the Anglo-German Foundation for

Industry. I met Campbell Fraser,* who had been talking to Shirley Williams about Neddy. She had said that it worked well when the CBI and TUC started talking to one another instead of making speeches at each other and that she thought there were increasing signs now of their willingness to do this.

Wednesday 20 October 1976

In the evening I went to a dinner at Quaglino's which was extremely boring even by the standards of trade association dinners. I came home to find that Doreen had been watching Harold Macmillan being interviewed by Robin Day. Apparently he was magnificent. His message was that with the country in its present crisis we ought to have a government of national unity – otherwise continued decline was inevitable.

Thursday 21 October 1976

I went to see Derek Mitchell at the Treasury. He was in a sombre mood but it is clear that the Treasury are simply hanging on until the IMF negotiations begin on 8 November. I doubt if things will hold till then – I would expect another run on sterling any day now. Derek seemed to agree with me that a fall to $1.50 is probable.

Later Doreen and I paid a quick visit to our bank in Trafalgar Square, which was somewhat incongruously giving a champagne party to celebrate Trafalgar Day. I then got into my boiled shirt and went off to the Mansion House for the bankers' dinner. I spoke to Tony Barber on the way in. He shares my view that if Callaghan and Healey are prepared to cut public expenditure the Tories will find it hard to vote them out. He said he thought Callaghan was doing well

---

* Chairman of Scottish Television.

and might get Conservative support if he followed national policies.

Healey made a quiet speech – moderate and quite sensible but not showing any awareness of the gravity of our crisis. He was followed by Nicholas Goodison of the Stock Exchange, who made a very good speech which showed that he understood the scale of our problems and wanted to be constructive about them. Gordon Richardson followed with a speech which I found disappointing. He looked extremely tired and his speech was very muted. He failed in my view to say what was required about the need for cuts in public expenditure. His reference to this was so hedged about with qualifications that it seemed to me to lose all force.

Monday 25 October 1976

I flew to Zurich, where Jimmy Reeve, the consul general, had arranged a lunch for me to meet some 'gnomes'. They turned out to be highly intelligent, friendly bankers – well informed about Britain and regular visitors to London. They told me when I arrived that the pound had fallen well below $1.60. We talked throughout lunch about Britain's difficulties, which they attribute, above all, to excessive levels of public expenditure on non-productive items. I was much struck by their friendliness to Britain. One of them said that if sympathy was all that was required sterling would be the hardest currency in the world and I think he meant it. They also said that the strength of the Swiss franc was based fundamentally on hard work – they are convinced that the Swiss work harder than anyone else in Europe, even the Germans.

Tuesday 26 October 1976

I flew back to London in the morning and after spending an hour or two at the office I went to the Hilton for a conference organised by the Food and Drink Industries Council. I sat next to Roy Hattersley at lunch. He is enjoying his new job as Secretary of State for Prices mainly because it gives him a seat in the Cabinet – he says the difference between being the senior minister outside the Cabinet (as he used to be) and the junior minister in the Cabinet is far greater than he had realised. In his speech after lunch he put a brave face on the fall in sterling but didn't carry his audience.

Saturday 30 October 1976

Ted Heath made a powerful speech today underlining the gravity of the present crisis.

Monday 1 November 1976

I called on Wass, Murray and Methven in turn to discuss the handling of Wednesday's Neddy meeting, which the PM is to chair. I had nearly an hour with Wass and came away from it feeling very depressed. I told him I hoped that in view of the gravity of the present crisis we should have some serious discussion at NEDC about the measures needed to get out of it. Wass was strongly opposed to this and said that such discussion as was needed could be much better handled in confidential, bilateral meetings between ministers and the TUC and the CBI respectively. He took a much more optimistic view of export prospects than I think was justified, especially in view of what I heard at Zurich. He is against any cuts in public expenditure because they would destroy the social contract 'and this would produce anarchy' (by which I think he meant anarchy in wage bargaining). If the borrowing requirement had to be reduced we could always put up taxes.

I then went to see Murray. Again I had nearly an hour with him and found him more relaxed than usual. He entirely agreed that we should discuss the crisis in NEDC and though he does not want to say so in public it is clear he fully understands how serious the situation is. I told him I considered that cuts in non-productive public expenditure were now essential but that they should be accompanied by measures – perhaps including constraints on imports – to maintain employment in manufacturing industry. Murray said this was more or less the line he was taking with the General Council and he thought that opinion there might be moving a little more in this direction. He also said he had read our nationalised industry study and found it 'very impressive'.

I had a shorter time with Methven. He was very depressed about the situation and said that the CBI had not seen any senior ministers for a couple of weeks – they seemed to want to talk only to the TUC.

I went on to have lunch with John Davies to discuss the work of his select committee on European legislation, which might be a pointer to ways of linking NEDO's work with Parliament. John said it worked well and that despite the very differing views on the committee it had never been necessary to take a vote on it. In discussion about the situation generally, he said that Margaret Thatcher was now convinced that the government would soon fall – perhaps before the end of the year – that there would then be a general election and that the Conservatives would be returned to power. He didn't think she had thought any further ahead than that.

After lunch I went to a meeting of Eric Roll's Committee on Finance for Investment. The Treasury had put in a very negative paper about the problems of administering a counter-cyclical investment scheme on the lines which Jeremy Morse's* group have been considering. Morse was clearly nettled by this and attacked the Treasury paper ferociously – an interesting process to watch as he is

---

* Sir Jeremy Morse was chairman designate of Lloyds Bank and formerly an executive director of the Bank of England.

usually so polite and not generally critical of the Establishment. Everyone then joined in the attack, which produced a good deal of harmony all round.

Wednesday 3 November 1976

The Neddy meeting went off very well. In reporting to the council on Monday's meeting of the sector chairmen I said that that side of things was going well but that the macro-economic environment was very unhelpful and that we hadn't begun to give manufacturing industry the priority to which we were in theory committed. This provoked a lively discussion in which Jack Jones took a constructive part. Just before the meeting we got the result of the US presidential election. The general view was that the hiatus caused by the change of administration would be unfortunate for us but that in the long run Carter's election might be helpful to us as he was more likely than Ford to reflate the US economy.

Callaghan chaired the meeting well and considering how much he must have on his mind seemed remarkably unruffled and relaxed.

Friday 5 November 1976

The Conservatives have won two of the three by-elections held yesterday. The result of Workington is staggering as there was a 74 per cent poll, which means that former Labour voters must have crossed the party lines in droves.*

The No. 10 press officer said that he had been instructed to tell me that Jim Callaghan was most displeased with the report I had

---

* The Conservatives won Walsall North and Workington, both of which had previously been considered safe Labour seats. Labour held on to Newcastle Central but with a much reduced majority.

given the press about his views on the US election. In fact I was very circumspect in what I said (in reply to pressing questions) and the reports seemed to me to come out quite all right. But apparently Reuters sent a report of what I said to the States straightaway and this beat Callaghan's formal message of congratulations to Carter by several hours. You can't win in my line of business.

As a consolation I found a copy of a letter which the consul general in Zurich has had from the chairman of one of the Swiss banks who was present at the lunch given for me. In it the banker referred to my views on the economic situation in the UK and on its international implications as 'most lucid, extremely well founded and therefore highly valuable'!

Monday 8 November 1976

This evening Thames Television did a programme on the industrial strategy in the Neddy council room. Lew Gardner was in the chair and those taking part were Eric Varley, John Methven, Len Murray, Charles Villiers, Dick Lloyd, Alex Jarratt and myself – all council members. We began with a ten-minute interview with Varley and this was followed by general discussion. Varley was good, quiet and very moderate. Methven and Murray were both convincing – Villiers waffled a good deal. He and I had a sharp exchange at one point – when he called the current Neddy sector work a paper-chase – and this enlivened the discussion. I took the line that we had to avoid deflation and maintain reasonable growth if we were to restructure the economy in the way we needed to. Len Murray told me afterwards that he was very grateful for this and agreed entirely with what I had been saying.

Doreen and I stayed up to see the programme, which came over quite well – more interestingly than I had expected.

Tuesday 9 November 1976

In the morning Ken Stowe rang from No. 10 to say that he understood I would be making a speech at lunch. He said that Callaghan
had been absolutely livid about my remarks about the US election
after last week's NEDC; he went on to say that he was sure the PM
would prefer it if I emphasised the positive aspects of our present
situation. I told Ken that it was too late to alter the speech now – I
realised it might provoke controversy but my intention was to be
constructive.

I delivered the speech to an audience of 200 or so BIM fellows at
the Savoy.* It was a distinguished gathering with a large number of
company chairmen and several permanent secretaries. I had taken a
lot of trouble over it. The general message was that we must cut non-
productive public expenditure now but that we should offset the
deflationary effect of this by taking various expansionary measures,
including a modest cut in direct taxation. This, I argued, was
essential if we were to redress the balance of the economy and give
manufacturing industry the priority we had promised it at
Chequers. The speech was a hard-hitting one and seemed to go
down well with my immediate audience.†

---

* Fellows of the institute (later designated Companions) were senior members who
had achieved distinction in industry or the professions.
† It included the following passage: 'It seems to me that an early cut in non-
productive public expenditure has now become imperative. The size of the cut will
need to be significant. Window-dressing reductions will not do and it would be
dishonest to pretend that an increase in unemployment can be avoided. But I am not
advocating savage cuts. My personal belief is that any action which convinced
foreign opinion that we really accepted the need to reduce the share of national
resources used in the non-productive sector – and that we would not go back on this
later – would have a disproportionately good effect on sterling. It is the refusal to
accept the need for this in principle which is so damaging to confidence ... It is not
a net reduction in activity we need but a transfer of resources within the economy
to the wealth-creating sectors. This is what the Chequers agreement was all about.'

There was a lot of press interest in the speech and Tom Rickett*
and I took immense trouble with the journalists to try to ensure that
they got the balance right and didn't simply say that I was advocating
a cut in public expenditure.

Robert Butler† rang about six to say that the TV news had had a
report of the speech and to congratulate me on it. Bearing in mind
his right-wing views that almost certainly means that the news
report got the balance wrong.

Wednesday 10 November 1976

My speech is prominently reported in all the newspapers. The
Express and the *Mail* represented it as a slashing attack on the
government but the heavies all got the balance exactly right. The
Guardian had a good leader calling it a courageous speech.

The *Today* programme put on an interview with me (which I
recorded last night) at 7.40 a.m., when a lot of people listen.
Fortunately the balance came out more or less right in this too.

At about midday I went to the BBC studios to be interviewed by
Jimmy Young, whose programme on Radio 2 is said to have about
six million listeners. He put me at my ease right away and it all went
off well. The line I took was to emphasise the need to switch
resources out of non-productive sectors (which I called the soft
underbelly of our economy) into the productive ones and give real
priority to 'the sharp end', i.e. industry. I said that the trade union
leaders were realists and understood the need to give industry
priority.

When I got back to the office I found that the TUC Economic
Committee, which had met this morning, had put out a statement

---

* NEDO's highly professional and proactive press officer.
† A retired Army officer and sailing friend.

criticising my speech and saying it was inappropriate for me to make it. In view of my call for cuts in public expenditure this was not unexpected and the statement did not seem to me to be very strong. After lunch Len Murray rang up to explain, half apologetically, why the statement had been issued. He said that everyone on the committee had been very angry and that he had had some difficulty in getting them to agree to a reasonably moderate statement. He said that none of them, including himself, had read the full text before the meeting – if they had it might have made a difference because there was a lot in it that they would have liked. Len said that he recognised that, like himself, I sometimes had to go out on a limb deliberately and th-t in such cases one had to take whatever consequences fo'.owed. It was a very friendly conversation and Len assured me that the incident had not damaged any personal relationships. For the rest of the day I refused to comment on the TUC statement – the only thing to do in these cases is to stand pat and keep one's head down.

In the late afternoon I drove to the management college at Ashridge, where we are holding a two-day 'retreat' for NEDO senior staff to think about our future role and aims. But before I left I telephoned Geoffrey Howe about the press reporting of my speech. I expressed the hope that the Tories would not make party political capital out of it at Prime Minister's Questions tomorrow since that would weaken the effectiveness of my message about public expenditure, with which I was sure the Conservatives would agree. Geoffrey said he fully took the point and would pass on what I had said.

Thursday 11 November 1976

The *Financial Times* has a very good first leader on my speech which emphasises that both the TUC and the CBI ought to be able to support my general thesis. This is very helpful and must be the handiwork of some of my friends on the paper.

My secretary rang from the office to say that Buckingham Palace had phoned to invite me to lunch with the Queen next month. To get a rap over the knuckles from the TUC and a summons to the Palace – presumably because of the same speech – makes a good combination.

Friday 12 November 1976

David Howell came down to Ashridge at eleven and stayed to lunch. He spoke very well and very frankly about the Conservative Party's views. The gist of his remarks was that things had gone so far down that the first task of a new government would be to take very harsh measures to restore external and internal confidence in the pound. These would involve a complete departure from the post-war tradition that every nasty piece of medicine had to be traded off against a concession to the people who would be hurt by it. David said he expected the collapse of the economy under the present government to be followed by a landslide victory for the Conservatives. Everything would then depend on whether the Conservative leadership was wise and mature enough to use its victory to move back into the middle ground, in which case it would probably receive support from all shades of political opinion except the extreme left.

Saturday 13 November 1976

I have received a sheaf of letters congratulating me on my speech, which has evidently struck a chord in a lot of people's minds.

Sunday 14 November 1976

Prince Philip is reported as having written an article for the *Engineer* in which he said much the same things as I said last week. There is a nice reference in the *Sunday Times* leader to a 'brilliant speech' by Sir Ronald McIntosh and my reference to the 'soft underbelly of the economy' is quoted in Sayings of the Week in the *Observer*.

The *Sunday Times* also has an exclusive story about our nationalised industries report with extensive extracts from my introduction. It is a bore that it should have leaked early – I would have preferred it to come out in an orderly fashion after the controversy over my speech had died down.

Tuesday 16 November 1976

I took Toby Aldington to lunch at the Thames. He confirmed that Ted Heath really would like to lead a government of national unity and gave me the impression that he (Ted) thinks he has a chance of doing so. This would explain a strange speech he has made criticising the Tories for their 'divisive' attacks on scroungers and their concentration on the growth of Marxist influence in the Labour Party.

Wednesday 17 November 1976

In the evening I was principal guest at the annual dinner of the Aluminium Federation. After last week's effort I wanted my speech to be relatively uncontroversial though I made it clear that the views I had expressed then 'are on the record and they stand'. I ended by saying that we should not look to governments to pull all our national chestnuts out of the fire. 'Our party political structure, with its quaint and out-of-date concepts of adversary politics, is not well fitted to regenerate a failing economy. The present numerical balance in Parliament, which in other countries would almost certainly lead the main political parties to seek more common ground, in Britain seems to accentuate the divisions between them and clouds the future with uncertainty.'

Friday 19 November 1976

All the papers feature our nationalised industries report very prominently. Most of them are against our proposal for policy councils, which the *Times* calls 'bizarre', but the report as a whole has got a good reception and come in for quite a lot of praise.

Saturday 20 November 1976

John Biffen is to be shadow minister for industry. This may affect the Conservative Party's approach to Neddy. I do not know Biffen well but he has the reputation for being a Josephite, anti-consensus sort of person.

Monday 22 November 1976

I discovered that last Thursday, in answer to a parliamentary question by John Pardoe, the Prime Minister said, 'The McIntoshes generally seem to have been causing a bit of bother lately. Regarding the views of Sir Ronald I thought that his speech was rather like the curate's egg: it was good in parts. There were some parts I found myself in agreement with more than others.'

Wednesday 24 November 1976

I have had a nice letter from Roy Jenkins today about my recent speeches in which he congratulates me warmly on my 'great courage and incisiveness'. This is the first time I can ever remember that he has paid me a compliment on my professional activities.

Thursday 25 November 1976

Ken Stowe rang up to say that there was to be a Cabinet meeting next Wednesday to discuss the IMF loan as they weren't able to reach any decisions on it today. We shall cancel next week's NEDC because of this – without regret on my part because it will deprive Jack Jones of the chance (which he would probably have taken) to attack me for my BIM speech.

Friday 26 November 1976

I flew to Glasgow in the morning. Willie Robertson of the Scottish Council for Industry met me to talk about his chairman's speech to the council's annual meeting. Robertson wants him to give strong support to Neddy in this and to say that our economic salvation can only come through everyone working together on Neddy.

I then called on Iain Lindsay-Smith, the editor of the *Glasgow Herald*. He is a youngish man with a pleasant personality and seemed both intelligent and constructive. He said that the paper had moved away from its right-wing position towards the centre under his editorship and that they tried to treat each issue on its individual merits. He also said he thought that the commitment of both the main political parties to devolution had now gone too far to be reversed, though he freely admitted it had no relevance to our national economic crisis.

I then went on to a conference arranged by the Church of Scotland. We talked about devolution over dinner and the same message came over that I had been hearing all day. This is that –

partly because of our economic failure and partly because of Whitehall's remote and 'faceless' attitudes – most Scots had wanted a larger say in running their own affairs. But after the SNP successes in 1974 the Labour and Conservative parties had both panicked and committed themselves to forms of devolution which were almost bound to lead in the end to separatism or a federal constitution. Few people in Scotland wanted this but it was impossible to go back on the commitments now, with the result that we should all be landed with a constitutional change to which most people throughout Great Britain were in principle opposed.

Tuesday 30 November 1976

We went to a big dinner at the Levers' for Anne Armstrong. When the politicians went to vote towards the end of dinner I sat next to her and had a long conversation with her. She is well informed and completely unpretentious. She and her husband Tobin, whom Doreen has sat next to at a number of dinners, make a good couple. She said that there was not the slightest hope of Congress agreeing to a large loan to fund the sterling balances which Callaghan is after.

Thursday 2 December 1976

I went to the annual lunch of the Metallurgical Plant Federation at the Savoy. Gordon Richardson was the principal guest. When I arrived he came up and congratulated me on my BIM speech, which he said was very good.

In the evening we went to a very nice dinner at the German embassy given by the von Hases for Roy and Jennifer Jenkins. I had a good talk with the widow of the man who had been German ambassador in Delhi when we were there. Karl-Günther von Hase made one of his splendid rambling speeches about Roy's contribution to international affairs and so on. Roy spoke well in reply and said that he hoped very much that as president of the Commission he would be able to help to reintroduce a sense of purpose into the EEC. Altogether it was a relaxed and very pleasant occasion.

Tuesday 7 December 1976

In the evening I went to Reading University to deliver my Mercantile Credit Lecture. I talked about the obsessive concern of our political parties with short-term issues and their destructive concepts of adversary politics and said that more and more people were coming to think that some realignment of political interests, which could provide a durable consensus on our industrial problems, might be needed if we were to regenerate our failing economy. I also said that at the Chequers meeting in November 1975, when a form of consensus planning was reintroduced into Britain, the Treasury were brought kicking and screaming into the 1960s.

Thursday 9 December 1976

In the evening I went to Chatham House to hear George Thomson give a lecture on his experiences as a commissioner in Brussels. He spoke with great authority and good sense and I thought that his general exposition was very good indeed. He said something not dissimilar to what I had said at Reading about the destructive effects of our two-party system and I see that in a speech to the Parliamentary Press Gallery Roy has also referred to the harmful effects of 'gladiatorial politics'.

Friday 10 December 1976

During Prime Minister's Questions in the House yesterday David Steel referred to what I said at Reading about adversary politics. He asked whether the PM agreed with 'the interesting remarks by the director general of NEDO about the structure of our political parties'. In his answer Callaghan said that 'Sir Ronald McIntosh seems to be straying a little beyond what is his proper concern at present and I may take the matter up with him'.

Sunday 12 December 1976

The *Sunday Times* Business News has a story on its front page headed 'Storm warnings for NEDO boss'. It says that 'relations between the government and Sir Ronald McIntosh have hit a new low following the Prime Minister's rebuff last week for McIntosh's outspokenness', adding, 'When asked to comment McIntosh was content to let the Reading lecture speak for itself.'

Wednesday 15 December 1976

I went today to a small lunch at Buckingham Palace. It was an informal and very delightful occasion – though unfortunately one to which spouses were not invited. The Queen and Prince Philip went out of their way to let me know that they thought well of my recent speeches. I told Prince Philip that I had been greatly cheered to find him saying very similar things in his own speeches. He said that he, like me, had been surprised at the publicity given to speeches which were doing no more than state the obvious.

I sat on the Queen's right at lunch. She talked to me for the first half of the meal – interestingly, informally and with great charm and naturalness. She had evidently discussed my BIM speech with

Callaghan, who had told her that it 'stated the priorities very clearly'. I was immensely cheered by her attitude and Prince Philip's towards it. The Queen has a nice wry sense of humour.

After lunch I talked again to Prince Philip who said he would be interested to pay another visit to Neddy – he spent a morning there in the late 1960s when Fred Catherwood was director general.

I then went on to the House of Commons to hear Healey make his statement about the IMF loan etc. Edna Healey sat next to me in the Distinguished Strangers' Gallery. She asked me if I would like to swap jobs with Denis and said that being Chancellor was an altogether impossible and unpleasant job, with unrelenting pressures from all sides.* The statement was complicated and hard to take in on first hearing – I expect this was deliberate on Healey's part. I doubt if it will do the trick – i.e. stop sterling from falling further in the new year. The government are to cut the public borrowing requirement by £1.5 billion next year but one-third of this is to come from the sale of BP shares. I should guess that foreigners will say we are evading the real issues again.

I went to the NIESR's Christmas party. Ken Berrill told me that he thought my Reading lecture gave the best account of what the industrial strategy is about that he has seen. He also said that the PM had read it all and had been 'much taken with it'. Douglas Allen on the other hand told me that the Prime Minister was very angry and I had better watch my step.

Monday 20 December 1976

After lunch I went to see Denis Healey at No. 11 at his request. He

---

* Healey, the toughest politician on the block, confessed in his memoirs, *The Time of My Life* (London: Michael Joseph, 1989), that the strains of this period nearly broke him.

said he thought both my BIM and Reading speeches were very good
and that he was circulating the latter to Cabinet. Certain passages in
both speeches had, however, offended various members of the
council; the TUC were upset by what I said in the BIM speech about
cuts in public expenditure and the Prime Minister (who had asked
Healey to speak to me) was annoyed by what I said at Reading about
adversary politics. I should remember that I was an appointed, not
elected, servant of the council and that it was my job to represent the
views of the council, not to express my own personal opinions.*

I said that with the country in its present very serious situation I
considered that people in public posts like mine had a duty to speak
plainly about our problems, provided they did so constructively. I
had prepared both speeches carefully and everything I had said and
done in recent weeks had been carefully considered. I said I had been
in public life for thirty years and had reached my own judgment
about my role as director general of NEDO and repeated that I
thought my duty was to speak plainly, provided I was always
constructive.

I added that I knew my BIM speech would probably provoke
public criticism from the TUC but that I had had private assurances
from them not to worry overmuch about this. Healey said that my
BIM speech had not been helpful to him in his efforts to persuade
the TUC to agree to cuts in public expenditure. He laid great stress
on the sentence in my Reading lecture about the Treasury being
brought 'kicking and screaming into the 1960s last year' – he said
this was a silly thing to say and diminished my influence. His
judgment, as elected chairman of Neddy, about my role mattered

* Neddy's founding fathers had a different idea of the DG's role and status. To
make sure that he was genuinely independent they made him a full member of
NEDC, whose appointment (or removal) required the agreement of all three parties
on the council. They also provided him with a staff of independent economists and
industry specialists, the result of whose work he was free to publish.

more than mine and it was his judgment that I would damage Neddy and myself if I continued to make speeches which clashed with the views of important members of Neddy. He hoped I would pay attention to his views – 'otherwise you might be forced to choose'.

I said I fully understood the position but my views were unchanged – one must reach one's own judgment about the director general's role and accept the consequences. The conversation lasted fifteen minutes or so. It was amicable but determined on both sides. Healey tried a little bullying but seemed anxious to avoid an argument. The main purpose of the interview was, I think, to get the fact that he had spoken to me on the record. His private secretary was present throughout and took notes.

Wednesday 22 December 1976

At lunch I sat next to Douglas Wass, who was very friendly and didn't seem to bear any resentment over my crack about the Treasury in the Reading lecture. He said it was the PM who decided that the lecture should be circulated to Cabinet.

Tuesday 4 January 1977

I corrected the proof of my Reading lecture (which is to be published in booklet form) and decided to take out the sentence about the Treasury which caused Denis Healey so much offence. I wrote and told him I had done this and expressed the hope in my letter that 1977 would bring happiness to him and prosperity to us all.

PART FIVE

SMOOTHER WATERS

14 January 1977 to 1 December 1977

The IMF loan agreed in December gave the country a breathing space. On the economic front it ushered in a period of reasonable stability, which lasted for the rest of my time at Neddy, and talk of an imminent national collapse was no longer heard. Politically, things were more difficult for the government, which in March 1977 had to make a deal with the Liberals (the Lib–Lab pact) in order to avert defeat on a Conservative motion of no confidence.

With the Prime Minister's unflagging support, work on the 'industrial strategy' continued. A growing number of people became constructively engaged in the work being done under the aegis of the little Neddies in individual industries, and the government took some useful initiatives to give the needs of manufacturing industry a higher priority in central policy-making.

Margaret Thatcher began to establish her position as a different kind of Conservative Party leader – and incidentally revealed her disagreement with her predecessor's handling of the TUC 'offer' made at the Neddy meeting on 9 January 1974.

In the trade union movement also, power began to pass to a new generation of leaders – most notably in the TGWU, where Jack Jones's long period of office came to an end. In line with this the social contract began to wither on the vine; and though the government and the TUC still talked about a new Phase 3, the days of the (to my mind) wrongheaded concept of incomes policies, which had been a central plank of Establishment thinking for so long, were clearly numbered.

Wednesday 5 January 1977

We had a fairly routine meeting of Neddy, which went off quite well. Whether because of my letter or not Denis Healey was very genial and no one made any reference to my recent speeches. Jack Jones was querulous, as he often is at NEDC, and had a few digs at me but generally speaking the meeting was quite constructive. Over drinks afterwards Healey was telling everyone who spoke to him that he couldn't wait to get out of his present job.

Friday 14 January 1977

I spent the morning at a conference of the GMWU people who sit on our various committees and working parties. There were twenty-seven of them, about half full-time officials and half shop stewards. David Basnett was in the chair and Eric Varley and I both spoke and took part in the discussion afterwards. I was very much struck by this conference, which was serious, well informed and constructive. I wish the TGWU would organise something similar.

Monday 17 January 1977

John Methven came to see me in the morning. He said the CBI were a bit concerned about my outspokenness, not because they disagreed with what I said but because it might endanger my position as director general of NEDO and they were particularly keen that I should stay on as long as possible. I told him of my various conversations with ministers and trade union people. I said I would take note of what he said but that I would go on saying what I thought about the country's economic situation and would no doubt from time to time offend one group or another among my shareholders. Methven repeated that the CBI very much wanted me to stay on as DG.

Wednesday 19 January 1977

I left with Doreen in the evening for Rome. We arrived about ten
and went straight to the Hassler, where we had a very comfortable,
old-fashioned room. It really must be one of the nicest hotels in
Europe.

Thursday 20 January 1977

I spent the day at a seminar in the Palazzo Venezia on 'public
enterprise in a mixed economy'. It was sponsored by IRI,* which is
under heavy fire in Italy just now. The other participants were all
academic economists. There were also a couple of dozen or so
observers from IRI and other Italian state enterprises, including
Professor Saraceno, who has been with IRI since its foundation
in 1933.

The proceedings were conducted in English. Each of us had to
make an opening statement and nearly all of these were interesting.
When my turn came I told them about the NEDO study of
nationalised industries and its main findings.

Friday 21 January 1977

We spent most of the day at the seminar. This proved to be quite a
success. All the contributions were of high quality and I think
everyone felt that they had learned something from the discussion.
This surprised the cynics, who thought the whole thing was a public
relations exercise put on by IRI to impress their critics in the Italian
parliament. There was a good deal of interest in our report – so

---

* Istituto per la Ricostruzione Industriale, the long-established Italian state holding
company on which the National Enterprise Board in Britain was largely modelled.

much so that I began to feel that even if the British don't accept our recommendations the Italians will!

Sunday 23 January 1977

We had lunch at the English College with the rector, Monsignor Cormac Murphy-O'Connor. He is a delightful man who will obviously be a bishop soon.

Monday 24 January 1977

In the morning I went to the embassy, where I had been asked to give a briefing to economic journalists about the social contract and other forms of co-operation between the government, employers and unions in Britain. This is a topical subject in Italy just now and our arrangements for tripartite consultation are much admired.

Tuesday 25 January 1977

Politically Italy is a very interesting country just now. I came there thinking that the Italian Communist Party was just like any other and would behave just as repressively if it came to power. Now I am not so sure. Clearly a lot of intelligent and middle-of-the-road Italians really believe that it is different from other Communist parties and that it can be relied on to operate within the framework of a democratic society. What does seem clear is that the Italian Communist Party does not believe (as many people on the left in Britain do) in encouraging the collapse of the capitalist economy so that they may build a socialist state out of the ruins. The Italian Communist Party really does seem to want to make the mixed economy work and to come to power democratically. But I still find it very difficult to believe that they would give up power willingly if the democratic vote went against them after they had formed a government. One of the difficulties in interpreting Italian politics is the complete disenchantment which exists about the Christian Democrats – a great deal of the Communist Party's strength must come simply from the fact that it is the only visible alternative to the corrupt 'Demo-Christians', who have been in power since the war.

Thursday 27 January 1977

I had lunch at the Bank of England. Gordon Richardson was interested to hear that the PM had circulated my Reading lecture to Cabinet – he said that Callaghan, who is often critical of the Bank in public, is always very pleasant in private. I gained the impression that Gordon thinks that the recent improvement in our economic situation is only temporary.

Both before and after lunch we gave informal briefings to the press about next week's NEDC. They seemed to go well – the press seems anxious not to be too cynical about the industrial strategy. They evidently want to believe in it and are half way towards doing so.

Monday 31 January 1977

I had lunch with the directors of Mobil (UK) – a relaxed group, mostly British. They say that in their negotiations with the government over North Sea oil the BNOC* is much more difficult than the Department of Energy. I explained to them that this was due to Tommy Balogh's desire to perform one last service for his adopted

---

* The state-owned British National Oil Corporation (of which Balogh was a director) was the government's chosen instrument for influencing the development of the North Sea oilfields.

country by screwing the American oil companies into the ground.

In the afternoon we had a meeting of the Group of 4. John Methven was in a negative mood. Douglas Wass seemed remarkably complacent about our underlying situation. Len Murray was the only one who seemed to want a positive outcome from Wednesday's meeting – but even he was pretty detached. In the evening I looked in at the Dorchester for a party which Terry Beckett was giving to celebrate the launch of a new Ford car called the Fiesta. Hugh Scanlon, who has just returned from a wonderful trip around the world – slaving away in the interests of his members, as he put it – buttonholed me about the Bullock inquiry. He said he regarded it as a complete irrelevance which should be 'kicked around until there was no life left in it'.

Tuesday 1 February 1977

I had a two-hour meeting in the morning with the chairmen of the EDCs and sector working parties involved in the strategy. It went very well. We had two strong newcomers – John Read, the chairman of EMI, and David Atterton, the chief executive of Foseco Minsep. Generally the sense of commitment in this group of thirty-odd people is now very strong. I came away much encouraged.

In the evening Denis Healey entertained the same group plus the ministerial members of Neddy to drinks at 11 Downing Street. This too went off very well.

I sent a letter to the Prime Minister about the handling of tomorrow's meeting urging the need to establish the credibility of the exercise more firmly by getting a positive outcome with a definite commitment to action.

Wednesday 2 February 1977

We had a long and disappointing meeting of Neddy from 9.30 until nearly one o'clock. We began on a sour note with an angry outburst by Jack Jones over Harold Watkinson's statement on Bullock. No one followed Jones. The Prime Minister said the government was committed to the principle of Bullock and after an uncomfortable moment we pressed on.

There then followed a ragged discussion. Jones took every opportunity to attack the industrial strategy, the sector working parties and NEDO. Scanlon was constructive and referred to one of our recent reports as 'courageous' but the other TUC people were muted (presumably because of Jones's attitude, with which they disagree). Healey was good and positive, but the CBI kept fairly quiet and the Prime Minister did not chair the meeting well. Everyone kept saying we had done enough analysis and what we now needed was action but when I proposed half a dozen areas to them where useful action could quite easily be taken they all retreated into generalities. The Prime Minister asked me how I thought the meeting had gone. I told him I was depressed by it – especially by Jones's attitude and the council's refusal to endorse the action they all said they wanted. Callaghan's only comment was that 'you can't expect to change the world overnight'. This after fifteen months of hard work on the strategy!

Thursday 3 February 1977

The Neddy meeting had quite a good press. A number of people who attended it think it went off quite well, though all my colleagues in NEDO were as depressed as I was about it. At least we have kept the show on the road.

Monday 7 February 1977

I spent a good deal of the day at a BIM conference on Bullock. Clive Jenkins* defended the majority recommendations in a serious speech with no histrionics. After lunch Jack Callard and Norman Biggs† explained their reasons for issuing a minority report and the meeting was then thrown open for discussion. It is clear that Bullock is the most divisive event to hit British industry since Heath's Industrial Relations Act. I feel confident that the majority recommendations will not be put into effect – with the trade union movement divided on them I doubt if the government could get the necessary legislation through Parliament.

Friday 11 February 1977

I took Arnold Hall to lunch.‡ He is a dedicated apostle of the market and against government intervention of all kinds but was at pains to say that he was not opposed to what we are trying to do – 'sometimes critical of NEDO but never hostile to it' was his phrase.

Monday 14 February 1977

I had a long lunch at Wiltons with Bill MacDonald,§ who is over from Canada. Like most Canadians whom I meet nowadays Bill was gloomy about the future of his country. On the other hand he said that almost everything I had forecast about Britain when I spoke at a

---

* General secretary of ASTMS.
† Chairman of Williams and Glyn's Bank
‡ Sir Arnold Hall was chairman of Hawker Siddeley and a distinguished member of the scientific/industrial Establishment.
§ W. A. MacDonald was a partner in a well-known Toronto law firm.

lunch in Toronto two and a half years ago[*] had come true – though I remember that at the time almost all my Canadian listeners believed I was being wildly optimistic.

Thursday 17 February 1977

I was taken to lunch at GEC by Ronnie Grierson, who spoke interestingly about our current predicament. He said that people on the Continent always feared the worst and prepared for it because they were used to seeing their savings wiped out by wars, inflation or revolution. They therefore bought land or salted their money away in Switzerland or made their dispositions in some other way. The English on the other hand were too naïve to do this – they went on believing that something would turn up and the middle classes cheerfully overspent their incomes and drew down their capital until soon they would have none left.[†]

Ronnie believes that we are in for a recurrence of very high (25–30 per cent) rates of inflation and that our economic situation will not come right until we have an authoritarian government prepared to introduce a Defence of the Realm Act.

After lunch we joined the GEC board for coffee. George Nelson said he had just written to me, in his capacity as chancellor of Aston University, offering me an honorary degree. Arnold Weinstock, whom I had expected to be very sceptical about our activities in NEDO, spoke sympathetically about them and wished me luck in what we are trying to achieve.[‡]

---

[*] See entry for 23 September 1974.

[†] Grierson (whose original surname was Griessmann) was born in Germany and came to Britain as a teenager before the war.

[‡] Lord Nelson of Stafford was chairman of GEC. Sir Arnold Weinstock was managing director and one of the most respected (and successful) industrialists in Britain. I much appreciated Aston's honorary degree.

Friday 18 February 1977

David Steel* came to lunch with me at the Royal Thames. I had not met him before but found him just as his TV appearances would lead one to expect – serious, moderate and likeable. He is in favour of having opposition parties represented on Neddy. He says it is appalling that we should have so few places where MPs of different parties can meet to discuss national issues outside Parliament. He thinks that 80 per cent of the British people are 'centrist' in their politics and that the biggest criticism one can level against politicians is that they completely fail, in their party battles, to reflect this national characteristic.

Sunday 20 February 1977

Tony Crosland† died today. When I was in the Cabinet Office from 1968 to 1970 I told Doreen that Tony showed himself as having the best intellect in the Cabinet – no mean feat considering that it also contained Roy Jenkins, Dick Crossman and Denis Healey.

Monday 21st February 1977

I had lunch at the *Economist*. I had not met Andrew Knight, the editor, before. He is a quiet, unassertive young man – very different from his bilious deputy, Norman Macrae. I said I was always struck by the difference in the tone of their articles about other countries, which are usually factual and objective, and those about Britain, which are so often caustic and destructive in their criticism. Knight was very defensive about this and I guessed that it was a subject of

---

* David Steel had taken over from Jeremy Thorpe as leader of the Liberal Party.
† He had been Foreign Secretary since March 1976.

controversy within the *Economist* – perhaps with Knight and Macrae on opposite sides. But altogether it was a friendly and pleasant lunch – much more so than I had expected as the *Economist* has never been an enthusiastic supporter of Neddy.

Tuesday 22 February 1977

I went to a lunch given by Peter Thorneycroft and Charles Forte at the Hyde Park Hotel. Ted Heath was principal guest. He made a very serious speech about world affairs – a shade pretentious for a gathering of that sort, I thought, but with some real meat in it. Once again he came out as a man of bigger stature than most of the leading politicians in either party just now.

In the late afternoon I went to see Len Murray at Congress House. He told me not to worry about Jack Jones's hostility to Neddy and our sector working parties: it was all to do with how little time he had left in office. I have never heard Len speak so freely about Jack Jones before; it shows that once a man is known to be on the last lap his influence really does diminish.

We had a useful talk about the relationship between Eric Roll's Committee on Finance for Investment and the committee Callaghan has asked Harold Wilson to chair on much the same subject. Len said that the TUC would press their political points in the 'political committee', i.e. Wilson's. This might mean Roll's committee would have to pack up, though the TUC had no wish to put it out of business if there was useful work for it to do. I said I was very anxious to keep the Roll committee in being so that if there was a general election this year and the Conservatives won we should have a committee in being which brought the City and the trade unions together. Len did not demur at this.

Thursday 24 February 1977

I had lunch with Jeremy Morse and Emmanuel Kaye* at Kaye's flat in St. James's. He showed us a batch of charts which he had had prepared – all of which showed that personal taxation is too high in Britain. Like all men who have made a fortune by their own efforts he is obsessed by the level of taxation and the amount which the state takes from those who create wealth by their drive and initiative. I think he is probably right – the removal of incentives by taxation and incomes policies may well be the most serious cause of our present troubles.

In the afternoon we had a good meeting of Eric Roll's committee. Len Murray made a very helpful intervention about the respective functions of the Roll and Wilson committees, in the course of which he said he thought it important to have a permanent committee in being which brought together representatives of the City and the trade unions.

Monday 21 March 1977

Refreshed by a fortnight skiing in France, we got back to find the country in the grip of a sudden political crisis. The Conservatives have put down a motion of no confidence in the government which is to be debated on Wednesday, and the signs are that it will be carried. This all blew up late last week and seems to have taken everyone by surprise.

---

* Sir Emmanuel Kaye was the founder of Lansing Bagnall, the leading manufacturer of fork-lift trucks.

Tuesday 22 March 1977

We went to dinner with André Philippe, the Luxembourg ambassador. All the talk was of tomorrow's confidence debate, in which Mrs Thatcher could bring the government down if the Liberals vote with her.

Wednesday 23 March 1977

During the day it was announced that David Steel has reached an agreement with Callaghan under which the Liberals will support the government in return for certain concessions, which include the Liberals' right to be consulted on matters of major policy and legislation before firm decisions are taken by the government. As a result of this the Tories' confidence motion was lost by twenty-two votes.

Thursday 24 March 1977

I set off with a party of thirty or so for my first Königswinter conference. This was initiated by Lilo Milschack, whose husband was mayor of Dusseldorf after the war and had a good anti-Nazi record. Robert Birley was in at the beginning and has been going to the conferences ever since, and the whole thing has developed into a friendly, quasi-family affair.

The British team included Bill Rodgers and Shirley Williams from the government, Tom King and David Howell from the Tories, plus Dick Marsh, Michael Clapham and a strong contingent of journalists. The Germans seemed equivalent sort of people though they included some SPD people who were further to the left than anyone on the British side.

The theme of the conference was 'Europe without Energy' and I thought the quality of the discussion was very high. Frank Chapple and John Lyons, two of the three British trade unionists present, intervened very effectively in the nuclear debate.

Monday 28 March 1977

I went to the last of Varley's meetings with selected sector working parties. Again it went off well and I was again struck by the degree of commitment there is in these working groups, especially on the part of the chairmen.

Tuesday 29 March 1977

After lunch I went to the House to hear the Budget. Denis Healey's speech was much shorter than usual and delivered in a low key with uncharacteristic humility. Margaret Thatcher spoke less well than last year, when her immediate response to the Budget speech was brilliant.

Thursday 31 March 1977

I went to see Derek Mitchell. This morning's papers have the news that he is to leave the Treasury to become a director of Guinness Mahon. This has attracted a lot of publicity, partly because Derek is well known from his days as Wilson's principal private secretary in the 1960s but more because his departure to the City follows hard on the heels of Alan Lord's move from the DTI to Dunlop. Derek said that although it was a wrench to leave the Treasury after thirty years he was glad to go because he found the internal atmosphere intolerable.

In the evening I gave a talk to the Bow Group at the House of Commons. There was a group of thirty or forty young men and women – all a bit like the 27-year-old estate agent who won the Stetchford by-election. The Conservative Party seems to consist largely of such people nowadays. I made a strong plea in my speech for the creation of formal links between Neddy and Parliament, preferably through a select committee which could call on EDC chairmen and the director general to give evidence to it.

Monday 4 April 1977

I had a visit from Peter Baldwin, who is Bill Rodgers's permanent secretary at Transport. He told me they would like to have a little Neddy for transport and that he personally strongly favoured the idea. It is a little ironic since Baldwin and his department have never previously given Neddy any support – the only reason they want an EDC now is that it might help them to avoid the national transport authority which Jack Jones is so keen on.

Wednesday 6 April 1977

We had a quiet, reasonably good meeting of Neddy. Most of it was taken up with discussion of the post-Budget prospects. The TUC are clearly unenthusiastic about Healey's tax proposals and showed it at the meeting. The other item was a discussion of David Stout's paper on the reasons why the depreciation of sterling cannot be expected to put our balance of payments right. This was generally considered to be an original and useful piece of work.

Tuesday 19 April 1977

Geoffrey Howe has written to me saying how pleased he was to read my remarks about Neddy and Parliament last week. The clerk of committees at the House has also written suggesting that I should send a copy of my speech to the Select Committee on Procedure. So perhaps we are making progress.

Wednesday 27 April 1977

I flew to Toronto for talks with the Ontario government, which had invited me over to tell them about Neddy.

Thursday 28 April 1977

Jim Fleck, the deputy Minister for Industry, launched me into a full programme of meetings with Ontario government officials. He is one of a small group of people in the Ontario government who are keen to strengthen the government's relations with business and labour, especially the latter. They are attracted by the tripartite concept, which is unfamiliar in Canada, and seemed interested to hear how we do things in Neddy. This seemed to arouse a good deal of interest. I was very favourably impressed by the provincial officials I met – they seemed fully up to the standard of Ottawa officials, who have always seemed to me to be a pretty able lot.

Saturday 30 April 1977

I flew to Washington, where I had a long telephone conversation with Peter Ramsbotham. He said that in the short term President Carter's moves on energy would slow down US economic growth and make it more difficult for the administration to press the Germans to reflate, but that it was time that someone took action on energy.*

Ramsbotham said that Denis Healey had just been staying with

---

* President Carter had introduced a national energy policy which included the removal of controls on domestic oil and gas prices to stimulate production.

him. He was impressed by Denis's steadiness and found him more modest and more realistic in his approach than a year ago. He asked me what the prospects were for Phase 3[*] and said the New York bankers were all relying on us to secure one. I said I was pretty sure that the resolutions passed at the TUC conference this summer would make it impossible for the leadership to negotiate a Phase 3 that had any real meaning and I suggested to Peter that he should begin to prepare the US bankers for this in order to avoid too big a feeling of let down later on.

I then flew to London in Concorde – 3 hours 37 minutes flying time.

Wednesday 4 May 1977

At 4 p.m. we had the monthly meeting of Neddy. It began with quite a good discussion of energy policy. This was initiated by Tony Benn, who shows an encouraging readiness to accept that the UK can and should have an energy policy, which none of his predecessors did.

The rest of the meeting was taken up with a discussion of the NEDO budget. I opened up with a careful statement about the role and accountability of the NEDO staff and the system I had developed for co-ordinating the activities of the people who serve on fifty or so Neddy committees. Len Murray made some mildly critical observations about NEDO staff, who must, he said, avoid pushing their own views, especially when these were likely to divide the parties, which led Jack Jones to deliver a rambling attack on NEDO and, by implication, on me. This pushed other members of the council to come strongly to our defence, including Denis Healey, who said that although he had had some differences of opinion with

---

[*] i.e. a voluntary agreement between the TUC and government to restrain wage increases.

me – and had told me so – he had always had the highest respect for the quality of NEDO's work. Jones got more bad tempered as he became more isolated – it was typical of the trade union movement that those of the TUC team who disagreed with him simply stayed away from the meeting. In the end the discussion went off rather well from our point of view – but it was a wearing and depressing episode.

Thursday 5 May 1977

I went to a small BIM lunch at the Connaught Rooms, hosted by Derek Ezra. He said he would like us to discuss growth and inflation and without warning asked me to lead off. I said that the AUEW, which had just voted overwhelmingly in favour of a return to free collective bargaining, had done us all a service by demonstrating so early on in the summer that there was no prospect of negotiating a meaningful third phase of incomes policy. This should prevent us from wasting any more time chasing a will o' the wisp and would force us to face reality. I said I thought that with high unemployment and responsible trade union leadership a return to free collective bargaining need not produce a wage explosion – provided we could work out some agreed parameters for the few sectors of the economy, like coal and electricity supply, where irresponsible use of industrial power could not be contained. This gave rise to a good discussion, in which the supporters and opponents of the proposition were about evenly divided.

In the evening I looked in at a party given by the Hungarian embassy for visiting trade union leaders who had spent some time at NEDO this morning. I exchanged pleasantries with Mick Costello – formerly the *Morning Star* correspondent who covered our activities and now industrial organiser of the CPGB. I also had a talk with Bill Sirs, the general secretary of the steel workers' union, who spoke with real enthusiasm about our iron and steel sector working party and the NEDO staff associated with it. This made a nice contrast to yesterday's criticisms from Jack Jones.

Wednesday 11 May 1977

Douglas Wass took me to lunch at the Reform. He was in a very gloomy mood – he couldn't see how we were going to pull out of our long decline and didn't think that any of our present policies were adequate. He doesn't accept the view that all the Treasury needs to do is to create the right environment and that the investment and productivity increases we require will automatically follow. This leads him to favour interventionist policies, though I don't think he is very clear what form they should take.

We went to a small dinner given by the Plowdens for Harold Macmillan. The old man was in good form, especially at the start when he was stimulated by the company of younger people. He slowed down a good deal as the evening went on but he had his wits about him and spoke well. In the conversation after dinner he talked a lot about times gone by – especially the First World War. But he made one pungent comment about the present political scene. He told Peter Carrington that when the Conservatives got back into power they would only last two years – 'and then, I suppose, there will be a national government'. He also said that in the 1920s and 1930s all that most Tory MPs wanted was to return to life as it had been in 1913. But he and a few others had realised that you could never put the clock back. They had, therefore, given a lot of thought to the ways in which society might develop and how the party should adapt itself to this – and by the time the Second World War came their ideas were reasonably well developed. No one in the Conservative Party seemed to be doing that kind of thinking now – they simply wanted to put the clock back to the 1950s.

It was delightful to see Macmillan. He seemed very much a figure out of history but his charm and force of personality are still evident and he is full of moderation and common sense.

Monday 16 May 1977

In the afternoon David Stout and I spent an hour with François Mitterrand's economic adviser, Jacques Attali. He is a personable, intelligent man of thirty-two and an economist of repute.* After we had explained to him how we handled industrial policy in Britain, I asked him whether this was a subject on which there would be differences of view within the coalition of the left. Attali said that there was no disagreement between the socialists and the Communists over goals but there were differences over means. I suspect this will apply to a good deal more than industrial policy.

Tuesday 17 May 1977

In the afternoon I went to see Siegmund Warburg about my future plans. He was full of compliments on the independent line I had taken at NEDO. He said he liked nonconformists and pressed me to join the board of S. G. Warburg, either full or part time as I chose.

Friday 20 May 1977

Bernard Asher and I spent a couple of hours at the House of Commons with Geoffrey Howe, Keith Joseph and David Howell. The meeting was arranged some time ago at Geoffrey's suggestion largely to enable us to explain our current activities to them.

---

* In 1991 he became the first – highly controversial – president of the London-based European Bank for Reconstruction and Development.

Bernard and I put great stress on the value of our sector groups' work and said that in our view it could be equally worthwhile under an interventionist or a non-interventionist government. We also discussed the role of the council and the possibility of linking its work with Parliament. Geoffrey and David were interested and constructive, but Keith was neither and I found it difficult to get on to his wavelength at all. He seemed to me to be judging everything we said against his own dogmatically held preconceptions and wasn't really prepared to listen to anything we said unless it fitted these. On this occasion at least he really did seem to be the 'mad monk'.

Wednesday 25 May 1977

I flew to Brussels at lunchtime. Roy's old police driver met me at the airport and drove me straight to the Economic and Social Committee in rue Ravenstein. The committee has not got a good name but it turned out to be, on this occasion at least, much better than I had been led to believe. When I arrived Frank Judd* had just started a long, but good and thoughtful, speech in which he gave a report on the British presidency and added some reflections of his own. During the discussion afterwards the British attitude to the Community was sharply criticised on all sides and the frankness with which people expressed their views seemed to me to be a sign of a lively committee.

I went on to see Donald Maitland, who confirmed that Britain is not popular in the community as a whole. Donald said that our manners had caused offence as well as our policies. The French pursued their national interests singlemindedly but they took care to do so at least ostensibly within the framework of the Rome treaty and when they won their point they referred to it as a victory for the

---

* Minister of State at the Foreign and Commonwealth Office.

Community. We on the other hand seemed to most Europeans to make a habit of calling in question the fundamental basis of the Community. This was particularly true of John Silkin's handling of agricultural issues, which had caused great offence within the commission. But it applied also to British civil servants. Most of them treated discussions in Brussels as just like any other international negotiations in GATT or the IMF. Officials from the other member countries on the other hand recognised that the EEC was a genuine community in which more was involved than the simple pursuit of national goals.

Thursday 26 May 1977

I went to see one or two people in the commission and then back to the Jenkins' house in rue de Praetère, where David Marquand* and I had lunch together. We talked, among other things, about the European Parliament. When I said that I might have tried standing for it but for the fact that I couldn't bring myself to support either Labour or Conservative policies for any length of time, David said that this was really why he had come to Brussels. He is completely disenchanted with British politics – as of course is Roy, who said that if there were an election now he really couldn't bring himself to vote for the Labour Party.

I called on Henk Vredeling, the Dutch Commissioner, who used to be Minister of Defence in Holland and now looks after labour problems and social affairs. He was very interested in what we are doing at Neddy and would like to see the tripartite sectoral approach adopted more widely in the Community. He was most friendly and welcoming.

---

* Chief adviser to the Secretariat General of the EEC. Formerly Labour MP for Ashfield.

Roy and I then went for a walk in the forest and had a long talk about the summit, the community and British politics. Roy is very critical of Callaghan for his behaviour towards him at the summit – he regards the decision to put him at the finance ministers' table and not with the heads of government or foreign ministers at the pre-summit dinner at No. 10 as a calculated insult. I said that Jim had never forgiven Roy for taking over at the Treasury and making a success of it after he himself had manifestly failed there.

Roy gave a pleasant dinner party in the evening. After dinner we sat up talking for a while. He said he might do only two years at Brussels; there was a risk that his appointment as president would not be renewed and he would not want to serve as a commissioner under another president. He also said, very wisely, that he had made up his mind that he would not worry about the renewal of his appointment – he would say and do what he thought was right even if this meant cutting across some heads of government. It was clear from what he said that he has already come into fairly sharp conflict with the French – and perhaps the British also. He also said that he had not given up all thought of returning to British politics. But he agreed that events would determine whether or not this was possible – he could not go back to British politics unless some structural change occurred, nor would he want to.

Wednesday 1 June 1977

We had a quiet Neddy meeting – longer than usual and with a better quality of discussion. There were three items – the prospects for investment, agriculture and trade with Japan – and each provoked a good debate. Hedley Greenborough of Shell has joined the CBI team as deputy president and is expected to succeed Harold Watkinson as president next year. He made a good impression.

Tuesday 7 June 1977

We went to St Paul's for the Queen's Jubilee service. It had rained a lot in the night but there were large crowds everywhere and everyone was very good tempered. The service was a magnificent piece of pageantry, which went off without a hitch and the Archbishop of Canterbury preached extremely well.

Wednesday 8 June 1977

In the afternoon the Japanese ambassador came to see me with a very senior man from the Japanese Foreign Office. We had a frank discussion about Anglo-Japanese trade and the reaction of British industry to the ruthless marketing of Japanese goods. The ambassador is a strong supporter of voluntary limits for Japanese exports of sensitive goods because he realises that without these Anglo-Japanese relations could deteriorate very sharply.

Friday 10 June 1977

I called on Douglas Allen and told him – for the time being in strict confidence – of my plans to leave Neddy in the autumn. He is very disenchanted and clearly wishes that he had left Whitehall before retirement age.

Monday 13 June 1977

I had lunch at Morgan Grenfell. Everyone was very pro-Neddy and pressed John Peyton,* who was the only politician there, to say that

---

* Conservative MP for Yeovil. He had been Minister of Transport from 1970 to 1974.

the Conservatives would give it their full support. He was encouraging but unspecific.

I drove John back to the House of Commons after lunch and we discussed the Conservative party's attitude to industry. He assured me that Keith Joseph's views were not shared by his colleagues in the shadow Cabinet and said he would not be given a top economic portfolio if the Tories came to power.*

Friday 17 June 1977

The political situation has changed a great deal this week due to two events. One is the government's defeat in committee on the Finance Bill as a result of two left-wingers voting with the Tories. The other is Callaghan's decision to allow Cabinet ministers to vote as they choose on the Bill on direct elections to the European Parliament. I think the second of these will prove very damaging to Callaghan as Prime Minister and to his reputation in the long run. Most people are doubtful if this government can survive beyond the autumn, though Richard Wainwright† told me yesterday that, even though they might well decline to renew their pact with Labour, the Liberals would do their best to keep the government in power at least until the New Year.

Moss Evans came in for a drink in the evening. He has won the election to succeed Jack Jones as TGWU general secretary and is therefore very relaxed. I think our talk will have helped a lot to restore good relations between the TGWU and NEDO.

---

* Sir Keith Joseph was Secretary of State for Industry in Margaret Thatcher's first administration.
† Liberal MP for Colne Valley.

Wednesday 22 June 1977

Doreen's birthday, but we couldn't do anything to celebrate it because today was the day on which the Prime Minister held the first of two conferences with people involved in our sector working parties. The conference was held in Lancaster House, with about a hundred people present from both management and unions. Denis Healey and three other ministers supported the PM on the platform, along with John Methven, Len Murray, Alf Allen and myself.

I thought the conference went well. It was realistic and constructive and Callaghan did not try to make party political capital out of it. He spoke briefly to newsmen after the conference but left the main briefing to me. All the participants to whom my colleagues and I spoke afterwards seemed to think the exercise worthwhile.

Friday 24 June 1977

I went to see Douglas Wass in the morning to tell him of my plans to leave NEDO by the end of the year. He was clearly taken aback and seemed sorry to hear my news. He even asked me whether I would be prepared to reconsider my decision, which was quite a turn around from a couple of years ago when we seemed to be so much at cross-purposes.

Tuesday 28 June 1977

An unforgettable day on which we were the guests of the Admiralty for the Spithead Review. At Southampton we went on board the Royal Fleet Auxiliary *Lyness* and we steamed down Southampton Water and out into the Solent, passing through the fleet lines to take up our station astern of *Britannia*. At 1430 *Britannia* weighed anchor and the review began. The royal yacht was led by the Trinity House ship *Patricia* and followed by HMS *Birmingham*, a missile cruiser which accommodated the Admiralty Board – then RFA *Engadine* with the press on board, then *Lyness*, followed by two other RFA ships with diplomats, MPs and other guests.

The weather was unfortunately cold and grey and we didn't see the sun all day. But it kept dry and we had a superb view of the whole fleet from the top deck of the *Lyness*. It was a great sight and a memorable day.

Wednesday 29 June 1977

I began the day with an hour's visit from a team of economists from Mexico led by the governor of the central bank. He was an intelligent and likeable man and I enjoyed the interview.

In the late morning I went to see Denis Healey to tell him of my plans. Like Douglas Wass he seemed surprised but made no attempt to change my mind because, he said, he had always been in favour of movement between the public and private sectors. He said some pleasant things about my work at NEDO and added that whatever differences we had had he had always maintained a high regard for NEDO's contribution. He said he thought my successor should probably not come from Whitehall. I agree with this – one doesn't want to get into a position where the DG of NEDO is automatically an ex-civil servant.* I told Denis I thought the principal qualities needed in the job were some knowledge of the trade unions, a thick skin and an ability to give leadership to the growing number of people involved in NEDO work. He agreed and said the third quality was now the most important.

---

* The first two directors general (Sir Robert Shone and Sir Fred Catherwood) had come from industry. Sir Frank Figgures and I were both former civil servants.

Monday 4 July 1977

I spent most of the day at the Festival Hall at a conference called 'London Looks Forward'. I found it all rather depressing. London is evidently losing population quite heavily, services are steadily deteriorating and nobody seems to have the least idea of how to deal with it. From that point of view the conference was a good idea as it brought together a group of people who ought to be thinking about these problems. There were about 400 people in all – mostly local councillors, planners and cranks.

Tuesday 5 July 1977

Again I spent a fair bit of the day at the Festival Hall. The Duke of Edinburgh, who provided the inspiration for the conference, intervened rather well in the discussion after lunch. He inveighed against what he called the 'nanny society' and said that in the old days all the people who wanted to tell other people how to run their lives used to go overseas and govern remote parts of the Empire – now unfortunately they stayed at home.

I was one of the speakers in the final session. I was given ten minutes and used it partly to suggest that London's role in the next twenty years should be as the pre-eminent city of the EEC. I said that even Paris – much less Bonn, Copenhagen or Brussels – couldn't really compare with London for the range of its financial, cultural, tourist and commercial activities; we ought therefore to aim consciously to make it the centre of the Community and spend the money needed to bring its services up to the required standard. This seemed to go down quite well, though the duke told me over drinks afterwards that he thought it too savoured a little of the nanny attitude.

Wednesday 6 July 1977

We had a good Neddy meeting. Peter Shore and Shirley Williams came to talk about how their departments' policies could be used to help the objectives of the industrial strategy. This stemmed from an initiative by Jim Callaghan, who really does seem to want to put the weight of the Cabinet generally behind what we are doing.

Peter Shore was positive and spoke well about the ways in which he was trying to get local authorities to give more priority to industry – e.g. by taking care not to disturb existing workshops unnecessarily when carrying through slum clearance schemes in city centres.

Shirley followed him with a brilliant exposition of the relationship between the educational system and industry and the things that could be done to bring the two into harmony with one another. Her talk, which lasted for about twenty minutes and was given without a note, gave rise to an unusually good discussion.

Altogether it was a good morning. At last people are beginning to accept that to stop our industrial decline we have to harness *all* aspects of policy to the task.

Monday 11 July 1977

I went to see the Prime Minister to tell him officially about my plan to leave NEDO and join Warburgs. He was friendly and affable and asked me for my advice on what Neddy's role should be in the future. He made it clear that he attached a good deal of importance to it and spoke pleasantly about my own activities. We then went on to Lancaster House together for the second of his conferences with representatives of our sector working parties.

This was a more heavyweight affair than the earlier one. There were four Cabinet ministers on the platform with Callaghan, plus Harold Watkinson, Hugh Scanlon and myself; and there were more company chairmen and trade union general secretaries than on the previous occasion.

After a rather slow and heavy start the conference got going very well and was in full flood when the PM brought it to an end at 6.30. Eric Varley and I saw the press together. It was clear from what was said over drinks afterwards that virtually all the participants thought it worthwhile – certainly I was encouraged by the strong commitment to the work which both management and trade union people showed. Callaghan was, I believe, delighted with it.

Tuesday 12 July 1977

I attended a sector working party meeting to introduce its new chairman, John Lyons. He is streets ahead of most trade union leaders in both intellect and personality and is correspondingly unpopular on the General Council.

Friday 22 July 1977

I went to see Len Murray at 9.30 and spent an hour with him. I told him of my decision to leave NEDO by the end of the year. I also said that I was going to join the board of a merchant bank, which Harry Urwin of the TGWU recently described as 'the social security system for top people'.

Len said he was sorry I was going – despite the ups and downs of the last year I had always retained the TUC's confidence. Len thought my successor probably ought not to come from Whitehall this time – the TUC would certainly not agree to the appointment of someone who could expect to go back to Whitehall after his time at NEDO was over. I agreed – one did not want to get into a situation where the post was assumed to be in Whitehall's gift. I also said I thought the new man should have some experience of dealing with trade unions – if only to avoid the trap which so many people who don't know them well fall into of taking them too seriously. I am glad to say that Len agreed with this.

Tuesday 2 August 1977

I chaired a meeting, arranged jointly by John Methven and myself, at which we discussed with representatives of twenty very large companies how far they could use their purchasing power to help their UK suppliers of components and machines to increase their efficiency.* This arose from a letter I sent to the chairmen of the companies concerned, which received a very encouraging response. The meeting was a good one and virtually everyone there was positive and constructive. The only exception was the man from GEC, no doubt reflecting Arnold Weinstock's views.

Thursday 4 August 1977

Dick Marsh came to see me at five o'clock to talk about relations between government and industry, on which he is chairing an inquiry for the Hansard Society. I said what I believe to be the truth – that the government machine has deteriorated sharply over the last fifteen years or so and has now become very inefficient. I said it seemed to me that the processes of internal consultation and discussion – through inter-departmental committees, Cabinet committees and so on – had become so convoluted and time consuming that ministers and senior officials had no time or energy left to listen to advice from outside the machine. Dick's report should make good reading.

---

* Marks & Spencer had pioneered this approach with considerable success.

Wednesday 17 August 1977

I had my portrait painted by John Bratby. He is an interesting chap who seems to think the country is going to pot because it doesn't value individuals highly enough. Perhaps he is right.

Friday 19 August 1977

We motored down to East Hendred for dinner through as heavy rain as I can remember seeing in August. We found Roy and Jennifer in good form. Roy in particular is more relaxed than I have seen him for some years; he gives the impression of being at peace with himself.

Tuesday 6 September 1977

The Rolls gave a dinner party this evening at Brooks's for Joe Peckman of the Brookings Institution and his wife. Apart from ourselves the other guests were Harold and Diane Lever, Bernard Donoughue and his wife and Douglas and Sybil Allen. I think Eric's original idea had been to have a general discussion about the state of the nation for the benefit of Joe Peckman. But Harold Lever launched out on a series of his usual, highly amusing auto-biographical anecdotes and Peckman left without hearing our views on the economy. Douglas was rather low – he feels he has wasted the last three years as Head of the Civil Service and now bitterly regrets taking the job on. He retires at the end of the year but told Doreen that he had done nothing about finding a post-retirement job as he did not want to get involved in the kind of controversy which surrounded William Armstrong's move to Midland Bank.

Wednesday 7 September 1977

I arrived in Blackpool for the Trades Union Congress about noon, in time for the start of the economic debate. Everyone was talking about the extraordinary events of Monday, when the TGWU delegation was temporarily suspended on the motion of the tiny union which represents pub managers. The pent-up resentment against the TGWU's heavyhanded tactics came out in this vote and all the unions who had suffered from their arrogant methods supported the motion for suspension. Trade union officials and journalists who had been attending Congress for twenty years all said they had never seen anything like it before.

The economic debate was almost entirely about incomes policy and whether the 'twelve-month rule'* should be continued. Hugh Scanlon spoke brilliantly in support of it, even though half his delegation ostentatiously disassociated themselves from his speech. In replying to the debate Scanlon took Clive Jenkins to pieces in a masterly way which gave great pleasure to all his listeners.

Thursday 8 September 1977

In the evening we gave our annual NEDO cocktail party. It was very well attended – most of the General Council were there except the TGWU people – and everyone was very friendly.

During the day I had a phone call from Arnold Weinstock, who is upset about a pamphlet published by a group of shop stewards in the heavy electrical industry. It evidently quotes NEDO as being in support of their policies, which include the 'social ownership' of

---

* This precluded trade unions from submitting wage claims at intervals of less than twelve months.

GEC's and Parsons' heavy electrical interests. I told Weinstock I would write to him and to the shop stewards pointing out that NEDO did not hold the views attributed to them in the pamphlet and that he could publish my letter if he liked.

Tuesday 13 September 1977

I took Leo Pliatzky* to lunch at the Royal Thames. We talked about politics and politicians, including Tony Crosland, whom at one time he knew very well. Leo said he had not kept up his political friendships – he did not think it right for civil servants to have close social contacts with active politicians. This seems to me an extraordinary – and wrongheaded – view.

Sunday 25 September 1977

Margaret Thatcher was interviewed on ITV for an hour today by Brian Walden. A great deal of the interview was taken up in discussion of relations between a future Conservative government and the TUC. Talking about the miners' dispute of 1973–4, she said, 'One thing Len Murray said which we have not given him enough credit for: when he offered to accept that the miners could be a special case. This was a very responsible proposal and in retrospect I am sorry that we did not follow it up.' So far as I know this is the first time a frontbench Conservative has ever publicly admitted that they made a mistake in rejecting the TUC's offer at the Neddy meeting in January 1974. Better late than never.

---

* Sir Leo Pliatzky had recently taken over as permanent secretary of the Department of Trade.

Monday 10 October 1977

We had a quiet but constructive meeting of Neddy. Denis Healey began with a balanced account of the economic situation: there has been a big improvement on the financial front but output and investment still remain very slack. The main item was a paper by our economists suggesting that a good deal of the surplus capacity in industry might be more apparent than real. It drew attention to the increasing evidence that shortage of skilled labour would hold back expansion at a much earlier point in the next upturn than in previous cycles. It also made the good point that some surplus plant capacity is idle simply because no one wants to buy the product it is designed to manufacture – such plant does not represent 'spare' capacity in any real sense. The paper was a good one and provoked a sensible discussion.

No reference to my resignation was made at the Neddy meeting but Denis Healey had a private talk with the TUC members after-wards and urged them to withdraw their objection to the appointment of a civil servant. David Lea told me later that they were reluctant to do this though they accept that it is up to them to propose a good alternative candidate. So far as I know the TUC attitude has not got anything to do with me – according to Douglas Wass they have been strongly anti-civil service for some time.

Tuesday 11 October 1977

I went to the Mining Machinery Exhibition in Sheffield, which my brother-in-law Richard Clark has had a big hand in organising. It is an impressive show which is a great credit to him.

Wednesday 12 October 1977

I released a statement to the press about my resignation. It is very nice to have the news out at last and Doreen and I both feel much relieved.

Wednesday 19 October 1977

Len Murray told me that the TUC are getting bored with the question of my successor at NEDO and will agree to a civil servant though they don't really want one. So the mandarins will as usual get their way.

Thursday 27 October 1977

I had a visit from Michel Rocard, who is a senior official on the secretariat of the French Socialist Party. He is an interesting chap who used to be an *inspecteur des finances* and he has seen Healey, David Owen, Gordon Richardson and Eric Roll while he has been over here.

We had a long talk about Neddy – then I asked him about relations within the coalition of the left in France. He said that the Socialists had no illusions about the Communists. Their purpose in entering a coalition with the Communists was to end the latter's political isolation, which had up to now enabled them to act as a permanent opposition party. Rocard thought that this was an unhealthy situation which led to undue polarisation between left and right. Since they had been working with the Socialists the French Communists had become much less Stalinist and had publicly committed themselves time and again to the concept of a multi-party state in which the party in power gave up office if defeated in a general election.

Wednesday 2 November 1977

We had a strange Neddy meeting. Denis Healey began by giving his views on the decision to let the pound float upwards.* He said it was the least damaging option open to the government. The TUC and CBI both seem to be opposed to the move but it seems to me to be both sensible and welcome.

We then went on to consider a paper which David Stout had written about world economic prospects and their implications for Britain. The paper was based on a report prepared for OECD by a distinguished group of economists and I thought it was rather good. I introduced it briefly and in a low key, hoping to stimulate a reasonable discussion about economic policy questions, which Neddy all too rarely considers. Harold Watkinson got us off to a bad start by saying he was fed up with general discussion and wanted action. This gave Jack Jones a chance to launch into a long diatribe against Neddy and all its works; ending up with the assertion that there were no problems which couldn't be taken care of in direct discussion between management and shop stewards at plant level. After a ragged discussion Eric Varley came in twice with a strong defence of NEDO and the sector working parties. Finally I got angry and laid into Jack for his constant denigration of Neddy and its sector working parties, which was highly damaging to the morale of the many people from trade unions and management who believed in the work they were doing and gave a lot of time to it. Jack made a grudging half-withdrawal – but it was a most unpleasant scene. I was, however, very pleased to have got my dislike of his attitude off my chest and I gathered afterwards that the other trade union

---

* Following the negotiations with the IMF a lot of foreign money flowed into London with consequent upward pressure on the exchange rate. The government had been intervening in the market to keep the rate down but at the end of October it abandoned this policy and let the pound find its own level.

members of Neddy enjoyed it (except for Len Murray, who seems unwilling to differ openly from Jack on anything, even though his time at the TGWU is so short now).[*]

I had lunch with Alf Allen, who said that Jack was in a minority of one on a lot of issues in the TUC economic committee and that they were all thoroughly fed up with him. It is clear that Hugh Scanlon takes the same view.

After lunch Doreen and I flew to Inverness for a Scottish Council conference. We travelled with Nick Morrison, the permanent secretary of the Scottish Office, who is an intelligent and civilised man, and then went by taxi to Aviemore. The driver was the same man as I had last year, when he killed a deer on the road. He showed us the place where it had happened and as he did so a deer crossed the road – fortunately without injuring itself this time.

Thursday 3 November 1977

I was the first speaker in the morning after Ronald Clydesmuir's formal welcome.[†] I had taken some trouble over my speech, which was about future problems of investment and contained a good deal about the growing threat from semi-industrialised countries such as Taiwan and Brazil which are becoming efficient producers of a rapidly widening range of goods. I was pleased to find that the speech went over very well.

In the discussion after my speech, I said it was deplorable that we should have reached the time when oil is going ashore in big quantities without having come to any agreement in the country about how the large revenues arising from it should be spent. A

---

[*] In his autobiography, *Union Man* (London: Collins, 1986), Jones said that the NEDC was a useful talking shop but that the sector working parties had little relevance to the shop floor. This is not a verdict I would seriously quarrel with.

[†] Lord Clydesmuir was governor of the Bank of Scotland.

Dutch industrialist urged us to avoid the 'Dutch disease', which led them to fritter away all the proceeds of their natural gas on higher consumption and welfare payments.

Friday 4 November 1977

George Thomson gave an excellent summing up. He strongly endorsed what I had said yesterday about the need for agreement on how to use the oil revenues, which he thought should have been done long ago.* My remarks on this are reported in the *Glasgow Herald* and the *Financial Times* and will no doubt flutter the dovecotes in Whitehall.

Friday 11 November 1977

I drove with Mark Bonham Carter† to Heathrow, where we joined up with the other British members of the Anglo-Hungarian Round Table. There were fourteen of us in all – academics, journalists and MPs.

On arrival at Budapest we were driven from the airport to Karl Marx University, where we were greeted by the rector, Ivan Behrend – a distinguished economist of great charm who has been invited to spend six months at All Souls. Most of the Hungarian members of the round table joined us at the university and we all set off by coach for Pécs, a charming city whose centre must have looked exactly the same under the Austro-Hungarian Empire at the turn of the century.

---

* In retrospect, the failure to devote the tax windfall from North Sea oil to improving the ageing national infrastructure (railways, hospitals etc.) was arguably Britain's biggest missed opportunity of the 1970s and 1980s.

† A former Liberal MP and chairman of the Race Relations Board from 1966 to 1970.

Sunday 13 November 1977

This was the main working day of the conference and the economic group (of which I was the British co-chairman) had three sessions. The quality of the discussion, which was entirely conducted in English, struck me as distinctly high. The British team was a strong one and the Hungarians more than held their own, intellectually as well as linguistically.

It is clear that many Hungarians want to develop their commercial and financial ties with the West because they see this as a way of reducing their political isolation. Hungary has what corresponds quite closely to a Western-style market economy and this, too, makes it easier for them to develop trading links with the West. At the end of the day Behrend told me that the discussion had left him feeling depressed. He said we had made it plain that we were concerned with the USA, the EEC and the developing world and we clearly put the development of trading links with eastern Europe near the bottom of our list of priorities. I suppose this is true.

Behrend made no secret of his dislike of the Soviet system and his desire to build really close links between Hungary and the West. I asked him how many of the Hungarian team at the conference shared his views and he replied, 'About 80 per cent.' I then turned to my neighbour, who was a party official of evident proletarian origins and clearly belonged to the other 20 per cent. He was a hard line pro-Moscow man who evidently regarded all Englishmen as upper-class exploiters.

We stayed up late after dinner chatting with some of the Hungarians. There are one or two convinced Marxists among them – including, oddly enough, a young man who went to school in London when his father was posted at the embassy there. But most of the Hungarian team clearly regard their colleagues in the Soviet bloc as second-rate barbarians and are desperately keen to become part of the Western world.

Thursday 24 November 1977

I went with Doreen to hear Roy Jenkins give the second Israel Sieff Memorial Lecture at the Royal Institution. It was a thoughtful lecture, looking back reflectively on thirty years in Parliament – full of historical references and, as always with Roy's compositions, beautifully phrased. It made plain his great disenchantment with party politics in Britain and was, I suppose, in a sense a farewell to them.

Monday 28 November 1977

At midday I called on Douglas Wass, who had seen Len Murray and John Methven about the directorship general of NEDO earlier in the morning. He told me that they had decided to advertise the post and to ask Bernard Asher, who does not want to be considered for the permanent job, to serve as acting DG until a successor is found.[*] He would be my choice for caretaker and is sure to do it well.

Tuesday 29 November 1977

I went to a big dinner at the Royal Lancaster Hotel. The Prime Minister made a very positive speech about his determination to give priority to manufacturing industry.

---

[*] Geoffrey Chandler, a director of Shell, was appointed director general in the new year.

Thursday 1 December 1977

Doreen and I drove to the University of Leicester. After a short reception at the university in the evening I gave my Alfred Herbert Memorial Lecture on Britain's industrial goals, under the auspices of the Institution of Production Engineers. The lecture theatre was bitterly cold – so much so that I had to stop halfway through to get an overcoat – but despite this it got a very good reception.

After my lecture we had about an hour's discussion, at the end of which I was presented with a handsome silver sugar shaker. There followed a speech by the president of the Institution's American counterpart, who – for reasons which entirely escaped me – presented our host with a full American Indian headdress. The proceedings, which had by now lasted for nearly two hours, ended with the strange spectacle of the president of the institution making a speech in an icy cold theatre with a magnificent array of feathers on his head.

And so I have my last major speech as director general of Neddy behind me, which is a great relief to both Doreen and me.

Afterword

As the Alfred Herbert lecture was my last speaking engagement I had decided to avoid issues of macro-economic policy, on which my views were liable to cause difficulties with some of my colleagues on NEDC. Instead, I concentrated on the rationale and objectives of the programme of work initiated at the Chequers meeting of Neddy on 5 November 1975.

The principal outcome of this meeting (agreed, however tentatively and with whatever reservations, by government, management and unions) was that the balance of national priorities should be altered – away from social objectives towards industrial ones. It was also agreed that a major effort should be made to stimulate improved performance in British industry, not by a top-down approach but by involving managers, shop floor representatives and government officials in a structured programme related to individual industries. The Prime Minister, James Callaghan, was a staunch supporter of this approach – or 'industrial strategy', as it was called – and put a lot of time into meeting and encouraging the growing number of people from industry who became involved in the work.

By the end of 1977, when I left Neddy, this programme had generated quite a head of steam and those who took part in it, both from industry and from Whitehall, seemed increasingly willing to play a positive role. The work continued in the new year but was gradually overtaken – and eventually swamped – by the events which led to the downfall of the Callaghan government.

In the spring of 1978 it became apparent that the prevailing mood in the trade unions had changed, as their members grew increasingly restive over the constraints imposed by various forms of incomes policy over the years. There was growing pressure among activists (not only on the left) for a return to unfettered collective bargaining. Both Jack Jones and Hugh Scanlon retired in 1978 and their successors were unable or unwilling to commit their members to the kind of understanding over wage restraint which ministers were desperate to secure.

By the autumn it was evident that the government's attempt to maintain a voluntary incomes policy of any kind had broken down beyond repair. The Labour movement's refusal to countenance any serious cutback in public expenditure meant that the government – already weakened by the Liberals' decision to withdraw from the Lib–Lab pact – had no counter-inflationary weapon left in its armoury. During the 'winter of discontent' which followed, this became blindingly obvious to the electorate, which drew the predictable conclusion and returned the Conservatives to power at the general election of May 1979.

This brought to an end a decade of decline, confusion and economic failure which had taken the country to the brink of collapse. It also closed a distinctive chapter of post-war British history – which had included the Attlee government's social reforms, the independence of India, the brief life of 'one nation' Conservatism and our accession to the EEC – as the national leadership passed to a new generation, with new ideas and values.

Somewhat ironically, it also ushered in the period of ten or more years of political stability (though not of consensus) which I had so often argued was a precondition of our return to economic strength. And as the new decade began, North Sea oil started to come ashore.

Index

378 CHALLENGE TO DEMOCRACY